Sleep with Spectators

Sleep with Spectators

Feminist Performance and Practice

Danielle Drees

MINNESOTA

University of Minnesota Press
Minneapolis
London

Excerpt from Laurel Rasplica Rodd's translation of Yosano Akiko's poem "Mountain Moving Day," from Laurel Rasplica Rodd, "Yosano Akiko and the Taishō Debate over the 'New Woman,'" in *Recreating Japanese Women, 1600–1945*, ed. Gail Lee Bernstein (University of California Press, 1991), 180; reprinted by permission of the University of California Press. Excerpt from Caryl Churchill, "A Poem for Irene Fornes," in *Conducting a Life: Reflections on the Theatre of Maria Irene Fornes*, ed. Maria M. Delgado and Caridad Svich (Lyme, N.H.: Smith and Kraus, 1999), xiv; reprinted with permission. Excerpts from Davóne Tines, *Vigil (an exercise in empathy)*, reprinted with permission.

A different version of chapter 3 was previously published as "Burnout Dramaturgy: Revaluing Sleep in Caryl Churchill's Sleepless Plays," *Journal of Dramatic Theory and Criticism* 35, no. 1 (Fall 2020): 45–59. A different version of chapter 7 was previously published as "Napping in Public: Feminist Practices of Care in Sleep Performance Art," *Frontiers: A Journal of Women Studies* 41, no. 3 (2020): 1–28.

Published by the University of Minnesota Press
111 Third Avenue South, Suite 290
Minneapolis, MN 55401-2520
http://www.upress.umn.edu

ISBN 978-1-5179-1849-1 (hc)
ISBN 978-1-5179-1850-7 (pb)

A Cataloging-in-Publication record for this book is available from the Library of Congress.

Printed on acid-free paper

To my grandmothers, Ann McMullin and Pat Drees

Contents

Part IV. Out in the World

Introduction
Sleep, Feminism, and Performance

Sleep, feminism, and performance are strange bedfellows. Sleep is associated with passivity and domesticity, qualities that feminists have long resisted. A sleeping performer also seems boring to watch—the opposite of dramatic action. Indeed, any hint of sleep appears anathema to live performance, where dozing audience members suggest a play has missed its mark. Although feminist performance has grown into an expansive area of research in theater studies, art history, and gender and sexuality studies over the past fifty years, *sleep* rarely breaks out as a key term in these fields. Yet sleep has emerged curiously often in feminist performance during this period, prompting formal innovation in myriad performance genres and facilitating artistic study of social practices as diverse as incarceration, labor exploitation, family life, care for chronic illness, and the use of public space. But sleep is a quiet act, easily overshadowed by more attention-grabbing elements of a play or artwork. Let's begin with an example, to spotlight the quiet presence of sleep in an ostensibly shocking work of art.

Throughout the dreary days of a mid-1990s winter, working-class British artist Tracey Emin hand-stitched 102 names into the yellow nylon interior walls of a hexagonal navy blue camping tent.[1] The names were spelled out in block capitals, each cut from richly colored fabric and stitched onto its own patterned rectangular backing. They filled the small interior space of the tent with colorful rows of patchwork blocks, attached to the walls as appliqués. Each name added fabric reinforcement to the tent, making it both more decorated and more durable. The names constituted a catalog of, in the artist's words, "everyone I have ever slept with" across her thirty-two years of life: not only different-gendered lovers but also friends and artistic collaborators, her grandmother, and two aborted pregnancies. In the finished artwork, *Everyone I Have Ever Slept With 1963–1995* (better known as *The Tent*), the names record a life history of sleep as a social practice. *The Tent* is a temporary but durable monument to a life spent sleeping alongside others.

The Tent also registers the feminist history that unfurled within the thirty-two-year span of sleep it encompasses. During these years, abortion was legalized in more than twenty countries; lesbian and bisexual women fought for women's sexual freedom; antiviolence campaigners sought to ensure legal protections against rape and abuse in the home; and feminist art historians and performance scholars argued for women's contributions to art and theater history—including their domestic craft labor, referenced in Emin's use of appliqué. Emin has at times disavowed feminism and, like many artists, is understandably opposed to having her work read only under the rubric of gender.[2] But the intertwined history of feminist theory and organizing—how feminists understand and act on their worlds—is everywhere in the story of sleep Emin's *Tent* tells.

The Tent became famous two years after its creation when it was included in *Sensation* (1997), a London exhibition showcasing provocative works from the collection of wealthy advertising executive Charles Saatchi. Nothing about *Sensation* was sleepy. *The Tent* appeared alongside a portrait of a convicted child murderer, a sculpture cast in human blood, and an image of the Virgin Mary crafted from oil paint and elephant dung.[3] *Sensation* brought together artists who made shocking mismatches between subject and medium, inserting murderers into the history of portraiture and bodily substances into the traditions of the bust and the religious icon. Sensationalism and shock value linked the British art scene of the 1990s to contemporaneous London theater, as plays with titles like *Penetrator, Blasted,* and *Shopping and Fucking* were smearing the Royal Court Theatre with what one critic described as a "disgusting feast of filth."[4] Shit, sex, and swearing emerged as strategies for young artists and playwrights to wake their viewers the fuck up.

In this context, *The Tent* is shocking because it seems to name a bold-faced list of Emin's sexual partners. The double meaning of "slept with" uses shock value to draw viewers in for a closer look. Yet when a viewer crawls fully inside the illuminated tent—the only way to see most of the interior appliqués—she encounters an intimate and not merely sexual space. Emin conceived of *The Tent*'s interior as a space for quiet contemplation, where a solo spectator would be beyond the view of other gallery patrons, sitting or reclining on a blue blanket stitched with its own appliqué message of interiority: "with myself / always myself / never forgetting."[5] Sheltered, in the quiet, the spectator might lay her own body across Emin's record of intimacy with the self, resting inside a soft monument to the social world of sleep.

Later events in *The Tent*'s story will make clear why I cannot describe crawling inside *The Tent* from firsthand experience. But the tools of performance studies allow for an imaginative reconstruction of the live experience of entering *The Tent* as a spectator, in order to examine sleep, a daily activity—and a frequent subject of the fine and performing arts—that rarely solicits our attention. In contrast to the shocking subject matter that *Sensation* foregrounded, sleep is easy to miss. While the word *slept* appears in the full title of Emin's piece, sleep is harder to locate in the artwork itself. *The Tent* draws attention to sleep's ephemeral, often-overlooked presence in our lives. Sleep happened in the past tense ("have slept"), and it happened in the now-vacant space of the tent's interior. As long as we are awake and conscious, sleep is never in the here and now. Instead, in queer utopian José Esteban Muñoz's words, sleep is "the trace, the remains, the things that are left, hanging in the air like a rumor," like *The Tent,* with its handsewn names of sleepers (and rumor of physical intimacy) but no visible sleeping body.[6] For Muñoz, the ephemeral is not only trace evidence of past events but also a hopeful gesture toward future recurrence. *The Tent,* with its flaps zipped open, might shelter sleepers again in the future. *The Tent* models how live art and performance can pause the ephemeral act of sleeping and situate this act in a waking, social world.

Although performance can pause and reconstruct sleep for an audience, sleep itself creates no conscious memories. While we might recall lying down in bed, waking up in the morning, or floating through fragments of dream, the hours-long substance of a night's sleep—what Anne Carson calls "that slab of outlaw time punctuating every pillow"—remains a blank in our individual recollection.[7] It is hard to know how to value an experience that we cannot hold in our memories, and this, perhaps, is why sleep is slipping away from us. Neuroscientists contend that sleep hours have declined in industrialized nations over the past sixty years to a level they characterize as "brutish."[8] The data they provide suggesting a trend of decreasing sleep hours point to our need to better understand the changing contexts and differing experiences of sleep, information that cannot be captured by electroencephalogram alone. We also need methods for studying sleep practices that leave only traces, with no lasting memories and incomplete material records. Following Muñoz and other performance scholars of recent decades in turning the lens of theater and performance studies toward examining ephemeral practices, I turn this lens on sleep, perhaps our most widely shared daily encounter with ephemerality. Live performance pauses and holds the ephemeral act of sleeping in a shared space and time, investigating the political implications and artistic possibilities of this contested segment of our daily lives.

A key political implication of sleep (one we often try to forget) is its insistence that we depend on other people. As art critic Jonathan Crary argues, "Sleep can stand for the durability of the social," for "sleep is crucially dependent on society in order to be sustained."[9] No matter how autonomous we feel, we spend roughly one-third of our time in a vulnerable, semiconscious state, implicitly dependent on local social relations and larger infrastructures of safety and care. But we rarely recognize how social sleep is. Crary suggests that our thinking about sleep is instead dominated by a psychoanalytic focus on dream narratives as the key element of sleep, with private, psychic wish fulfillment as the individualistic purpose of those dreams. Theater and performance scholarship, too, has tended to interpret dream scenes—from Mercutio's dream of Queen Mab to the dream ballets of mid-twentieth-century musical theater—without attending to the sleep that enrobes and enables them. Too narrow a focus on the individualistic dream world of the sleeper, Crary posits, leads us to overlook the social and political implications of sleep as a time when we do not actively participate in the laboring and consuming world of capital.

Yet Sigmund Freud developed his psychoanalytic theory of dream in a dynamic relationship with his understanding of sleep, as feminist critic Jacqueline Rose has emphasized. In short, sleep was harder for Freud to pin down than dream. It is, quite simply, "not easy to think about." Sleep, in Rose's reading of Freud's *Interpretation of Dreams,* "brings dreams closer to psychosis than neurosis," bridging the distance between disruptive and merely everyday psychic challenges. Sleep is the terrain on which the everyday can be radically transformed—perhaps into something mad. Most important, in Freud's theory of dream, sleep is the beginning of an unpredictable voyage: "We never know what will happen—or where exactly we are going—when we go to sleep."[10] Despite the thorough interpretation of dream instigated by Freud and pursued by many performance scholars and literary critics, sleep itself remains an underexamined territory connecting our everyday social world to its as-yet-unimagined transformation.

The Tent reveals the everyday social world of Emin's sleep, showing us sleep as a social practice, stitched into a network of co-sleepers.[11] When we view sleep as a social practice in artworks like Emin's, we let go of the idea that sleep is universally solipsistic and instead examine how it is context dependent, biopolitically differentiated, and shared with others in relations of interdependence. Sleep is context dependent in that the particular practices and meanings people associate with sleep are specific to their place and time.[12] The dates embroidered on the exterior of *The Tent* (1963–1995) mark Emin's sleep as situated in a discrete historical moment, and the tent itself suggests the qualities of that context. A tent is portable, temporary, comparatively inexpensive shelter. A tent evokes both the freedoms of outdoor rest and the physical dangers and social stigma of sleeping outside the recognizable, long-term structures of private property.

These different meanings of sleeping in a tent—camping versus homelessness—also illustrate how sleep is biopolitically differentiated. While mainstream sleep scholarship, like the neuroscientific research cited above, presents a generalized picture of declining sleep quantity, feminist scholars of temporality pose a different reading of diminished sleep. When it comes to our time, Sarah Sharma argues, “inequitable investments are made along [the] lines of class, race, gender, and sexuality,” and this includes inequitable investments in sleep time. Late capitalism’s accelerations do not fall on each of us in the same way, for states invest in the lives of some populations and not others, as Michel Foucault proposed in his lectures on biopolitics.[13] First articulated in the 1970s, these arguments about accelerationism and biopower form the warp and weft of our uneven experiences of time passing, and they are the backdrop to the sleep performances in this book. Although we may not participate actively in capitalist labor and consumption while asleep, sleeping conditions are part of political economy. When and where we sleep, how much sleep we get, how safe and restoring that sleep is, and how sleep affects our waking lives all reflect and reinforce uneven social and political commitments seen in hierarchies of social difference.

Emin’s titular double entendre “slept with” calls for careful interpretation, signaling that the social world of sleep stitched into the walls of *The Tent* rewards close reading. “Slept with” is the phrase that spelled sex to Emin’s reviewers, who then turned their attention away from the artwork itself to their own commentary on sex in women’s art. But the awkwardness of this dangling preposition should make us examine it a second time. Like a line of Shakespeare with an extra syllable, this syntax calls out for the viewer to slow down, setting aside one meaning of the phrase—and setting aside assumptions about Emin’s intentions—to linger and wonder about its ambiguities. Almost every playwright and artist discussed in this book has been written off, at some point in their career, as a weirdo attention-seeking dilettante or a relentless single-issue nag. It is the whore/saint binary of feminist performance. In an archive of work by women and nonbinary artists, close reading at its most basic means reading what they actually wrote, listening to what they actually said. Close reading is my method for what poet Adrienne Rich calls “re-vision,” a feminist strategy of re-seeing, of paying close and curious attention to what authoritative interpretations have overlooked.[14]

At its roots, close reading analyzes the relationship between content and form: With sleep performances, close reading is first a method for noticing sleep as content, for attending to sleep as thematic material that might be overlooked as boring or brushed off as incidental. Anthropologist Anna Lowenhaupt Tsing characterizes the "arts of noticing" as "look[ing] for what has been ignored because it never fit the time line of progress."[15] Noticing sleep in feminist performance asks us to be "agnostic" about accepted chronologies—both the familiar wave narratives of feminist activism and dormancy and the expected tempi of live performances. Once we start to notice sleep hiding in plain sight as a theme of both canonical and lesser-known performances, it emerges as a productive formal challenge, a wrench in the gears whose unsuitability to performance prompts creative innovation in the artworks themselves. Putting sleep in performance changes the form of the performance: its relation to audience, its fit with genre, its strategies of representation, and its reproduction of the offstage world. Read closely, these sleep performances demand that feminist theory reexamine political experience surrounding sleep—bodily exhaustion alongside militant energy, the refusal of work alongside the labor of activism, slowness alongside speed. At its best, close reading is a slow method. Sleep seems like unsuitable content for feminist theory, but its presence productively challenges and revises the forms of feminist thinking.

Making sense of sleep, the traces of this ephemeral practice, is also a shared act—not a solo but a collective reading. We do not remember our own experiences of sleep, but we know a lot about how others sleep. Like Emin, we have all spent our lives witnessing other people—roommates, children, friends, partners, and strangers—sleep and, at times, interpreting that sleep to answer questions: *Why does the baby keep waking up? Why are you snoring? Is that man on the subway okay?* State power also interprets our sleep, from police deciding which sleepers in public spaces to harass to municipal governments choosing which neighborhoods to invest in protecting from noise and light pollution and which homeless encampments to raze. With *The Tent,* Emin suggests that a lifelong experience of sleep might be better understood through its social relations than through a representation of the sleeper herself. When the spectator crawls inside the tent to see the names sewn on its interior, she joins the experience of witnessing, remembering, and interpreting traces of that sleep. The shared interpretive context of the performance site is uniquely suited to a close reading of the unevenly distributed conditions and effects of sleep. *The Tent* combines textual, visual, and performance elements, with spectators who climb inside the tent providing the live interaction that brings it under the rubric of feminist sleep performance.

Sleep performances ask spectators to participate in sleep as a social practice, whether they are witnessing the sleep of an actor or artist or attempting to sleep themselves. When a character in a play or opera sleeps onstage, she cues social interactions shaped by uneven vulnerabilities. The audience watches other characters drug her, steal from her, care for her, sing to her, molest her, or murder her. Performance and installation artworks about sleep reveal parallel relationships of vulnerability and interdependence, drawing spectators' attention to the sleeping conditions on public streets, in immigration detention centers, or in a camping tent. Thus, the sleep performances in this book stage sleep deprivation as much as they do restful slumber. People with less power—poor and overworked people, sick people, people of color, people who fear abuse in the home or violence intruding from outside—sleep less and worse. In performance, sleep loss marks the social world's intrusion on sleep. Sleep loss is both an aggravating physical reminder that the biological imperative to sleep cannot override all other demands on our bodies and minds and a prompt for dramatic action when the social world interrupts the body's plan.

The interrupted sleep of beautiful, young, white women has been particularly well represented in the performing and fine arts. The Sleeping Beauty trope makes the primary social relation of sleep a one-sided heterosexual romance between the exposed, passive female subject and the voyeuristic, creative male artist (and anticipated viewers); the trope is a cornerstone of gendered dynamics of Western cultural history that have been thoroughly skewered by feminist critics and artists. But to see the hand-stitched traces of Emin's sleeping partners, the spectator must relinquish her distanced view of the artwork. *The Tent,* therefore, participates in a late twentieth-century feminist project that uses diverse aesthetic strategies to intervene in the too-familiar opposition of sleeping female subject and awake male artist/viewer.

Out of the unexpectedly vast archive of sleep performance, this study focuses on performances where this feminist intervention in the gendered relationship between performance and spectators interacts with another major feminist intervention of the late twentieth century, the turn to socially reproductive labor as a serious area of study and activism. Socially reproductive labor does not produce commodities but instead sustains lives, through household maintenance, child- and eldercare, and other forms of work that make our homes clean, comfortable, reliable places to sleep. Read in conversation with feminist schools of thought that are invested in uprooting and remaking our social world, sleep performances imagine how the maintenance of daily life might become more valued and more sustainable, especially for those people who are most endangered by exhausting living conditions. Scholars, activists, and artists who are more skeptical of the promises of employment—particularly those shaping the fields of crip/disabled, queer/trans, Marxist, and abolition feminisms—have grappled most creatively with how to make restful sleep accessible to all. (But, as I will address later, Betty Friedan also rooted her foundational feminist text in women's everyday exhaustion.) The word *feminist* indicates this commitment to transforming the structures of daily life, both imaginatively and practically, toward ways of living in which care for one another and liberation for oneself are sustainably and equitably shared.

In this book, feminist sleep performance encompasses a wide-ranging and idiosyncratic archive of live, time-based media, including plays, solo performances, operas, participatory events, and performance and installation artworks like *The Tent.* The book's mixed-genre archive emerges from the playwrights and artists themselves, who borrow artistic techniques and strategies for financial survival from each other's fields. Some of these artists, such as Laurie Anderson and Regina José Galindo, have worked in multiple art forms, and their works have been taken up as objects of study by scholars of music, communication, and media, among other fields. Others, like playwright Sarah Kane and composer Philip Venables, find themselves working on the same material—Kane's text *4.48 Psychosis*—in two different stage genres, first as a play and then as an opera. In search of venues that are welcoming and appropriate for their work, artists like Navild Acosta and

Fannie Sosa have bounced between performance spaces and art museums, following in the footsteps of playwright María Irene Fornés, who pioneered "site-specific" staging in an unused apartment in the 1970s.[16] At times, solo performer Peggy Shaw and artist Sakiko Yamaoka seem to have traveled wherever funding and space were available—a necessity for many playwrights and artists whose work is not palatable or profitable for mainstream venues. Too narrow a disciplinary focus can lead scholars to overlook generative sites of comparison, like the proximity of Anderson and Shaw, who began their careers cheek by jowl in the artistic foment of downtown New York in the 1970s, or Emin and Kane, two young women who repulsed establishment London critics with their vulgar art amid the antifeminist backlash of the 1990s. Attending to the breadth of performance forms that play with sleep invites readers to think across genres, resisting the disciplinary separation of theater studies from art history in favor of noticing overlapping political concerns, artistic strategies, and material conditions of production and circulation.

At street level, these performances circulate in university, regional, and alternative theaters; multipurpose, nonprofit art and performance venues; and borrowed public spaces—including, in Yamaoka's work, actual street corners. At the global level, most of the performances circulate across national borders: They were constituted in transnational markets and address transnational political concerns. They all have iterations in North America—and at least some documentation in either English or Spanish—but they also travel among major cosmopolitan cities with significant arts scenes, from New York, San Antonio, Seattle, and Toronto to London, Madrid, and Tokyo. (And documentation travels beyond the performance sites themselves, ending up, for example, in an archive in Hong Kong or a museum in Washington, D.C.) Yet despite the globalized arts scene, the context of sleep performance matters, and these relocations have significant and unpredictable consequences. Churchill's play *Far Away,* which ends in a state of global warfare, had a much more engaged critical reception after it transferred to post-9/11 New York than it did when it premiered in London the year before. Acosta and Sosa's installation *Black Power Naps* faced unexpected controversy when it moved from smaller venues to New York's canonical Museum of Modern Art, where two

Black patrons were asked to leave an installation designed specifically for Black audiences. To represent these performances accurately, my archive exceeds the borders of North America, following the global migrations of feminist sleep performances.

And the conditions of globalization, of course, affect sleep. This is a prominent theme in Galindo's performance art piece *America's Family Prison,* which stages the sleeping conditions of a migrant family incarcerated at the U.S.–Mexico border, and in Yamaoka's participatory performance *Best Place to Sleep,* which uses public napping to interrupt bank patrons' access to the global flow of capital in ATM lobbies. Read alongside one another, these two performances measure the skewed velocities of global capitalism: Migrant families spend night after night stuck in place while money streams easily across borders. But the effects of globalization on sleep also haunt performances like Churchill's play *Fen,* which is set entirely in rural Britain and stages the parochial family dramas of women farmworkers. Even as the farmworkers dig potatoes on the same patch of land their ancestors cultivated, the pace and demand for their labor are accelerated by international investment, so that a British farmhand can be exhausted into desperation by a real estate deal executed by a multinational corporation. The global politics of immigration laws and international financial deregulation are materialized as the personal, bodily feelings of fatigue and burnout.

Within feminist activism, fatigue and burnout have by now become near clichés of feminist failure. The predominant metaphor of feminist waves suggests women care about their own liberation more in some moments and tire of politics in others. Yet fatigue, burnout, and periods of dormancy are manifestations of a genuine need for rest, evidence of both the round-the-clock ardency of activism during feminism's peaks and the vast structural resources mobilized by antifeminist opponents. Historian Sara M. Evans sees habitual, periodic disavowals of feminism as counterintuitive evidence of the power of feminist visions of change:

> The stereotype that women's liberation activists were "shrill" and "ugly" points us to the militancy of the women's liberation movement, and the radical, utopian, sometimes apocalyptic, expectations of a particular moment in the New Left,

> both in the United States and around the world: the belief that *everything could change, perhaps overnight.*[17]

To Evans's description of women's liberation in the late 1960s, political theorist Verónica Gago adds the "indeterminate potencia"—the dynamic power—of international feminist movements of the 2010s, "expressed as *the desire to change everything.*"[18] Tired clichés of feminists as unlikable and uncompromising belie their visionary power and wholehearted commitment to uproot and remake the world, for themselves and for others, and to do it as soon as possible. When you can almost grasp this future in front of you, who has time for sleep?

The feminist sleep performances discussed in this book emerged from the conditions of living in a world that did not transform overnight but instead changed incrementally and fitfully. Beginning with Anderson's performance-photography project *Institutional Dream Series* (1972–73), these feminist sleep performances strive to make sense of or feel their way through the distance between a particular vision of a revolutionary future and the frustrating knowledge that it has not arrived overnight. This making sense of and feeling through is exhausting, and feminist sleep performances examine how various iterations of feminism have grappled with this exhaustion—and simultaneously how they imagine and briefly enact less exhausting ways of living out feminist commitments. The subtitle's reference to "feminist performance *and practice*" signals my hope that this book will contribute to the work of a constellation of feminist writers who study sleep and allied forms of rest as collective, direct-action practices.[19] These practices intervene in systems of gendered, racialized capitalism whose growth depends on exhausting disempowered and disabled people out of the will to resist. This writing foregrounds the vernacular theory of people who reclaim rest from histories of slavery, colonial extraction, and labor exploitation, who forge networks of caring and activism from bedroom to bedroom. The ensuing chapters interweave the particular tactics and capabilities of performance more fully into this conversation about sleep, politics, and aesthetics.

But the story of *The Tent* is not quite over. *The Tent*'s life as an art object at the turn of the twenty-first century can be read as a potent fable about the need for feminist interventions in the social structures that shelter sleep. The artwork was purchased by Charles Saatchi, the collector who bankrolled *Sensation*. Along with his prodigious art collecting, Saatchi is best known as the cofounder of the advertising firm that catapulted Margaret Thatcher into power in the United Kingdom with the campaign slogan "Labour isn't working." Like many of Saatchi's acquisitions—and many artworks across the high-end global art market—*The Tent* was tucked away in a warehouse, London's Momart storage facility. When the warehouse caught fire on the evening of May 24, 2004, *The Tent* was destroyed.[20] Emin never re-created *The Tent*.

Read in the context of a wealthy nation like the United Kingdom at the turn of the twenty-first century, the story of *The Tent*'s immolation asks us to consider the threats to sleep posed by austerity politics.[21] Saatchi is hired to get Thatcher elected; she goes on to lead a government that cuts social welfare programs, crushes unions, and interferes in postcolonial states already impoverished by imperial extraction. By the time *The Tent* debuts in 1995, Britain's New Labour leaders are embracing deregulated market economics at the cost of public safety. *The Tent* perishes in a fire that an underfunded social service, the London Fire Brigade, cannot reach in time. This fire will pale in comparison to the Grenfell Tower fire of 2017, which kills seventy-two Londoners as they sleep in public housing that, owing to continued deregulation, is covered in flammable cladding and has been failing fire risk assessments without consequence for five years.[22] In a world where systems of shelter and care have been so inequitably distributed, sleep can be fatal for the most vulnerable among us. Yet, except in these brief moments of disaster, the conditions of sleep remain out of sight and out of mind, behind closed doors or beyond closed eyes. Feminist sleep performances ask spectators to confront sleep not just as a biological need but as a social practice that reveals existing inequities in unexpected ways—and that might indeed be put to work to change the world.

Falling Asleep at the Theater

Sleep performance can seem like an oxymoron. Sleep is when we are least likely to be "performing" and are most exposed as ourselves.

Perhaps because sleep strikes us as nonperformative, we often overlook sleep in theater—only to realize, when prompted, that sleep is everywhere in the history of staged drama. From Aeschylus to Shakespeare to Calderón to Wagner, scenes of punishing insomnia, revelatory sleepwalking, elaborate dreams, and supernatural slumber have filled our amphitheaters and corrales and opera houses. But in the late nineteenth century, with the advent of a professionalized European proscenium theater staging naturalist drama, new dramatic conventions that disciplined spectators' bodies and behaviors made sleep a practical problem for audiences. It became easier than ever for a spectator to fall asleep in a dark theater where one was not supposed to speak or move. Sleep became an unexpectedly common concern in the professionalizing European theater and the twentieth-century Anglophone drama it influenced, and sleep appeared as a favored act in performance art from the early days of the art form. At the same time, a rash of new plays arrived to grapple with problem women. August Strindberg's 1888 play *Miss Julie* puts the late nineteenth-century "woman question," the danger of sleeping spectators, and the new conventions of modern drama together onstage. Theater scholars often turn to Strindberg's famous preface to *Miss Julie* to unearth the troubling class and gender politics of his influential naturalist staging conventions. Sleep is an overlooked connection between the preface's theory of theatrical form and the story of the play, which unfolds over one midsummer night. In this play and its preface, we see that modern dramatic forms, feminist politics onstage, and sleep at the theater are not merely coincidental: They mutually constitute one another.

Just a few lines about sleeping habits in *Miss Julie* reveal the central dynamic among the play's characters: the cook Kristine, who has fallen asleep; her fiancé Jean, the valet; and their mistress Julie.

> **JULIE:** What a pleasant wife she'll make! She probably snores, too.
>
> **JEAN:** No she doesn't, but she talks in her sleep.
>
> **JULIE:** *(cynically).* How do you know?
>
> **JEAN:** *(audaciously).* I've heard her! *(Pause, during which they stare at each other.)*[23]

As soon as Jean reveals Kristine talks in her sleep, we assume they have slept together. Julie's sexual jealousy, hinted at when she suggests that Kristine snores, becomes full-blown. Jean's provocative revelation has succeeded. Later in the scene Kristine indeed speaks in her sleep, and Kristine and Jean's sexual relationship is confirmed. If sleep is a part of life in which we cannot perform but must instead be ourselves, then Kristine's somniloquy is firm evidence. Unlike the elaborate, highly artificed performances of seduction that Jean and Julie enact, Kristine's sleep is real.

The plan for modern drama that Strindberg lays out in his preface is formed by the limits of spectatorial attention. The preface is a theoretical statement in which Strindberg holds up his play as an exemplar for a new kind of theater practice aimed at political instruction. He sets the length of *Miss Julie* at ninety minutes, concerned that "our dwindling capacity for accepting illusion is perhaps further disturbed by intermissions" and landing on ninety minutes as not "too tiring" for spectators to handle.[24] The ninety-minute, no-intermission play remains a conventional dramatic form today. Strindberg, moreover, worries that audiences at intermission may break free of the "suggestive influence of the author-hypnotist": He wants his audiences attentive but not free to think as they will. Indeed, this is Julie's fate in her eponymous play. Having spent all of the night of midsummer's eve awake, plotting unlikely escapes from her father's estate with Jean, she realizes her only realistic exit will be like that of a spectator seeing "a hypnotist in the theater" (941). The hypnotist would instruct a hypnotized ("sleeping") spectator to sweep with a broom. "Here's the broom!" Jean says as he hands Julie a sharpened razor. "I'm going now to rest!" Julie responds, and she marches out the door, razor in hand. So Julie and the audience of *Miss Julie* are in the same position, awake straight through a night collapsed into ninety minutes and yet, paradoxically, "sleeping" under the influence of the author-theater-hypnotist as the morning dawns onstage and the curtain falls across the proscenium. Julie is "going now to rest," but the spectators will actually go to rest, leaving an evening at the theater for their beds at home.

Yet Strindberg's modern dramatic form—naturalist drama—does not intend to promote spectatorial sympathy with Julie. In his preface, Strindberg calls Julie "a modern character," but also a "man-hating half-woman" and "a retrogressive step in evolution." It is the job of naturalist drama to "dissipate" this character and instruct audiences in "happiness . . . for the strong and skillful species" of humans.[25] In the play, Julie is explicitly the daughter of a feminist, a woman "brought up believing in social equality, women's rights, and all that," who refused to marry and got caught up in a romantic (and not at all naturalist) tangle of hysteria, adultery, arson, and belated insurance payments (935–36). Julie's mother's story parodies the plots of Henrik Ibsen's contemporaneous plays *A Doll's House* and *Ghosts.* Whereas Ibsen writes characters like Julie's mother, facing problems common to women in an unequal society, as the centerpiece of his naturalism, Strindberg makes Julie's mother a cautionary tale unsuited to the naturalist form that relays it. (Like Konstantin's mother in Anton Chekhov's *The Seagull,* Julie's mother is stuck in the wrong dramatic form, as naturalism moves forward without her.) Julie's mother's story is a parable that instructs spectators in the unsuitability of women to advance the race, while Strindberg's ninety-minute naturalist form holds them in a state of receptive attention. Be hypnotized like Julie, in order to learn not to *be* like Julie.

While Julie spends midsummer's eve both awake and hypnotized, the cook Kristine actually sleeps in her chair in the kitchen. And at some point, stage directions indicate, Kristine "*awakens and shambles sleepily off right to bed*" (930). Yet, unlike Strindberg's otherwise precisely timed directions, this particular note allows Kristine to wake, exit, and fall asleep again offstage at any point over twenty-five lines of dialogue. The timing is up to the actor playing the role. Kristine, unlike Julie, does not move at the hypnotist's command, and she is unwilling to be audience to Julie and Jean's performance of seduction. Unlike Kristine, the real audience at Strindberg's modern drama would have found it hard to get up and walk out. In service of a pedagogical naturalism, a naturalism that hypnotizes spectators despite their diminishing attention spans, Strindberg inadvertently creates the staging conventions of modern drama that lead some spectators to fall asleep mid-show. In contrast to a large thrust stage, which would tend to spill more light onto the audience seating, Strindberg calls for "complete darkness during performances" on "a *small* stage" and in "a *small* auditorium."[26] With more specific, focused lighting technology now available, Strindberg also turns off the footlights that had made all the actors' faces more visible across the width of the stage. He even nixes late seating for spectators whose pre-show dinners run long. Strindberg thus plunges spectators into a cramped, completely dark house, after a rushed, early dinner, and forbids the temptations of intermissions and well-made-up actresses—creating the conditions for audience sleep even as he strives to make audiences pay closer attention. Many theaters today continue to follow this model of proscenium staging and spectatorial behavior, and many audience members still fall asleep at the theater.

But the spectators who did not fall asleep watching Strindberg's new form of modern drama could learn something from new plays *about sleep*. Beyond the archive I have gleaned under the rubric of feminist sleep performance, sleep plays a surprisingly meaty role in the history of modern drama. Playwrights use sleep dramaturgically, to intervene in dramatic structure and theatrical conventions, and thematically, to illustrate political concerns.

Along with the nineteenth-century women's rights and social equality movements represented by Miss Julie's mother, ideas from Charles Darwin, Karl Marx, and Sigmund Freud inspired modern dramatic innovation, and these legacies also come to light in how playwrights use sleep onstage. In turn-of-the-century naturalist and social realist theater, sleep often symbolizes failing regimes of power. Chekhov's *The Cherry Orchard* ends as the aging servant Firs, born a serf, lies down for a nap. Left behind when his employer finally sells her family estate, Firs falls asleep—or perhaps dies—just as the aristocratic landholding class who determined the conditions of his existence is forced to retire their social control. George Bernard Shaw also uses sleep to mark the failures of a political regime in *Heartbreak House,* translating Chekhov's technique to an Anglophone context, and Samuel Beckett lifts sleep-or-death out of its naturalist origins entirely for his absurdist apocalyptic play *Endgame. Endgame* ends with the character Hamm alone onstage in his wheelchair, his eyes covered. This may be just another nap—or it may be the death of the last living creature in the world.

Throughout the twentieth century, U.S. theater about class and racial divides continued to deploy sleep as an onstage indicator of political apathy or exhaustion. The uneven distribution of rest in these plays parallels the division of labor within the professional theater, which makes the working day (or working evening) of the actors and crew contiguous with the leisure time of the audience.[27] In the midcentury musical *The Pajama Game,* members of the Sleeptite Pajama Factory's labor union stay up all night negotiating with their boss for a seven-and-a-half-cent raise. When they achieve a contract, they celebrate with a plant-wide pajama fashion show, and then the leader of the union grievance committee, Babe, heads off to sleep, splitting a set of pajamas with the factory foreman. (Babe wears the pajama top; the foreman gets the bottoms.) Sleep marks an accord—or a compromise in labor values. In Adam P. Kennedy and Adrienne Kennedy's play *Sleep Deprivation Chamber,* sleep enters the play in name only. Sleep is an absent peace, missing when Adam, a Black man, is beaten by a white police officer but then arrested for assault. Kennedy and Kennedy forge a direct link between racial policing and Black exhaustion.

While naturalists and their heirs developed sleep onstage as a social critique, sleep onstage freed the surrealists to explore the associative, elliptical structures of dream logic as a new dramatic form. The paradigmatic example is Strindberg's *A Dream Play,* adapted more than a century later by Caryl Churchill. Dream is a powerful tool for theater artists to match the playing space to the human psyche, as Marjorie Garber argues in *Dream in Shakespeare,* which proves the richness of psychoanalysis for dramatic criticism.[28] Freudian readings of dreams entered commercial U.S. theater in the 1930s via the dream ballet, a device of musical comedies.[29] Dream ballets are discrete dances that interrupt the narrative to show off virtuosic performance skill. These choreographed sequences express a character's repressed, unspeakable desires through symbolic dance rather than dialogue—and they can also redistribute the labor of playing the dreaming protagonist between two performers. In some dream ballets, the actor playing the sleeping character lies down or exits the stage while a trained dancer takes over to perform the choreography. With this substitution, the dream ballet fills a practical theatrical need for rest through the division of labor, allowing the actor playing the dreamer to take a break while the action continues. The revelation of a character's deepest wishes can, paradoxically, materialize via the body of a stand-in dancer in a sort of theatrical Freudian displacement.

In some queer dramas, the relationship between personal desire and social risk coalesces in the political implications of the shared bed. When the musical *Falsettos* opened off-Broadway in 1979, it was perhaps the first time mainstream U.S. theater audiences saw two men sleep in the same bed onstage, outside an explicitly gay venue. In the same year, Martin Sherman's play *Bent* opened in London with two men sleeping beside each other in Berlin on the Night of the Long Knives. Their slumber is the last moment of protected queer life afforded by the twilight of Weimar Germany before the play follows its protagonist to Dachau. And sleep is the medium for new forms of relationality in Tony Kushner's *Angels in America.* While the ways gay men in the play meet each other are reshaped by the AIDS crisis, sleep allows for other, maybe queerer, meetings: between a man and his ex-boyfriend's new lover's wife in a shared dream scene, and between that same man and a majestic, bureaucratic angel who crashes through the ceiling above his bed. The line between dream encounters and real social relations blurs.

The shared bed is also, of course, a fruitful site for comedy. In modern musical comedies, the bed becomes the site of forbidden (or at least discouraged) romance. Mary Rodgers's musical *Once upon a Mattress,* based on Hans Christian Andersen's story "The Princess and the Pea," finds a scheming queen complaining in song about her "sensitivity" to lumpy mattresses before she realizes that she might use this sensitivity to prove her son's would-be bride is not truly a princess.[30] A stack of twenty mattresses, a strong sedative, and a single pea strike her as a fair test of the princess's claim to royal blood. (The 1959 Broadway production of *Once upon a Mattress* contended with its own relationship prejudices: For the role of the queen, biracial actor Jane White was asked to lighten her skin, so that the production could avoid an apparently interracial marriage with the white actor playing the king.)[31] The princess ultimately spends a long night counting sheep and passes the queen's test—with some help. A sleepless night offers similar proof of the power of love, or at least infatuation, in the face of prejudice in Jeanine Tesori and Lisa Kron's musical *Fun Home.* The character Medium Alison, a first-year college student agog at the pleasures of lesbian sex, belts out her plan to "chang[e] her major to sex with

Joan / with a minor in kissing Joan" as her new lover snoozes in her dorm room bed, miraculously oblivious to the noise.[32]

Along with performances that deploy sleep as a symbol or dramaturgical device, some performances make sleep their central theme. Yoko Ono and John Lennon's *Bed-ins for Peace* argued for the political potential of staying in bed rather than going to war; two years later, Vietnam veterans would perform Ono and Lennon's song "Give Peace a Chance" alongside the cast of the musical *Hair* before camping out illegally on the Washington Mall in their own antiwar sleep performance.[33] Ultimately, many performance artworks, from Chris Burden's *Bed Piece* to Cornelia Parker's *The Maybe* to Trajal Harrell's *The Ambien Piece/Tickle the Sleeping Giant,* put sleeping people into galleries as artistic objects. Sleep performance art also overlaps with the genre of durational performance, as in the yearlong performances of Tehching Hsieh, which, by virtue of their length, involve significant manipulation of sleep. Like performance art, theater about sleep in the late twentieth century made personal sleep experiences public, dramatizing neuroscientists' newfound access to the inner workings of sleepers' brains. In the 1980s, Harold Pinter's one-act play *A Kind of Alaska* adapted a popular nonfiction study of people living with encephalitis lethargica, or sleeping sickness. The Living Theatre's devised work *The Archaeology of Sleep* took its structure from then-novel research into human sleep phases (such as REM and non-REM sleep), staging a grab bag of sleep material, from experiments on sleep deprivation in cats to the actors' recollections of their own dreams (many of which concerned arriving late to rehearsal). Although at least one reviewer of *The Archaeology of Sleep* found it irredeemably soporific, plays like it strive to dig up the drama immanent in sleep research.[34]

But—as Strindberg's preface cautions—the characters onstage are not the only people who might be sleeping at the theater. In her study of theater audiences, Susan Bennett describes spectators who fall asleep as "refus[ing] the collective contract" of theatergoing, albeit in a "less dramatic" way than exiting the theater entirely.[35] Whether to fight or cede to the quiet refusal practiced by a snoozing spectator is a question at the heart of a cluster of immersive performances at the turn of the twenty-first century. Immersive theater-makers are, like Strindberg, concerned with reshaping audience behavior and attention. In the British company Punchdrunk's immersive piece *Sleep No More,* for example, audience members were encouraged to run around a multistory set, chasing after the performers as the action moved from room to room. The title of the piece, lifted from *Macbeth,* spells out how hard the performance worked to keep the spectators awake and active.[36] Other recent immersive performances have tried to use the theater to induce sleep. Queer theater troupe Duckie's *Lullaby* and choreographer Jim Findlay's *Dream of the Red Chamber* both filled performance spaces with beds or cots and immersed spectators in dream worlds populated by giant animal puppets or mesmerizing modern dancers. Tricia Hersey's Nap Ministry workshops and Diana Oh's sleepover *Infinite Love Party* took a more targeted approach, intervening in the uneven distribution of sleep by crafting opportunities for restful sleep for historically oppressed populations.

Outside the theater or gallery, sleep sometimes takes on the qualities of a performance as part of an intervention—conscious or unconscious—in the social world. In 2018, a church in the Netherlands conducted continuous religious services, twenty-four hours a day for ninety-six days, in order to maintain the church as an inviolable space of sanctuary under Dutch law. By sheltering one immigrant family from deportation, this ongoing religious vigil provoked the Dutch government to agree to reassess the deportation orders standing against seven hundred families.[37] In Sweden, hundreds of children of Roma and Uyghur families fell into a mysterious, long-term slumber when their families' asylum claims were rejected. They became "apathetic," unresponsive, and dependent on feeding tubes. Many of the children's families received Swedish residency status as a result of a child's endangered health, and, once their immigration status had stabilized, the apathetic children recovered.[38] It is hard to know whether to classify these traumatized children's supernaturally long sleep as performance. No one suggests the children were consciously feigning sleep, as an actor does onstage, but they defied neuroscientists' understanding of sleep in that their unresponsive bodies seemed prompted to sleep—sometimes for years—only by social and environmental circumstances, rather than a biological need for rest. At some deep level of their brains, they may have been *acting* asleep.

At the end of the day, sleep and theater are both daily, repetitive, often-ritualized practices. Sleep biologists identify sleep in animals by looking for a cluster of repeated behaviors, such as "circling, yawning, [or] nest-making," that recur roughly once every twenty-four hours.[39] Bits of behavior enacted repeatedly is one definition commonly offered for *performance*; repeated ritual behavior every night certainly sounds like *theater.* We could find any number of analogous nightly rituals between theater conventions and at-home sleep habits: In the theater, for example, lowering the house lights signals the beginning of the show, while at home, turning off lights is a part of getting ready for bed. Plugging in the ghost light at the end of a night's performance might be compared to switching on a security light or a child's night light at home—lighting a single bulb to create a sense of safety in the vast dark.

And backstage at any professional theater in the United States, the "Equity cot," a labor union requirement, gives actors a place to nap during long technical rehearsals or two-show days. The Equity cot was dreamed up by Broadway dancer Jeanna Belkin in 1946, when a fellow performer with menstrual cramps needed to lie down.[40] Belkin's activism on her colleague's behalf anticipated larger claims about women's health and women in the workplace that would be staples of 1960s and 1970s feminism. Rather than diminishing menstrual pain as merely a woman's problem, Belkin wielded the Equity cot as a practical response to the bodily need for rest, the hard work of theatrical performance, and the potential of organized labor to protect theater workers from exhaustion. Any Kristine in a professional U.S. production of *Miss Julie* can "shamble sleepily" offstage to bed—and then actually lie down on the cot backstage until her next entrance. Like *Miss Julie,* the story of the Equity cot braids together sleep, feminism, and performance—with a shift of focus from the drama onstage to the artistic labor that makes that drama possible.

Waking Up, Burning Out, Discovering Possibilities

Like sleep and performance, sleep and feminism have a long and perhaps counterintuitive history together. Arguing that women are neither essentially weak nor inherently attuned to the domestic sphere, feminists hardly seem to benefit from admitting any special interest in sleep. Yet premodern and early modern writings by women, such as Sei Shōnagon's *The Pillow Book* (eleventh century) and Juana Inés de la Cruz's *First [I] Dream* (1692), make formally innovative, evocative use of the material culture of the bedroom and the peregrinations of the sleeping mind. By the mid- to late nineteenth century, self-identified feminists in many parts of the world were writing in pursuit of political change—and sleep became a curious part of this body of work. Not making headlines as a prominent campaign, sleep still appeared, sporadically yet reliably, as both a material issue and a set of generative metaphors, in the work of writers affiliated with quite varied, and sometimes conflicting, feminist projects. From their late nineteenth-century origins onward, feminists have used *awakening* as a metaphor for coming to feminist consciousness while also naming *fatigue, tiredness, exhaustion,* and *burnout* as material effects of the overwork, discrimination, and violence underwritten by social injustice.

In feminist writings, sleep traverses the blurry border separating the material from the metaphorical, linking a nightly private experience to widespread conditions of living. In her 1964 speech "I'm Sick and Tired of Being Sick and Tired," civil rights leader Fannie Lou Hamer names the material conditions of exhaustion, in the face of ongoing anti-Black violence, as the defining metaphor of her existence. She begins by saying that she does not live but merely "exist[s]" in the town of Ruleville, Mississippi, where she has been evicted by her white landlord and beaten by white police for organizing Black voter registration. Hamer yokes the ways life in Ruleville has made her physically ill and exhausted to an existential fatigue, a tiredness she can neither escape nor live with. "After we would work ten and eleven hours a day for three lousy dollars and couldn't sleep," she says of her fellow sharecroppers, "we couldn't do anything else but think. And we have been thinking a long time. And we are tired of what's going on."[41] Hamer calls on her audience in Harlem to see that their freedom is tied to her freedom in Mississippi, to see that as long as she is physically and existentially exhausted by U.S. racism, their lives too remain circumscribed.

Hamer's titular claim, "I'm sick and tired of being sick and tired," is an epanalepsis, a phrase repeated after intervening words. An epanalepsis in speech is an intentional echo; the figure begins and ends with the same sounds. Like many classical rhetorical figures, it has auditory power. Like a people's microphone at a rally, the repetition of the epanaleptic phrase, of "sick and tired," amplifies it and anchors it in the audience's memory. But Hamer, a skilled rhetorical performer, also refracts this repeated phrase into two distinct meanings: The first is metaphorical; the second, material. (Like Emin, Hamer draws her audience's attention to the literal experiences of rest and exhaustion underwriting a commonplace expression with a double meaning.) Hamer's tiredness is brought on by external material conditions—by exhausting labor and a pervasive climate of violence and injustice—but it takes root and grows inside her mind and body, becoming the kind of fatigue that keeps her up at night. Hamer's wakefulness might be what Christina Sharpe describes as a Black American experience of being "in the wake." Being in the wake has many meanings, but one is "*the state of wakefulness; consciousness,*" consciousness "of the unfinished project of emancipation," consciousness that comes from "a position of deep hurt and deep knowledge."[42] Wakefulness and fatigue become political motivations even as they shorten Hamer's life, for this fatigue cannot be solved by sleep alone.[43] In calling on her audience in New York to join the work of the Mississippi Freedom Democratic Party, Hamer asserts that her ill health and exhaustion are neither accidental nor her fault, and she cannot fix them on her own—she depends on collective political action that pursues a future in which she does not merely exist but can live.

Both alongside and against such accounts of women's fatigue, feminists speak of awakening. The oblique pain of coming to recognize one's own oppression is figured as both inexplicable tiredness and persistent insomnia in the most famous white middle-class woman's account of feminist awakening, Betty Friedan's *The Feminine Mystique* (1963). Writing only a year before Hamer's speech, Friedan recounts an epidemic of "housewife's fatigue" among 1950s suburbanites. She conjures up the archetypal not-yet-feminist housewife as insistently awake, "[lying] beside her husband at night . . . afraid to ask even of herself the silent question—'Is this all?'"[44] In recent years, researchers have used "awakening" to characterize large feminist political movements in sites as far-flung as Rwanda, Argentina, and China; the metaphor has a global reach.[45] But the meaning of awakening is unexpectedly slippery.

On the surface, feminist awakening indicates a moment of conversion to feminist consciousness—opening one's eyes to a new way of seeing the world. Yet the metaphor of awakening, which is also used widely beyond feminist contexts, can suggest an absence of critical reflection, a thoughtless compulsion to action, as involuntary as the bodily phenomenon of waking up in the morning. Crary points to the Nazi rallying cry "Deutschland erwache!"—Germany awake![46] Indeed, there is nothing specifically feminist or specifically liberatory about awakening as a metaphor for a change in political consciousness. It can connote mindless and inexplicable political transformation; on its own, therefore, the act of awakening does not capture the full story of feminist engagements with sleep and rest.

On the heels of stories of awakening come stories of feminism itself as a source of very real fatigue. It is commonplace to read activist burnout (along with trashing, infighting, and factionalism) as indicative of feminism's many failures, and these histories do represent real problems of racism, classism, homophobia, transphobia, and other harms. But burnout is also evidence of feminists' desire, and deep need, to change their lives.[47] The sleep performances examined in this book emerge from this distance between how particular performers or onstage characters imagine feminism can change their lives and the slow, frustrating, sometimes deadening process of working to get there. In their groundbreaking pamphlet *Women and the Subversion of the Community* (1972), Mariarosa Dalla Costa and Selma James exhort their readers to fight for a way of living in which women's socialized skills in childcare and housework are not exploited to power capitalism. "Women must completely discover their own possibilities," they proclaim, "which are neither mending socks nor becoming captains of oceangoing ships," but an as-yet-unimagined future beyond the sexual division of labor.[48] This process of discovery often involves a reckoning with structural change and collective action, with forging connections between individuals and larger activist projects, audience members, or fellow artists.

The following preview of upcoming chapters ties these experiments in discovering possibilities to key themes of feminist sleep performance. The book's four sections spotlight sites where the thematic entanglements of feminism and sleep repeat across my archive: the unreliable body, the family and the household labor it demands, networks of care among queer and trans friends, and public spaces remade into places for rest. I pair sleep performances that share a thematic focus but emerge in different times and places, so that sleep—this odd recurring character in feminist performance history—can illuminate multiple ways of understanding and reimagining some of feminism's foundational concerns.

Part I, "In Our Bodies," opens with sleep performances that reconsider the sleeping woman's body as an aesthetic object. The first chapter situates U.S. multimedia artist Laurie Anderson's *Institutional Dream Series* amid feminist body politics of the early 1970s. *Institutional Dream Series* is an early-career performance series documenting Anderson's sleep in public New York City sites. Although Anderson's project initially looks like a conventional exploration of the passive woman's body exposed to male-coded institutional power, *Institutional Dream Series* skews this gendered binary as Anderson's experiments with public sleep instigate unexpected dramas. From the premise of an artistic project in which the artist herself cannot see what is happening to the presence of a hidden artistic collaborator (unseen in the performance documentation), *Institutional Dream Series* transforms quiet, brief public naps into flashes of insight into the performance potential of a woman asleep. Chapter 2 turns from asking how a spectator views a sleeping woman to consider how U.S. theater artist Peggy Shaw keeps her audience *from* sleeping in her solo performance *Menopausal Gentleman* (1997). Picking up 1990s queer theory debates between futurity and nihilism, Shaw's sleep performance establishes a feminist disability project of *self*-reproduction aimed neither at future generations nor annihilation but instead at survival until the near future of the next morning. *Menopausal Gentleman* dramatizes Shaw's own menopausal insomnia in order to test whether Shaw, as she ages, can hold her audience's attention without a climactic scene of violence. Read in conversation with Audre Lorde's and Eve Kosofsky Sedgwick's autotheoretical narratives of breast cancer, *Menopausal Gentleman* becomes a performance about the nonviolent, nondramatic story of a woman coaxing her restless body toward sleep.

Part II, "At Home," turns to the unavoidable figure of the mother in feminist theories of fatigue. Chapter 3 looks at the work of Caryl

Churchill, a key playwright of the socialist feminist movement, to excavate the reproductive labor lurking in the genre of domestic drama. In each of the Churchill plays *Three More Sleepless Nights* (1980), *Fen* (1983), and *Far Away* (2000), a central housewife character becomes conscious of her domestic workload when she becomes unusually unable to sleep. This sleeplessness becomes a powerful destabilizing force with formal repercussions. Read as part of an ongoing engagement with the feminist analysis of social reproduction, these plays translate the underrealized potential of overworked housewives as a political class into an uprising against the formal conventions of domestic drama. Whereas Churchill's housewives are trapped in their family homes, chapter 4 explores a feat of endurance art that asks what particular power mothers might have to stop the suffering of a family beyond their own households' walls. In the twenty-four-hour performance *America's Family Prison* (2008), Guatemalan body artist Regina José Galindo spent the night in an immigration jail cell with her partner and young child, restaging the experience of real incarcerated migrant families. I read this performance in conversation with another drama of maternal politics at bedtime, Bertolt Brecht's *Mother Courage and Her Children,* to compare performance tactics for activating maternal solidarity across militarized borders. Galindo ventures away from familiar endurance performances of virtuosic bodily suffering and into less charted territory, risking the comfort of her own sleeping family to urge her spectators toward anticarceral action.

Part III, "Among Friends," looks to plays that exploit sleep and theater as twinned sites for confronting what cannot be faced in the conscious, offstage world. The performances addressed in this section are, it follows, the craggiest of the book: They self-consciously evade interpretation, slipping away from any sort of triumphal feminist claims and reminding us that sleep onstage is the realm of the shadowy and the subconscious, the modernist and the surreal. Chapter 5 examines fantasies of reciprocal queer care in staged dreams in Cuban-born playwright María Irene Fornés's drama *Enter THE NIGHT* (1993). The play brings together three friends whose relationships with each other have become limited to tasks of caretaking in the face of heart disease and HIV/AIDS. When the friends fall asleep, they enact dream fantasies of libidinal and aesthetic richness, drawing on a dense tissue of shared camp references, from films of the Chinese Exclusion Era to the Theatre of the Ridiculous. Unlike contemporaneous AIDS plays in which white gay men care for one another through illness, cementing a proud gay cultural lineage, Fornés's play approaches care and death through fantasies of racial-sexual transformation, of shedding identities rather than celebrating them. The scope of care dilates to include a caring work of theatrical adaptation in chapter 6, which reads British playwright Sarah Kane's insomniac play *4.48 Psychosis* (2000) in conversation with its first adaptation, a chamber opera created by British composer Philip Venables (2016). *4.48 Psychosis* dramatizes mental illness and gender dysphoria as chronic, existentially threatening sleep loss. Against the grain of Kane criticism, I read *4.48 Psychosis* as a trans/queer archive of both care and death. Venables's opera adaptation is at the crux of late twentieth-century feminist and queer opera studies, which battle over whether opera is an antifeminist spectacle of violence against women or a lavishly queer celebration of antinormative sexuality. Read as an act of intergenerational trans/queer care for Kane's text, the opera both marks a turning point in how theater history regards this posthumous play and intervenes in the operatic convention of Black soprano death onstage.

Part IV, "Out in the World," follows sleep performance out of the theater and into a twenty-first-century world in which sleep itself is increasingly accepted as both political and monetizable—and not as far outside the realm of capitalism as we might hope. The final chapter examines two participatory, transnational artworks that ask spectators to nap in public in order to reclaim space and time for sleep. In *Best Place to Sleep* (2007–12), Japanese performance artist Sakiko Yamaoka led participants in group naps at sites of global capital flow, such as luxury shopping districts and bank lobbies. In *Black Power Naps* (2018–23), Latin American multimedia artists Navild Acosta and Fannie Sosa created an installation of fantastic beds that invite Black and Indigenous people to reclaim public daytime rest. Amid myriad participatory sleep performances in the 2010s, these pieces are uniquely attuned to the etiology of lost or poor sleep in the syncopations of global capital and the long historical reverberations of slavery. Yet, even as the performances discussed in this book mobilize sleep as a tactic of feminist survival and sustainability, untimely deaths haunt their production histories. My coda appraises the close resemblance between sleep and death onstage. I counterpose two sleep performances across a span of four hundred years: William Shakespeare's late play *Cymbeline* (circa 1611) and U.S. opera singer Davóne Tines's short music film *Vigil (an exercise in empathy)* (2020), created after the murder of Breonna Taylor. These two performances sit at the troubling crossroads of sleep and violent death. When audiences watch a performance like this, what makes their spectatorship an act of political witness rather than one of mere voyeurism? By returning to this enduring question of political spectatorship, I ask what role sleep performance might play in the as-yet-uncharted future of feminist imagination.

Feminist theory and theatrical production share a fascination with the basic practices of daily life. The live, three-dimensional, time-based capacities of theater and performance make acts of everyday living—embracing a friend, swallowing a pill, nursing a baby, stopping by the bank—objects of rapt attention. Among these daily acts, sleep is unique because we cannot observe ourselves enacting it; watching sleep onstage offers privileged access to a daily event that dims our senses and obscures our memories. But, while sleep is unique in this way, it is not at all disconnected from the politics of the waking world. Sleep indexes the inequities of our lives both within the volatility and exhaustion of late capitalism and after more than fifty years of ardent feminist intervention in the world. Attending to sleep in performance opens a gateway to attending to all that is overlooked or unregarded in daily existence, to questioning the fundamental given conditions of how we live out our days among one another. Sleep puts theater to the test, demanding that playwrights and artists fully exercise the faculties of this art form to hold a mirror—or perhaps a microscope—up to what goes unnoticed in daily life and to experiment with ways of coexisting that we have not yet fully grasped.

Part One

In Our Bodies

One
Not a Sleeping Beauty
Feminist Visual Culture in the Early Performance Art of Laurie Anderson

The poem "The Day the Mountains Move," by Yosano Akiko, is an eight-line call to feminist action. Written for a Japanese women's magazine in 1911, it announces: "The day the mountains move has come." Although "for a long time the mountains have been asleep," in the past they "danced with fire." Akiko alerts her audience that this slumber is coming to an end: "All the sleeping women / Are now awake and moving."[1] In the early 1970s, the founder of the Chicago Women's Liberation Rock Band, psychologist Naomi Weisstein, revised Akiko's lyric into a propulsive refrain for her song "Mountain Moving Day," in which the band members chanted, "All sleeping women now awake and move / All sleeping women now awake and move."[2] In Akiko's original and Weisstein's adaptation, the sleeping woman is not the conventional figure of feminist awakening, a woman sleepwalking through her life until something shakes her awake to political consciousness. Instead, Akiko's and Weisstein's sleeping women are storehouses of banked power, dormant volcanoes who will dance with fire again. Akiko's poem, written from a volcanic archipelago, is a weather report. The women are moving, and, as with tectonic plates, their movement is not under human control, nor is it on a timescale within human experience. In reaching back to a time long ago, before the mountains were asleep, Akiko conjures premodern feminisms against a narrative of men's natural and age-old power. The poem is also a performative utterance: If I publish a poem saying the sleeping women are now awake and moving, I am one of the awake and moving women, part of the volcanic eruption. And in Weisstein's rock song, the lyric is an imperative: You women listening to me, wake up and *move.*

Weather reports, rock music, sleeping women, the 1970s: This chapter could only be about Laurie Anderson. Perhaps no performer has explored sleep as a source of embodied knowledge about the world, and its weather, more thoroughly and imaginatively than Anderson. A multimedia performance artist who would eventually sign a record deal with Warner Bros., Anderson began her interdisciplinary career in 1972 with the little-known sleep performance *Institutional Dream Series.* In this work, Anderson experimented with her own sleeping body as a powerful, finely calibrated technology for perceiving and reimagining the social and material conditions of her world. For this performance, Anderson slept alone in public spaces in New York City at a time when "the whole city was so broke and so unsafe," yet *Institutional Dream Series* is not a straightforward illustration of the bodily vulnerability of a sleeping woman in public, male-coded space.[3] Instead, the sleeping Anderson is, like Akiko's sleeping mountains, a kind of dormant volcano, deeply attentive and responsive to shifts in her environment, even as she appears insensate. And, like the music of Weisstein and the Chicago Women's Liberation Rock Band, early Anderson performances are in conversation with the eruption of feminist performance forms in the late 1960s and early 1970s. *Institutional Dream Series* set the stage for Anderson's lifelong interrogation of the world around her through the unconventional epistemological wellspring of the performing—and sleeping—body.

The body is a battleground, as Barbara Kruger would later say, and the body became a formative battleground for feminists by the 1970s.[4] No battle cry makes this clearer than the title chosen for the revolutionary health textbook collectively researched, written, and published by women, for women, from 1969 to 1973: *Our Bodies, Ourselves.*[5] But "our bodies, ourselves" was also the spirit of the day in the emerging field of feminist performance: Performance artists and theorists from Yoko Ono to Laura Mulvey were naming and contesting the role of the passive woman's body as a source of visual pleasure for presumed-male audiences. And across many spheres of daily life, feminists were claiming bodily sovereignty in myriad ways, both individually and collectively, taking their bodies back from institutions they were coming to call patriarchal (and, often, capitalist, racist, and homophobic). If a society dominated by men understood women's bodies as physically weaker, prone to hysteria, vulnerable to assault, and made for procreation—as a natural explanation for women's second-class social position—then reclaiming the value of their bodies for themselves was a powerful move for women seeking liberation. Their principles of bodily sovereignty, self-knowledge, and self-representation have reached far beyond their powerful early formulations in women's movements around the year 1970.

Feminist discussions of embodiment become unexpectedly animated and complex in feminist discourse and performance about sleep. Sleep often appears in feminist writing about the body as fatigue, as the moment when the inescapable needs of the body rear up and make themselves known, derailing other imperatives. *Our Bodies, Ourselves* cautions women not to "use energy in a way that leaves us exhausted"; Silvia Federici describes the "nervous and physical exhaustion" experienced by women tasked with family care work; and Audre Lorde reckons with "the devastating effects of overextension" that fill her daily life and accompany her activism.[6] But, as much as fatigue denotes the inescapability of the body's needs, sleep itself offers a temporary yet substantial shift in our experience of the body. Sleep is a nightly event in which our ways of knowing and interacting with the world through the body are radically changed. We process sensory information in different ways, filtering out some sounds while remaining hypersensitive to others; moving our eyes but not seeing through them as we fill in our visual environment with dream content; and existing in an altered awareness of the people and events around us, including both friends and potential threats.

While sleeping, performers like Anderson turn off their conscious brains and sense of vision and filter their particular sleeping environments—including their small discomforts and serious dangers—through altered senses of touch and hearing that give the performers and their audiences new ways of understanding the social relations and material world around them. When Anderson began experimenting with sleep in performance, she was freshly graduated from Columbia University with an MFA in sculpture. She was in the early years of what would become a lifelong career as a multimedia performer fascinated with the body as a technology for perceiving the world anew through sensory experience and transmitting that altered sense of the world to her audiences. *Institutional Dream Series* combines elements of autobiographical art, street art, and body art, all parts of a downtown artistic culture in New York City circa 1970 that was insistently interdisciplinary.[7] Anderson shares her focus on the body with many of her peer downtown artists and feminist artists of the 1970s, but her persistent fascination with sleep, along with the length and disciplinary breadth of her career (spanning visual art, live theater, recorded music, and virtual reality) bridges the divide between performance art and theater. While Anderson's later, larger works, such as her live epic performance *United States* (1983), have received substantial critical attention, *Institutional Dream Series* has attracted less commentary, perhaps because of its small scale and quiet nature.[8] Yet reading *Institutional Dream Series* as part of the genre of sleep performance demonstrates the importance of sleep to Anderson's career-long exploration of the body as a perceptive and communicative technology. In *Institutional Dream Series,* the power of Anderson's body is not defined primarily by either her visibility or her own capacity for vision. Instead, Anderson's sleep performance expands her nonvisual aesthetic abilities to sense and remake the world around her.

Anderson's name for the body as an aesthetic technology is the "nerve bible": a powerful book (or recording technology) for capturing and transmuting raw sensory experience. She pictures the nerve bible as a "sensory homunculus," a depiction of the human body with "the relative proportions of sensory neurons as they're represented in the brain"—big ears and a big mouth, but not big eyes.[9] The nerve bible is a body that is finely attuned to certain sensory experiences. While Anderson has reworked the idea of the body as nerve bible throughout her career, her first experiments with the body as aesthetic technology appear in her early explorations of sleep and feminist intervention as performance actions, also seen in her 1970s artworks *Fully Automated Nikon* and *Talking Pillows.* Sleep, in Anderson's work, is a powerful practice for reclaiming the body—not just *from* the male gaze or a male-dominated social sphere but also *for* the artist, as a technology that lets Anderson sidestep visual art's prioritization of eyesight. In *Institutional Dream Series,* Anderson collaborates with her friend the photographer Geri (Geraldine) Pontius, transforming the solipsism of sleep into a shared experience. Through experimenting with sleep as a bodily technology for sensing and remaking social and material surroundings, Anderson's performances expand the feminist project of reclaiming the body by demonstrating the epistemological power of a body at rest. By paying attention to sleep, we can better know ourselves and our worlds.

She Tucks Her Contact Lenses Under Her Tongue

Institutional Dream Series was a sequence of quiet and unadvertised performances in which Anderson attempted to sleep in public or semipublic spaces in New York City in 1972 and 1973. She was accompanied and photographed by Pontius and wrote brief records of what she experienced and what she dreamed while sleeping in each location. Pontius's black-and-white photographs focus closely on Anderson's body: She is a small and unremarkable-looking white woman, clad in long pants and long sleeves, often wearing a stocking cap over short hair. Only one photograph—of Anderson's final *Institutional Dream Series* performance, on a desolate winter beach—shows much of Anderson's surroundings. Anderson's written records are similarly sparse. She struggles to sleep well in these public spaces, and her dreams are not fantastic, surreal narratives but instead brief transformations of her sensory impressions, such as fluorescent lighting or loud waves, into alternate images, sounds, and feelings. *Institutional Dream Series* is an early example of Anderson's exploration of the body as an aesthetic technology. The first brief performance in the series, in which Anderson slept in a university library, demonstrates her practice of de-emphasizing eyesight in favor of other senses and in contrast to institutional habits of visual surveillance.

Fifty years after performing *Institutional Dream Series,* Anderson chose this performance as the earliest artwork included in her self-curated career survey *The Weather* (2021–22). Spanning several museum galleries, *The Weather* foregrounded Anderson's enduring project of using her body—and inviting her audience members to use their bodies—as a technology for sensing the social and material environment in ways that go beyond the visual across a variety of media. Anderson calls this sensed but barely seen world "the world of multimedia, music, theater, and performance, where stories unfold through sound and action, often in darkness," conditions in which sight cannot be the primary sense for the aesthetic encounter.[10] In her installation *Salute,* for example, a corridor of large flags moved in robotic, unison semaphore, creating a series of breezes that museum visitors could not see but only feel, haptically, on their skin. In *Habeas Corpus,* Anderson projected a larger-than-life video image of former Guantánamo Bay detainee Mohammed el Gharani, who now lives in Ghana and cannot enter the United States, onto a colossal sculpture of a sitting body. Audiences in the United States will never be able to see el Gharani face-to-face, but they could instead come in contact with an immense version of his bodily presence. As these examples from *The Weather* demonstrate, Anderson's aesthetic experiments with the body-as-technology have political implications, suggesting that there is more to be sensed and known about a patriotic waving flag or a hidden former prisoner than just what we are able to see.

For *The Weather,* Anderson wrote a new introduction to *Institutional Dream Series* in which she suggests several reasons for experimenting with sleep performance:

> I decided to sleep in various public places to see if they would influence my dreams. . . . Initially I wanted to do this because I was interested in taboos. Public sleeping is discouraged, although not illegal; it seems to violate an unspoken social contract that requires awareness. People who are unconscious are obviously very vulnerable.[11]

While we might think of several reasons public sleep is taboo—including laws that punish and restrict the freedom of unhoused people—Anderson highlights the less obvious "social contract that requires awareness," a sense that individuals in public are supposed to stay alert, to assume personal responsibility for their own safety. In other words, we should keep our eyes open. (In New York City, Anderson's longtime home, this social contract was later made explicit with the post-9/11 policing catchphrase "If you see something, say something.") In *Institutional Dream Series,* Anderson uses sleep to free herself from this social contract of awareness, which implies acute visual attention, and instead perceive the world around her through other sensory means.

When Anderson cultivates her sleeping body as a sensory technology for perceiving her environment in novel ways, her live sleep performance contests the Freudian argument that sleep is a solipsistic experience, a time for the sleeper to disengage from the outside world and burrow into her own unconscious, reworking existing memories and desires. In Freud's theory of dreaming, the dream "acts like a conscientious night-watchman," guarding the sleeping mind from any external influences and maintaining its focus on the internal, repressed emotions and desires of the sleeper.[12] While Freud argues that dreaming is necessary and meaningful psychic activity, technological experiments in the field of consumer sleep goods have exploited a more loosely Freudian sense that the sleeping brain remains cognitively productive—and therefore can be put to work. One of these consumer sleep technologies has particularly fascinated Anderson: a language-learning device called the Pillow Speaker. The Pillow Speaker aims to optimize sleep time through technological intervention by playing German language tapes into a pillow, enabling the user to learn the language passively while sleeping. (There is no evidence that this is a successful method for language learning.) For her performance *Talking Pillows* (1978–79), Anderson removed the Pillow Speaker microphone from inside the pillow, recorded over the German tape with a violin solo, and put the microphone in her mouth, using her mouth movements to make live alterations to the recorded sound. In *Talking Pillows* Anderson incorporates the sleep technology into her body; she has remarked that "the potential for electrocution" by the speaker as its circuitry is exposed to her saliva is "always a thrill."[13] Here, Anderson asserts the power of the human body not as a passive recipient for German language lessons but as an active (possibly even electrified) manipulator of technology. Sleep holds a particular attraction for Anderson as a site where technology and performance can transform what we know about the world around us—whether that is our knowledge of the German language or, more consequentially, in *Institutional Dream Series,* the conditions of public sleep in New York City.

Like *Talking Pillows,* which borrows an educational tool and makes it a technology of the body, *Institutional Dream Series* begins in a site of education: a Columbia University library. In the first photographed performance of *Institutional Dream Series,* in April 1972, Anderson slept on a couch near the women's restroom of the university's Schermerhorn Library, covering her face with a notebook for three hours in the afternoon. It is hard to imagine that Anderson looked too out of the ordinary in this setting; she could have been just another student dozing off while studying or catching up on sleep after pulling an all-nighter.[14] (Her collaborator, Geri Pontius, taking photographs of the sleeping Anderson in a library, might have attracted more curiosity.) Anderson reports that, during these performances, she tucked her contact lenses under her tongue to preserve them for later wear. With her face obscured by her notebook, her contacts removed from her eyes, and her eyes themselves closed in sleep, Anderson positioned herself as both asleep and emphatically unseeing.

Although closing one's eyes and ceasing to see might seem to be an obvious part of any sleep performance, Anderson's emphatic choice to turn off her capacity for sight marks a jumping-off point for several key interventions, not only in Anderson's own career but also in the field of visual art and in feminist theories of the body. Eyesight would seem to be *the* necessary sensory capacity for a visual artist. In her study of blind museumgoers and artists, Georgina Kleege finds that Western philosophical and critical writing about artists tends to paint the visual artist as either a "superman of seeing" or a "romantic" figure engaged in "mortal combat" against blindness—whose victory arrives when he finally overcomes a metaphorical blindness in order to see beauty come to life on the canvas before him.[15] Film and media scholar Sean Cubitt adds that over the past few decades media technologies have increasingly prioritized audience members' sight above other senses, such that "we become 'all eyes' . . . [and] we lose any sense of the rest of our bodies."[16] So the ideal artist and the ideal art audience are both imagined as seeing with particular acuity, their other senses lagging far behind. Yet Kleege, herself a blind arts writer, points out that museums often overemphasize the visual in conceptual art, with photographic or video documentation overshadowing the idea at the center of the artwork and downplaying the other senses that artwork engages. An overemphasis on the visual can be a problem in museum representations of Anderson's own performances. As Anderson says, seeing an art performance is nothing like viewing the camera documentation of it: "The eyes can't zoom, pan, or dolly very well," but instead rely on the mind to "fix up" the sensory information they receive.[17] The body is not a camera and does not see like one.

Alternate, noncamera bodily technologies of perception emerge in Anderson's written record of her dreams from the library performance. Sleeping on a bench near the library's restroom, Anderson "dream[s] that the library is an open-air market and all the stacks are stalls stocked with vegetables."[18] The dream narrative remakes the existing sensory cues of the library—its shelves laden with books available for the taking, along with the presence of other students—into stalls laden with vegetables available for purchase, along with other market shoppers. It is not a particularly fantastic or fascinating dream. It is also a much more direct translation of Anderson's immediate, recognizable surroundings into a dream environment than Freud's theories of condensation and displacement would lead us to expect. Of course, the dream narratives are a part of the artwork, not necessarily direct renderings of Anderson's real dreams. (Indeed, all waking retellings of dreams involve the sleeper applying linearity and language to the dream form.)[19] Anderson's interest in the weather remains consistent in all the *Institutional Dream Series* dream narratives, which repeatedly translate interior settings and human-made objects into more natural analogues, like the books turned into vegetables. And in each dream narrative, Anderson accomplishes a recognizable translation of the sensory details of her real surroundings—in that performance's selected "institution"—into an imagined alternative setting. Her dream narratives are not escapes from reality but remakings of it.

The aesthetic ability to remake the world of daily life, of vegetable markets and library shelves, through sleep is one of the key capacities that sleep performance offers for feminism. We might think of acute vision not just as a sense appropriate to visual artists but also as a powerful tool of institutional male dominance, from the visual power suggested by the era of the Enlightenment to the expanding state capacity for surveillance conjured by

Foucault's panopticon to the male gaze that feminists of the 1970s were pinpointing in film, medicine, and other institutions.[20] In the early 1970s, in a moment when U.S. women's movements were interrogating every corner of daily life to imagine how it could be remade to liberate women, performances like Anderson's offered sleep as a technology for perceiving one's environment and remaking it into something different. *Institutional Dream Series* suggests that feminist artists or activists do not need to ape or master the all-seeing vision of male dominance to know themselves and their world meaningfully. And, as in the work of many of her peer performance artists, Anderson's sleep is a strategy that simultaneously reclaims the epistemological power of the body and experiments with the politics of bodily vulnerability in visual culture.

The Judge Makes a Show

The vulnerable sleeping woman, often painted nude, is a seminal object in the history of visual art, an object made and disseminated by men. The sleeping woman epitomizes a familiar gendered logic of Western visual culture, in which women are passive objects exposed for male artists and presumed-male audiences across the spectrum from high art to film to popular culture to advertising to pornography. This is the "split between active/male and passive/female" that organizes our "pleasure in looking," as articulated by film critic Laura Mulvey in *Screen* in 1975.[21] Feminist interventions in the arenas of both visual culture and health activism in the late 1960s and early 1970s worked to reclaim women's bodies for women, using myriad tactics to disrupt this gendered logic and putting the means of producing "pleasure in looking" into women's own hands. Yet some of the earliest aesthetic representations we have of sleeping women are sculptures from ancient Maltese grottoes that may have had oracular functions.[22] The aestheticized sleeping woman is, then, a contradictory object, both exposed to voyeurs or greater threats and imagined as a site of atypical power whose oracular capacity comes from a perspective on the world not limited to what can be seen—not limited to the very power the artist and audience exercise over her. Anderson's performance of *Institutional Dream Series* in a Manhattan night court, which included an unexpected confrontation with a judge, exploited this contradiction. The night court performance participated in the vulnerability—not only gendered but also classed—made more evident by the court's nocturnal schedule. At the same time, this performance disrupted the organized hierarchy of the courtroom when the judge's misinterpretation of Pontius's photographs of the sleeping Anderson proved more histrionic than Anderson's own performance.

Anderson's performance of *Institutional Dream Series* in Manhattan's night court began at 10:30 on a late December evening in 1972 and lasted until the early morning. Anderson looks a bit vulnerable in Pontius's photograph from the performance, but she is not clearly gendered. In the night court photograph, Anderson wears a shapeless jacket and pants, her body fully covered and curled into a molded bench, head tucked down, hands clasped awkwardly over her lap. Pontius's camera looks slightly upward at Anderson, so that Anderson's head, leaning against a wall behind her, is tilted away from the viewer, and Anderson's right arm is the largest part of the image, ineffectually shielding her body. Anderson looks uncomfortable. She reports she only slept for around forty-five minutes, even though this is the sole iteration of *Institutional Dream Series* that actually took place at night. The photograph is a familiar image of a public sleeper making do with a city's inhospitable architecture.

As when Anderson napped in a university library, we might assume that a woman dozing off in night court would not attract too much attention or appear out of place. New York City's night court was in fact founded to manage women who were out at night, behaving improperly—in the eyes of the law—without male supervision on city streets. When the court opened in 1907, any woman charged with a crime outside business hours was sent to night court; business was so brisk that a separate women's court, for prostitution and intoxication arrests, opened three years later in Greenwich Village. In practice, almost all the women sent to these courts at night in the early twentieth century had been arrested for prostitution. As historian Hugh Ryan notes, a woman walking on her own at night without a man could be flagged by police as a sex worker, and this meant that queer working women were especially vulnerable to arrest because they were less likely to travel with male companions. These women were, in Ryan's words, arrested for being "improperly feminine," for behaving in public in ways that were acceptable for men yet newly criminalized for women in the early twentieth century.[23] In this context, Anderson's public sleep performance in night court enacted a woman's taboo public behavior against the court's founding goal of disciplining women in public.

The contradiction between the photographic and written records of *Institutional Dream Series*—between vulnerable, passive sleep and active artistic imagination—places *Institutional Dream Series* in an unusual position within the feminist artistic project of reclaiming the vulnerable, passive, or, indeed, sleeping woman's body from its role as visual art object. As in the library performance, when Anderson sleeps in night court, she turns off her sense of sight (covering her eyes with a stocking cap to block out the light) and dreams she is in an environment that remakes her real surroundings. Anderson reports she dreamed of "dark clouds . . . scudding through the courtroom about twelve feet from the floor." Upon waking, she recognized that her stocking cap "alternately obscures and reveals the bright lights which hang about twelve feet from the floor," so the combination of stocking cap and bright lighting became clouds moving across a light sky. As with the previous dream narrative, Anderson substitutes a natural entity, clouds, for the human-made light fixtures. Sleep is, again, a technology for Anderson to remake her surroundings based on her sensory experience without the dominating influence of sight. Anderson's written record of her dreams deploys sleep as a creative technology for remaking the world around her, even as Pontius's photograph depicts the sleeping Anderson as a somewhat vulnerable figure, finding little comfort or protection in the night court's hard surfaces and bright lights.

Understanding that the logic of visual culture tended to set up women as vulnerable, passive objects of artistic creation and men as active creators and viewers, many feminist performance artists of the 1960s and 1970s were, like Anderson, reclaiming an active role, becoming both creators and viewers of their own exposed or vulnerable bodies. At the vanguard, Japanese artist Yoko Ono's 1964 performance of the event score *Cut Piece* at Carnegie Hall made the aesthetic work of exposing a woman's body explicit by inviting audience members to cut away as much of Ono's clothing as they chose.[24] Austrian performance artist Valie Export has also described taking a cut-out approach to exposing her body, inventing crotchless "action pants" that could be worn to confront audience members at a cinema screening a pornographic film. Export envisioned "challeng[ing] the voyeurism of cinema" by "develop[ing] a completely new, non-voyeuristic approach to the female body as something other than a visual object."[25] If audiences went to the cinema to view beautiful women's bodies, Export considered what would happen when a woman artist put her real body in their field of vision and in the audience, simultaneously.

Along with confronting men through a direct and incisive analysis of the narrow conditions under which men liked to view women's bodies, feminist body art was also often directed toward women's self-knowledge, toward women's seeing themselves rather than being seen. In 1973, North American visual artists Judy Chicago and Miriam Schapiro theorized "central core" imagery, the proposition that an earlier generation of women artists, like Georgia O'Keeffe, "defined a central orifice whose formal organization is often a metaphor for a woman's body." Again, foregrounding the body—the "central cavity," not merely the genitals—is a strategy for disrupting the gendered binaries of subject and object or active and passive. Central core imagery was an artistic strategy not only for resisting phallic forms but also for women to better know themselves—their "personal, sexual identity"—by seeing themselves more clearly and fully, through their own eyes rather than another's gaze. "Where is the mirror," Chicago and Schapiro ask dramatically, "to reveal who I am?"[26] Taking a different approach to mirroring the gendered body, Japanese artist Yayoi Kusama's 1965 installation *Infinity Mirror Room–Phalli's Field* filled a mirrored room with "phallus-like stuffed objects . . . convey[ing] the illusion of a continuous sea of multiplied phalli expanding to its infinity."[27] Work by these artists suggests the ways that the woman's body in art history is simultaneously over- and underexposed. While audiences desire a prone or passive female art object, they are confronted or put off by women taking control of their own exposure, and women artists in the 1960s and 1970s both created and sought models for knowing themselves as artists who could see and represent bodies of various genders and genital configurations. Feminist artists reclaimed nudity and mirrors as tools for asserting artistic control over their own bodies—and over bodies as a foundational object of visual culture.

The mirror, instrument of self-portraiture, was also a key tool for U.S. women's health activists at the beginning of the 1970s, as they responded to the male-dominated medical industry in ways parallel to feminist performance artists' resistance to a visual culture organized around men's creation and spectatorship. *Our Bodies, Ourselves* advocates "us[ing] a mirror to see ourselves." The self-help clinic movement, founded by abortion-access activists Carol Downer and Lorraine Rothman in 1971, toured the country with mirrors and specula, encouraging women to examine their own vulvas and cervixes. Self-viewing as self-knowledge equipped women to provide themselves with abortions, using Downer and Rothman's Del-Em extraction technique or other approaches, when abortion was not legal or affordable.[28] Like many feminist artists, women's health activists disrupted the gendered viewer/viewed, active/passive binary in medical institutions staffed by male physicians and researchers: "We discovered that you don't learn very much when you are just a passive recipient of information," the Boston Women's Health Book Collective wrote. "Whatever we need to learn now, in whatever areas of our life, we know more about how to go about it."[29] The direct line these activists drew from mirrors to health research to abortion linked seeing to knowing to exercising power over the body.

In 1973, at the same time she was working on *Institutional Dream Series,* Anderson experimented with the link between artistic tools for seeing and the exercise of power over the body in her performance-photography series *Fully Automated Nikon.* For this project, Anderson photographed men who commented on her body in public places, particularly on the street. "As I walked through the Lower East Side with my fully automated Nikon," she later wrote of the project, "I felt armed, ready."[30] Anderson responded to the threat of men making claims on her body with what she articulated as a more powerful weapon—a camera used like an assault rifle. In what we now see as a classic feminist move, she turned the artist's gaze back on the men, with the camera as a sign of the artist's power to control what is seen. Yet these men "seemed flattered" by Anderson's aesthetic attention, not distressed by the camera as weapon.[31] As with another explicitly feminist project

Anderson made in the 1970s (*A Feminist Bestiary,* discussed at the end of this chapter), this performance did not have the effect on her immediate audience that Anderson says she desired—which does not mean that Anderson did not enjoy executing the performance. But this reversal of the street's hierarchy of seeing and seen via the camera was not straightforward. Attention on the street was not threatening to the men Anderson photographed because it did not index a larger system of violence exercised with impunity in public spaces. Instead, the camera wielded as part of Anderson's larger performance prompted men to become unpredictable yet telling participants in that performance's examination of visual control, as would happen with Pontius's camera at night court.

As I have suggested, Anderson does look somewhat vulnerable in the photograph of her sleeping in the night court, but this vulnerability seems less specific to her gender and more generalizable to anyone stuck waiting for a municipal court hearing at midnight in Manhattan. In Anderson's narrative, however, Pontius's camera is cast in an unexpectedly threatening role. *Institutional Dream Series* participates in the feminist interrogation of the vulnerable female body as art object—including the particular power of the camera—while developing a unique intervention in this chapter of art history through Anderson's rejection of sight as the artist's primary tool (or weapon). Anderson's narrative of her dream at the night court performance concludes, "I wake up just as the judge is confiscating our camera. 'You understand, of course, blackmail is illegal,' he is saying." In Anderson's story, the judge believed Pontius was taking pictures in order to blackmail one of the night court defendants with evidence of their court appearance; Pontius eventually convinced him she was an architecture student merely studying the court building's design as part of her degree. Ultimately, Anderson writes, the judge "only makes a show of taking the film out of the camera and then hands it back" with the film still intact. Without realizing a performance is taking place, the judge "makes a show" of his own.

Anderson's story of the judge's spontaneous participation in *Institutional Dream Series* illustrates how live sleep performance expands the possibilities of a feminist response to a gendered visual culture. The judge's visual read of the situation is completely askew: He does see vulnerability, but it is the vulnerability of a nonexistent victim of extortion. He sees the power of the camera, but this particular power of the camera (as a source of evidence for blackmail) is not one Anderson and Pontius are trying to exercise. Quite reasonably, it never seems to occur to the judge that Anderson's sleep is the object of the photography, or even that this sleep might be staged. In the way that sleep, as an artistic technology, lets Anderson reimagine her environment—remaking the courtroom as a cloudscape in her dream—sleep performance remakes the situation of the sleeping, vulnerable woman art object (Anderson, being photographed) and the institutionally empowered male viewer (the judge). Sleep performance generates novel and unexpected power dynamics in the night court, prompting the judge to imagine his own dramatic noir scenario in which Anderson and Pontius are vigilante blackmailers, weaponizing their camera to extort Manhattan's criminal underworld. And Anderson and Pontius emerge victorious, not only retaining their film but having remade Anderson's initial experiment with the vulnerability of public sleep—photographed as quiet, passive, and solo—into a spontaneous participatory performance. Rather than straightforwardly reversing the gendered binary of who sees and is seen (as in *Fully Automated Nikon*), *Institutional Dream Series* demonstrates that sleep, as a performance, remakes social relations in less predictable ways.

In remaking social relations, *Institutional Dream Series* also demonstrates that sleep is a social practice. Sleep, in other words, is contingent on and shaped by the terrain of social relations that surrounds it. Seeing public sleepers as "obviously very vulnerable" (in Anderson's words) shows us the expectation of immanent violence in Anderson's sleeping environment. Since their founding, night court and the similarly nocturnal women's court have in fact been venues where wealthier New Yorkers have gone slumming for cheap evening entertainment; online travel guides continue to recommend night court to tourists.[32] The logic of both high art and popular visual culture surrounding Anderson in the United States in the 1970s indicates that this immanent violence toward sleepers is gendered: that men positioning, watching, and exerting control over exposed or unaware women is a common visual trope, a familiar representation of the world in which Anderson performed *Institutional Dream Series*. Like several of her contemporaries,

Anderson intervenes in this gendered visual logic by being simultaneously artist and art object, by choosing how to position herself as the sleeping figure and directing her friend with the camera. But Anderson's use of performance, specifically, invites the social world to participate in her sleep in unexpected and telling ways, with the judge attempting to assert an authoritative male surveillance of and control over Anderson's sleep—which Anderson ultimately incorporates into the performance itself.

She Wakes Up at the Right Time

The final performance of *Institutional Dream Series*—on a desolate Coney Island beach in January—looks initially like a rejection of the social relations of sleep.[33] In comparison to other photographs of *Institutional Dream Series,* Anderson's body is smaller in the Coney Island image, dwarfed by the emptiness of the beach in the foreground and a Ferris wheel and other rides on the distant horizon. No one else is on the beach or at the nearby amusement park in winter. No judge is going to interrupt Anderson's sleep here. Yet this photograph is just one, partial record of the performances that constitute *Institutional Dream Series.* Contradictions among Pontius's image, Anderson's written dream narrative, and the live conditions of Anderson's final public nap point to the persistence of social relations within even this emphatically solo iteration of the performance, exposing a tension between the isolation the photograph depicts and the essential presence of a friendly collaborator in executing Anderson's sleep performance. Even as feminist theories of the body in the 1970s articulated women's bodily sovereignty, Anderson's sleep performance participates in a more complex feminist exploration of the uncoerced exercise of passivity.

At first glance, the Coney Island performance of *Institutional Dream Series* seems to explore different themes than the earlier iterations in the library and the courtroom. In comparison to those capital-*I* "Institutional" settings, peopled sites full of surveillance and social hierarchies, the Coney Island performance might mark the beginning of Anderson's career-spanning interest in "the weather"—as suggested by her decision to include *Institutional Dream Series* as the earliest piece in *The Weather,* her retrospective exhibition. Anderson's written record of her experience sleeping on the beach focuses on her direct interaction with the natural world, as she endures "bitter cold," "damp" sand, and "frozen feet" covered by the incoming tidal waters. She wakes up when she hears "a giant wave . . . rolling toward shore." Upon waking, Anderson realizes that it is not a wave but a "large helicopter . . . hovering directly overhead." She writes, "I jump up and start to run."

The story of this performance, as recorded in Anderson's written journal and Pontius's photograph, is of a lone artist confronting an impersonal natural world, a world beyond the scale of the human. *Institutional Dream Series,* I have argued, participates in a feminist project of reclaiming the body, as Anderson creates a performance in which she is simultaneously the artist and the sleeping woman object of the artwork, a performance that ropes in and wrong-foots the night court judge, destabilizing a legacy of male power through visual surveillance. But is the feminist project of reclaiming the body aimed solely at leveling the playing field with men? Gaining access for women to the empowered social roles that men hold was certainly a project of feminist movements, and it had particular successes in the first two settings of *Institutional Dream Series*: the university and the court of law, two institutions where women have gained much more access to positions of power (as faculty, administrators, lawyers, and judges) than they had in the early 1970s. Yet sleeping is a bad strategy for gaining this kind of power. Anderson's performance brushes up against the sites of institutional power some feminists were climbing toward in the 1970s, but her sleep performance instead moves toward a kind of self-knowledge that reorganizes social relations rather than ascending them.

Perhaps the most important social relation in *Institutional Dream Series,* the relationship between Anderson and her friend and photographer Pontius, almost disappears from written and visual records of the performances themselves. The photographs and write-ups make *Institutional Dream Series* appear to be a solo performance, but the existence of the images (and Anderson's recollections of making the art piece) reveals it as a two-person show, with Pontius playing the more traditionally artistic role of photographer. Sleep performance, like many kinds of performance, is ephemeral: Although it can be recorded in static forms, as Anderson does with photography and written journals, some aspects of the performance are experienced only live, as they unfold in time. And sleep itself, on the border of consciousness, is an ephemeral experience, one we remember only unreliably, in brief waking moments and bits of dream. The record we have of the Coney Island performance of *Institutional Dream Series* is particularly shaped by this ephemerality because the written and photographic records diverge in important ways. The photograph is of Anderson facing toward Coney Island's amusements, with no water in sight and with Anderson's feet pointing *away* from the shoreline, not being covered with water, as Anderson describes in her narration. The horizon line is high in Pontius's photograph. Anderson is in the foreground, head toward the camera, and the open beach stretches across the middle ground of the image, until we see scant evidence of Coney Island—one Ferris wheel, one tower of some kind—in the top quarter of the image. The photograph also does not capture the helicopter, so although Anderson does look vulnerable and abandoned on the shore, the sources of danger are not in frame. And then, beyond the image and text, there is the performance itself, in which Anderson was not alone but had Pontius there watching her, taking pictures. Pontius ran interference between Anderson and the suspicious judge in the night court and presumably would have woken Anderson if she had been about to be engulfed by a wave.

Pontius's photograph, Anderson's written record (ostensibly based on semiconscious memories), and our own knowledge of the performance conditions are not fully reconcilable, and these ambiguities invite divergent readings of the Coney Island performance. In one, Anderson's written fears that this attempt to sleep in public is a "crazy idea," along with Pontius's photograph of Anderson completely alone on a vast expanse of beach, support the claim that Anderson was unable to sleep because of the potential dangers around her. She set out to experiment with the vulnerabilities of public sleep and found her limit on a desolate shorefront in the middle of winter. As in her earlier performances, Anderson sensed a transmuted version of the world around her—the sound of the helicopter above transformed into a giant wave by Anderson's sleeping brain—but the bodily technology Anderson had cultivated throughout the performance series remained an accurate sensor of a threat. The helicopter hovering overhead shows the likelihood that a vulnerable woman, sleeping alone in public, will be interrupted with unwanted attention.

The helicopter might even remind readers of images from the Vietnam War, a larger political context lying behind Anderson's early 1970s performance series and other performance art of this era that critiqued U.S. military imperialism. In 1971, a protest by antiwar Vietnam veterans led to a court battle about the legality of sleeping overnight on the Washington Mall, and the close timing between this event and *Institutional Dream Series* suggests Anderson may have been aware of the court case's contribution to the taboo on sleep in public places.[34] The helicopter becomes male state violence, an overdetermined symbol of the visual, the masculine, the imperialist, the physically and technologically powerful. These themes recur throughout Anderson's career, which includes critiques of how U.S. hegemony turns technology toward its own ends. Art historian RoseLee Goldberg describes Anderson's oeuvre as a project of responding to U.S. technological hypercontrol with "subject matter that underlines human frailty: melancholic and frequently surreal tales of animals, dreams, families and angels."[35] When read in this vein, Anderson's decision to relinquish her sight and perform sleep exaggerates the divide between her vulnerability and the helicopter's surveillance, the institutional power and visual dominance of the night court judge made bigger, louder, more anonymous, and more potent. The Coney Island sleep performance confirms the vulnerability of the sleeper (possibly gendered female) to the threat of visual, technological state power.

Yet Anderson "jump[s] up and start[s] to run." The sleeping Anderson in Pontius's photographs looks vulnerable. She occupies a much smaller portion of the image in the Coney Island photograph than in others in the series, but in Anderson's description, her physical power returns instantaneously. After "a couple of hours" asleep, Anderson hears a loud noise and accurately senses that she might be in danger. She wakes up at the right time. We might imagine that Pontius does not intervene because she trusts her friend's ability to take care of herself. Through sleep performance, Anderson cultivates her own body as a sensitive and powerful technology—not for control but for knowledge of herself and her world. By cultivating her self-knowledge through sleep performance, Anderson does not merely "awaken" to the sexism and other inequities around her, as the development of a political consciousness is often described. Instead, she finds herself able to rest, to sleep, and to know when she should wake again. Although Anderson describes having the most difficulty sleeping on Coney Island, she also sleeps longer there than in any of the other *Institutional Dream Series* performances (according to her own record, for two hours). Knowing the body well enough to know how to rest is Anderson's ultimate achievement in *Institutional Dream Series.* Anderson's project mirrors that of her peers in the Boston Women's Health Book Collective. In their opening chapter, "Our Changing Sense of Self," the authors write collectively about their evolving relationship to what they call *passivity:* "Although in our past we were passive and not able to act when we wanted, now we realize that we can act, but it is nice to choose not to at times. . . . Now we can choose to be dependent, and we see this as a strength, because intimate relationships are dependent relationships."[36] When you know yourself and your body, you can experience healthy passivity: The decision to rest or sleep, dependent on the social relations that surround you, becomes not vulnerability but intimacy.

And I like imagining Anderson and Pontius's working artistic relationship as an intimate one, as Anderson trusting a good friend with a weird early art project, as two young artists rapidly expanding their sphere of aesthetic experimentation from their own university library to the outer boroughs. Pontius collaborated with Anderson on several artworks in the first decade of their post-MFA careers, including as a performer in the short film *Dearreader* (1974), which critiques stereotypical female characters in film.[37] Anderson's much-lauded capacity for endlessly inventive performance and incisive critique might have been fueled by the safety and camaraderie she felt in the intimacy of this early collaboration. *Institutional Dream Series* shows us a feminist resistance to bodily vulnerability that moves not in the direction of completely independent control over the body but instead toward intimate dependence. One way we can know this dependence intimately is by really knowing what it is to sleep while trusting a friend to watch over us.

Anderson's work poses two key interventions that define feminist sleep performance: interventions in the history and study of performance and interventions in feminist projects in major cosmopolitan cities after 1970. When Anderson performs sleep in *Institutional Dream Series,* she experiments with the body as a technology for knowing the self that works only if the sleeper can depend on caring, healthily intimate social relations. Sleep performance requires that social relations be reconfigured with intimate dependence as their priority. In requiring this reconfiguration, sleep performance temporarily remakes the institutions where it happens, letting witnesses to the performance imagine these institutions functioning in fundamentally different ways. In Anderson's recorded dreams, she tends to remake densely urban institutions into outdoor spaces: The university library becomes an open-air market, and the lights on the courtroom ceiling become a cloudscape. Anderson's dreams are open to the weather. And in the full performance of *Institutional Dream Series,* Anderson not only imagines these institutions changing but also temporarily remakes their social relations. Sleep performance makes Anderson's body, her "nerve bible," sensitively attuned to social relations that might otherwise go unnoticed. Anderson shifts the balance of surveillance and power in the courtroom, participating in a larger feminist project of changing the gendered visual culture of the United States in the 1970s, and she turns the solo endurance performance of sleeping on a desolate winter beach into a practice of dependence on her friend and artistic collaborator. Although Anderson began *Institutional Dream Series* with the goal of seeing how sleeping in public institutions would "influence" her dreams, her public performance of quiet, vulnerable, passive dependence influenced those institutions in return.

Institutional Dream Series originated, in one telling of the story, in what might be the most common and underappreciated way that sleep intervenes in any given performance: with Anderson falling asleep in the audience. While an MFA student, Anderson says, she found herself napping through art history lectures. Like many other students, she nodded off in the darkened environment of the lecture hall, and she noticed that the artworks from her professors' slides mingled with other parts of her life in her dreams.[38] When Anderson went to sleep in art history class, she turned off her eyesight and remade the history of Western art in her dreaming brain. *Institutional Dream Series* expands on this initial, accidental intervention, demonstrating that performance art can change the gendered logic of visual culture and even challenge the priority of eyesight itself. Many of the artistic and performance innovations for which Anderson became known appear in nascent forms in *Institutional Dream Series,* including her fascination with the body as a technology; her wide-ranging, sidelong critique of American institutions; and her experiments with sleep and dream as a way to access the "nerve bible," the communicative capacities of the body beyond what the conscious brain registers. Anderson's influence on other performers and artists starts, we might say, with her falling asleep in art history class.

Like Anderson's far-reaching exploration of performance, her engagement with feminism has also been expansive and idiosyncratic. Anderson's autobiographical storytelling, in performances and artist books, records various experiments with feminist action, especially with women as visual objects and actors. In the early 1970s, these included *Fully Automated Nikon* as well as a demonstration at the Playboy Club for which Anderson drew the pamphlet *A Feminist Bestiary,* reclaiming the words "bitch" and "bird" along with "the female breasts" as "the symbol of motherhood and its attributes of love, nourishment and protection." Anderson reprinted *A Feminist Bestiary* in collections of her later work alongside her story of a conversation she had with a Playboy employee (a "Bunny") at the protest. The Playboy employee encouraged Anderson to let the Bunnies continue to earn a good wage at the Playboy Club and to go protest worker exploitation at a textile factory instead.[39] The pamphlet and the much-recounted fable of the Playboy protest contain many seeds of now-familiar conflicts within feminist movements: between women of different economic classes, between pro- and anti-sex work stances, between feminists focused on representation and those focused on material conditions, between an essentialist reclamation of the female body as inherently good ("the symbol of motherhood and its attributes of love") and a skepticism about reducing a political movement to a particular kind of body.

Anderson's early career coincided with the early days of a resurgent U.S. women's movement, a time when Anderson was one of a huge number of feminists figuring out what they could do if they claimed their bodies as their own—and *the body* as a subject of their work. Along with the interventions in women's health care and women's role in visual art addressed in this chapter, we might see the project of women reclaiming the body as central to various and conflicting political projects, including campaigns to end violence against women (Anderson's public sleep performances share some elements with Take Back the Night marches), to legalize abortion and protect reproductive freedom, to critique women who participate in pornography and sex work, to form separatist all-women utopias, to ensure transgender people access to affirming and lifesaving medical care, and to harm trans women by treating them as usurpers of the female body. Although many of us would not claim all of these projects as part of our specific feminism, they have all traveled under feminist flags.

What draws me to Anderson's particular project of reclaiming the body is her use of the sleeping body as a technology that intervenes in the social relations around it and, at the same time, openly acknowledges a dependence on social relations to sustain it. It is only a sleep *performance* when Pontius is there to watch it happen: From Anderson's intimate dependence on Pontius comes Anderson's early practice of knowing her body through sleeping, of learning to sense the world around her precisely and imaginatively. This practice produces unpredictable, momentary interventions in that world. And this is a pattern across the feminist sleep performances discussed in this book—solo performer Peggy Shaw, performance artist Regina José Galindo, and opera composer Philip Venables, among other artists, find themselves working with unexpected collaborators and undermining claims to solo artistry when they confront sleep as a theme and a tactic of performance. The sleep artists in upcoming chapters turn their sensitivities and imaginations toward larger aesthetic and political endeavors, but *Institutional Dream Series* lets us begin to understand how performers have used sleep in idiosyncratic feminist projects aimed at changing the world.

Two
Fluorescent Bedrooms
Peggy Shaw's Menopausal Gentleman Wakes Up Her Audience

In reading Laurie Anderson's *Institutional Dream Series,* I have argued that her public sleep performances intervene in a gendered visual culture in which men like to depict and view sleeping women. The fantasy of a sleeping woman's body as public spectacle is a fantasy of a woman who is attractive in the eyes of those who create and consume her image. This chapter turns to another sleep performance about the body—this time, the body as aging, sweaty, sick, restless, tired, and lustful, with "lumps," "stretch marks," and "blue veins" (91).[1] This is the body as described by theater writer, actor, and producer Peggy Shaw, put onstage in her 1997 solo performance *Menopausal Gentleman.* Shaw invites her audience to spend a sleepless night with her, "from the dusk to the dawn of the nighttime in my body" (71). This body is not the hypervisible body depicted in voyeuristic fantasies of sleeping women; instead, it is a body—queer, sick, poor, and aging—that has been encouraged or even coerced to stay out of public sight. Through campaigns to keep trans and queer people out of public spaces, through failures of accessibility and public health that keep disabled and chronically ill people trapped in their homes, and through laws and architecture that limit unhoused people's access to public space, the United States has forced all kinds of people to keep their bodily needs in private or hidden spaces.[2] In the face of this push back to the bedroom, Shaw spends fifty minutes alone onstage detailing how she sweats, seduces, and even occasionally sleeps in her bed at night. She makes the bedroom of a menopausal butch lesbian a public space. In doing so, Shaw participates in a lifesaving tradition of queer, trans, and disability activism that claims public space and refuses to yield it. But in focusing primarily on the quotidian and often private problem of insomnia—rather than a more acute issue like terminal illness or civil rights—Shaw raises the question of longer-term survival, of sustaining herself in a nation not invested in her life.

As Shaw's title suggests, her insomnia is a product of menopause. At night, she gets hot flashes that lead to night sweats that lead to sleeplessness. Shaw has described herself as "really upset and freaked out" by menopause.[3] Her candid discussion of her bodily experience is of a piece with her other solo work and with the conventions of the genre of solo performance, especially solo performances by queer artists. Shaw's candor about menopause reflects queer and disability strategies of publicizing the sick or otherwise nonnormative (possibly "sick," as in inappropriate or depraved) body, as seen in activism and writing from the 1980s and 1990s, particularly activism around breast cancer and HIV/AIDS. These activists put their bodies, bodies that they had been told to hide away—one-breasted bodies, bodies emaciated by wasting syndrome, bleeding bodies, even the remains of AIDS victims—into public spaces. In doing so, they brought the root of their suffering and early deaths, a homophobic, misogynist nation with a wildly unequal health care system, into public discussion.[4] But in bringing this candor about the body to menopause rather than a terminal illness, Shaw reflects the distressing ways that the body—even the "healthy" body, aging in a "normal" way—is unpredictable and uncontrollable. In *Menopausal Gentleman,* sleep is ground zero for the unstable body: "Menopause is all it's made up to be," Shaw threatens. "I'm insane, I don't sleep. If I was president I'd blow up the world" (76).

Claiming the exhausted or bedridden woman's body as a site of feminist power is perilous terrain, but ignoring this epistemological perspective is an equal risk. The rest cure, memorialized in late nineteenth-century feminist writing, was typically prescribed in response to a diagnosis of hysteria. Women's increasing participation in public life, including feminist activism, launched a vogue of gendered hysteria diagnoses in the Euro-American middle and upper classes. Literary critic Elaine Showalter argues that the hysteria diagnosis was thoroughly exploited for its dramatic potential in turn-of-the-century European theater, via hysterical characters in Henrik Ibsen's plays and physical reenactments of hysteria symptoms in French cabarets. In turn, physicians claimed that some hysterical women were performing—feigning—their symptoms like actresses.[5] Essentialist, antifeminist myths about women's inherent weakness both insist that women as a group need more rest than men do and delegitimate individual women's claims to fatigue as psychological fantasies or actorly performances. Feminist writing from these bedrooms unmasks the sexism behind hysteria diagnoses and the abusive nature of the rest cure while simultaneously exposing the lack of real treatment for often-gendered conditions like mental illness, postpartum sleep loss and depression, and persistent insomnia.

While Shaw is distressed by her insomnia, she is happy that menopause heralds the end of biological reproduction. "They say women have a certain amount of eggs to use up in a lifetime," Shaw remarks. Then, triumphantly, "I DID IT!" (85). Shaw's celebration of no longer being at risk of future pregnancy and childbirth is a novel contribution to the well-known debates within queer studies at the turn of the twenty-first century pitting antirelational or antisocial theories against theories of queer futurity. In short, does a queer politics reject any investment in the future as a hegemonic fantasy about the reproduction of the heterosexual nuclear family, that idealized moral and economic unit of late twentieth-century life? Or does a queer politics invest in imagining a radically different future, sketched out but not yet nailed down via the ephemeral nature of queer performance?[6] Shaw's solo performance about menopause draws our attention to a third possibility: *reproducing the self* as a queer political project, one focused on the very near future of the next day. In *Menopausal Gentleman,* Shaw has her hands full just getting herself through the night. She is constantly fending off threats to her own sleep: sweat, sexual desire, anxiety, loud noises, flashing neon clocks, sad memories, the fear that she forgot to feed the parking meter. Every night is a minefield, and Shaw dramatizes sleep as a battle for her own survival. In Shaw's deft performance, reproducing the self through menopause is shot through with the history of women, queer and trans people, and poor people who have been violently cast aside for their failure to keep themselves together.

In this menopausal sleep drama, the project of reproducing the self each night meets the question of what the theater reproduces onstage every evening. In other words, when an artist invents a new performance, drawing on all the things they have witnessed or could imagine people doing, how do they choose what to put on the stage and repeat for an audience, over and over again? What parts of life, real or imagined, do they want to *re*produce, to make happen repeatedly in front of spectators, in order to make their living? Shaw has an answer to this question, articulated in her essay "How I Learned Theater":

> Doing non-traditional theater—not like the white man's linear theater from the past—you do realize that three-quarters of the way through, instead of having a rape or a war or a woman killed or something, you do have to do something to wake up the audience. So that's when you do something more exciting than what you've been doing for the last forty minutes. . . . That's my formula.[7]

Shaw's theory (her "formula") of theatrical reproduction is aligned against white male "linear" dramaturgies that hold the audience's attention by staging violence, especially violence against women, in the form of rape, war, or murder. In order to avoid reproducing violence against women, Shaw has to find new strategies to "wake up the audience." Since she refuses to use violence against women onstage to keep her audience awake, she tests how engaging her plays are by performing them for her grandson and revising the places where he falls asleep. Shaw suggests that keeping one's audience awake by harming women onstage is a cheap trick. By instead using her young grandchild as a barometer for audience attention, she holds herself to a more rigorous creative standard.[8] By dramatizing menopausal sleep, Shaw sets aside two (related, familiar) plotlines about women, as objects of violence and as reproducers of children, and keeps her audience awake by exposing the eventfulness of coaxing her body to get the rest it needs to keep living. In attending to the political value of sleep, Shaw finds plenty to wake us all up.

Night Sweats

Menopausal Gentleman is a one-person performance, written by Shaw (in collaboration with director Rebecca Taichman) and performed by Shaw, speaking in the first person. *Menopausal Gentleman* was first staged in 1997 at Dixon Place, a downtown New York venue for new experimental art, and then transferred to off-Broadway and toured to other cities (69).[9] Shaw speaks directly to her audience, inviting us to travel with her "from the dusk to the dawn of the nighttime in my body," through one night of hot flashes and insomnia that prompts her to share other stories from her life experience as a queer woman who dresses in men's clothing in public (71). For the fifty-minute performance, Shaw performs as a version of herself, making no particular distinction between who she is offstage and who is she is in the show. Since Shaw offers no straightforward way to distinguish between her character onstage and her self offstage, I refer to her simply as Shaw throughout this chapter.[10] Shaw calls herself "lesbian," "butch," "queer," "woman," "anarchist," and "in debt"; I use these words—her words—to describe her politics and her affinities.[11] In *Menopausal Gentleman,* Shaw draws on her experiences making queer theater through hard work—especially through physical labor—to fuel her care for herself as she ages. Shaw figures this care for herself as *sweat,* the physical evidence that her body is experiencing menopause in the form of nightly hot flashes and also that Shaw is working hard to perform this care for her body in front of her audience.

Sweat interacts dynamically with Shaw's high drag masculine presentation, via costuming and props that both constitute and clean up after Shaw's sweaty onstage body. Shaw performs on a simple stage, with a bench as her only scenic element, so the focus is on her costume, a men's suiting ensemble inspired by the 1940s. This anachronistic costume evokes the decade of Shaw's birth, a time of sharper distinctions between women's dresses and men's tailored suits. Stage directions note that Shaw, from her short hair down to her shined shoes, is achieving the "*full 'passing' effect.*" Beneath the "*double-breasted*" suit, Shaw's breasts are bound (71). Men are expected to be the sweaty gender; in the 1940s style of Shaw's costuming, only a man would sport a visible handkerchief, mopping his sweat in public. Shaw's handkerchiefs are a part of her tightly rehearsed presentation: "I keep fresh handkerchiefs by my bed. I wash them every day and iron them and neatly fold them." Dressing well as a man of the 1940s takes work, but the reward is that the tailored suit holds Shaw's body in check. Yet Shaw's night sweats exceed the capacities of the ironed and folded handkerchiefs. Every night, Shaw "throw[s] off the covers and look[s] for water" as "beads of sweat" rise along her scalp "like bugs" (73). Shaw, in well-practiced drag, expertly deploys the visual markers of masculine confidence and continence, a suit that holds the body in and shoes that seem to slough off the very dirt they walk through, while delivering a story about her body as profoundly beyond her control. She wears a suit in the day, but she can't sleep at night.

Sweat, then, not only blurs Shaw's studied masculine presentation but also marks the limits of her bodily discipline as a working actor. Shaw can prompt sweat to appear in her performance by wearing heavy clothing and moving in vigorous and exaggerated ways, and she can signal sweat to her audience by mopping her brow with a handkerchief, but the actual sweat that glistens on her forehead under the stage lights and disrupts her sleep is not a performance she can cue. "Sweat is big, lots of sweat," Shaw proclaims. "I can't sleep. I'm all wet" (72). Shaw's sweat onstage is overdetermined—"big"—a symptom not only of menopause but also of labor, gender, embodiment, and stage performance. Onstage, this unstoppable sweat threatens Shaw's ability to make a living from acting, if she can no longer keep her body disciplined and responsive, as a professional actor must. She runs the risk of not being able to perform the same show every evening. Offstage, overnight, that professional risk becomes an existential threat, as sweat prevents the sleep Shaw needs to carry on the next day.

Shaw announces her sleeplessness as a symptom of menopause while also suggesting sleeplessness as an effect of sexual pleasure, the triumph of physical desire over fatigue, figured through a body that transforms at night from a sleepless menopausal human into a seductive tiger on the prowl. Shaw invites her audience into her body at night: "Let me try and describe it to you . . . what it all looks like, and how it all takes place inside my body" (71). In her recorded 1998 performance, Shaw pops the opening *b* of "body" and stretches out the first vowel so the word sounds like "bawdy," a tough-guy, midcentury New York pronunciation that draws attention to Shaw's body onstage. In sound and appearance, she is a gentleman on the rise, a working-class guy whose confidence, charisma, and snappy wardrobe promise a big, self-made future. But the story she tells is of a *bawdy* body, "lewd, obscene, unchaste," betrayed as exceeding its bounds.[12] Shaw calls four o'clock in the morning, when she is least able to sleep, "Tiger Time." She punctuates "Tiger Time" by leaping into a tiger's stance, arms stretched high above her head, mouth gaping open, tongue out, growling. When Shaw is in tiger mode, more of her body emerges: We see her wrists and open palms, we see her jacket splayed open to reveal the shape of her midsection under her white shirt, we see her tongue and teeth and the inside of her mouth. We hear a raspy growl in place of Shaw's practiced, low vocal pitch. And we see the comedian under Shaw's drag king facade, the hammy performer getting a laugh out of the audience. The sweaty tiger overpowers the cool, precise masculine presentation with which Shaw began the show. She drags her claws down in front of her body, then she shakes out her wrists and straightens her lapels again.

The story of Shaw's experience of menopause cannot be neatly divided between a disciplined, masculine, public presentation during the day and an incontinent, feminine, private night because the tiger of Shaw's sweaty nights is not private. Shaw's tiger "looks up into the night and sees the blue blue sky . . . and doesn't HAVE to fuck it / own it / grab it / wish it / change it / hold it / touch it / paint it / or please it. . . . But"—Shaw sticks out her tongue again, panting like a tiger—"it would be fun to try" (74). Shaw grins. She is not merely holding it together against the tiger's eventual overpowering force; she is seducing her audience, giving them little glimpses of the tiger inside. A reviewer of Shaw's 1997 performance described her "flirt[ing] outrageously with the audience" at Dixon Place. In turn, Shaw's audience "leave[s] with a taste for surrender, seduced by the rough treatment and hungry for more excavation of the menopausal mystery and the fascinating woman both sharing and creating it."[13] The sweat Shaw wipes from her brow marks the labor of this carefully crafted and rehearsed seduction. This labor belies Shaw's gentlemanly costume as much as her menopausal body does. Shaw calls herself "the hardest-working gentleman in show business" (78). She works to lower her voice, shine her shoes, fasten her cufflinks, and wolf-whistle convincingly at women. Shaw figures her sweaty menopausal nights as physically energetic creatures and sites of hard work: Along with tiger time, she compares night sweats to a captive beast, a wolf, a furnace, and an engine room. In *Menopausal Gentleman,* Shaw makes her drag king performance a kind of unalienated physical labor: hard work, but work she loves to do, work that helps her feel less estranged from what it reproduces, her own aging, changing body.

Physical labor is central to Shaw's own descriptions of her origins and success as a queer theater-maker. After growing up in a working-class Massachusetts family, marrying young, divorcing, and moving to New York with a toddler in tow to work for the Bureau of Child Welfare, Shaw stumbled upon drag queen Wilhelmina Ross, singing—serendipitously, in Shaw's telling of the story—"The Welfare Blues."[14] Leaving one form of socially reproductive labor as a child welfare worker, Shaw started her performance career doing another kind of reproductive work: maintenance labor as a driver and painter for Ross's drag cabaret group Hot Peaches. Shaw's behind-the-scenes labor became essential to Hot Peaches' nightly work of putting on a show. In interviews, she has described both the pleasure and the difficulty of theater as physical maintenance labor. Of founding the WOW Café, Shaw says, "It was a real pleasure to have my own theater and wash the floors."[15] Shaw brings the same attention and precision she devotes to maintaining her theater to the development and delivery of her theatrical productions: "The reason people liked our shows," she told interviewer Craig Lucas in 1999, "is that we rehearsed!"[16] Shaw understands making theater—washing the floors and rehearsing the shows—as the physical, sweaty labor of maintenance and reproduction. She reckons with the night sweat produced by menopause by incorporating it into her work, trading her unsatisfied desire for sleep for the satisfactory pleasures of seducing her audience.

Menopausal Gentleman, written and first performed in the late 1990s, emerged from a transitional moment in both Shaw's career and the overlapping fields of feminist and queer performance studies and queer theory more broadly—a moment for which sleep performance is an apt dramaturgical metaphor. The late 1990s was a time when queer downtown performance was growing dormant, past its heyday. Shaw's artistic career is intimately enmeshed in

New York's queer downtown performance scene of the late twentieth century. She is well known for her solo performances and her collaborative work with artistic partner Lois Weaver in their cofounded ensemble Split Britches, as well as for her work with other queer or feminist troupes and venues, including Spiderwoman Theater, Hot Peaches, and WOW Café Theater. Shaw's theater work also motivated significant early scholarship in feminist, lesbian, and queer performance studies, which developed in tandem with this academic discipline in the 1980s and 1990s.[17] In the late 1990s, Shaw was moving away from her more overtly collaborative work with Split Britches and the WOW Café and toward more frequent solo performance. Solo performance can adapt to a lack of public arts funding: Solo performers often have low production costs and can travel light, operating as independent contractors and surviving on commissions from arts venues and universities.[18] Shaw developed her first solo performance, *You're Just Like My Father,* in response to a performance commission from Hampshire College (for its parents' weekend) that arrived when Weaver was out of the country; *Menopausal Gentleman* is Shaw's second full-length solo work.[19] At the same time, in the late 1990s, queer and allied organizers who responded to the AIDS crisis with groundbreaking, lifesaving works of activism and care seemed to be turning the volume down. This was partly a result of their many successes (such as expanding the CDC's definition of AIDS to include women's symptoms, pushing for research on effective treatments, and bringing sexuality studies into the university) and partly due to a need for recovery after continued assaults from the religious right and a generation of untimely deaths.[20]

But alongside dormancy, sleep performance offers a vehicle for thinking through practices of sustainability for people whose gender and sexual politics put them in frequent antagonistic relationships with structures of power. Shaw's solo performance about menopause is perhaps an unusual path into this era of queer activism because it is about older age. Against a backdrop of organizing for breast cancer and AIDS to be taken seriously by the U.S. government and medical research institutions, along with an urgent awareness of high suicide rates among queer youth and the general violence faced by queer people in a vocally homophobic nation, it is remarkable that Shaw lived to—and through—menopause. As

Eve Kosofsky Sedgwick wrote in 1993, "I look at my adult friends and colleagues doing lesbian and gay work, and I feel that the survival of each one is a miracle."[21] Shaw is a miraculous performer: an anarchist, in-debt, working-class, queer single mother who has become a "grand-butch-elder" of queer theater in downtown New York.[22] *Menopausal Gentleman* presents us with Shaw's sweaty menopausal night as a moment in which Shaw's body and the theatrical world Shaw helped to create are aligned in their loss of youthful energy and engaged community. Feeling alone and exhausted, Shaw reorients toward the more personal goal of sustaining her own body through sleep.

Body Work

In order to sustain herself through one night of sleep, Shaw reins herself back in from the seductions of tiger time to focus all her energy on her own body. After a lifetime of community building with other people, Shaw's need to care for herself forces her performance to explore the more self-oriented, or even selfish, strains in feminist and queer theories of the body, sex, and illness. To start, Shaw attempts a classic exercise, borrowed from nineteenth-century theater training, to relax each part of her body progressively until she falls asleep. On a bench at center stage, Shaw lies gingerly on her back and arranges her body "*in an impossibly tense posture*" (80). She contracts her muscles as if she is performing an abdominal crunch: neck curved up so she can look down toward her feet, shoulders lifted off the bench, knees bent and pulled in toward her belly, feet hovering above the bench, and toes pointed up at the ceiling. "When I start feeling tired at night," she cautions, "I'm real careful . . . so I won't wake myself up" (80). Shaw splits in two again, now not by gender but by part of speech: the Shaw "I" and the Shaw "myself," both subject and object of the sentence.

Yet as Shaw describes the exercise out loud, she further divides herself into independent parts—toes and ankles and legs, each with its own agency to sleep or not—so that Shaw becomes not just a two-part self but an assemblage of independently functioning body parts that must be enjoined to collaborate for her multiple self to fully sleep. Shaw "start[s] at my toes and I say, okay toes, / you just relax and take it easy . . . time to go to sleep" (80).

Shaw's toes and feet relax, angling down to rest on the bench, and she moves up her body to her ankles. Shaw describes her different body parts helping each other relax, as well: "Thighs I want you to join the rest of the leg and foot / and set a good example for my belly and my hips" (81). As Shaw approaches her head, her coaxing grows less pedestrian and more abstract, turning from calming the joints, muscles, and organs to settling the mind. Shaw takes a "*long pause*" before turning to her own thoughts: "Okay brain! Hello brain, that's it, / we're almost all asleep" (82). Shaw continues to contract only her neck, hovering her head just an inch or two above its resting place. Two concerns hold her brain back from falling asleep: "I know I don't have any health insurance" and "I know I wasn't a good mother" (82).[23]

While Shaw's approach to falling asleep is a widely recommended physiological practice for getting out of the brain and relaxing the body, the specific concerns in Shaw's brain draw attention to *Menopausal Gentleman*'s particular exploration of how gender and class meet up with aging. Shaw answers her own concern about health insurance with "It's okay, I'm not gonna get sick" (82), yet at the time Shaw was writing *Menopausal Gentleman*—and experiencing menopause—menopause itself was being studied as a form of illness that might benefit from medical treatment. Menopause, like homosexuality, was first named and pathologized by nineteenth-century doctors. The widespread use of synthetic estrogen as a medical treatment for menopause began much later, with the 1966 publication *Feminine Forever,* written by a male physician whose research was funded by the pharmaceutical company producing the hormones.[24] In the early 1990s, the U.S. National Institutes of Health began to consider women's experiences of menopause more directly with their first study of women's illnesses and death, as distinct from men's. Around the same time, in 1992, two major books on menopause were published by women, American journalist Gail Sheehy's *The Silent Passage: Menopause* and idiosyncratic Australian feminist Germaine Greer's *The Change: Women, Aging, and the Menopause.*[25] Beginning in 1993, when Shaw was forty-nine, the NIH Women's Health Initiative Hormone Therapy Trials studied the long-term effects of synthetic estrogen and progestin on various medical conditions among menopausal and postmenopausal women (ages fifty to seventy-nine). These trials were famously stopped early in 2002, when all participants were told to cease using hormone therapy because of a heightened risk for several life-threatening conditions.[26]

Feminists continue to spearhead investigations into understudied bodily exhaustion in forms as varied as chronic fatigue, depression, autoimmune disorders, long-term side effects of chemotherapy, and psychological burnout.[27] Yet a dearth of similar scholarship or advocacy in the realm of *men's* fatigue—or even fatigue without gender—makes it appear that women have sleep problems while men's sleep sets the norm. Perhaps bad sleep, or fatigue that persists despite sleep, is more common than we are led to believe. In her struggle to sleep as she worries about her flaws as a mother and her lack of health insurance, Shaw registers how little medical researchers have cared about women in her age bracket—past the point of active biological reproduction (as mothers) and so (until the possibility of pharmaceuticals was raised by hormone therapy) largely outside the concerns of medical research. Although Shaw tells herself she is "not gonna get sick" as she tries and fails to fall asleep, menopause reads as an impairment—Shaw's anxiety and nightly hot flashes prevent her from attaining the sleep she desires. If Shaw here is divided both between parts of speech (subject and object) and among body parts (toes, ankles, legs), she is also divided between the body she describes relaxing and the body onstage performing relaxation. The body Shaw describes relaxing is slowly giving in to leisure, but the body onstage performing continues to labor throughout the sequence, precisely flexing and extending different muscle groups to deliver a stylized rendition of the body falling asleep.

Shaw's sense of bodily dissolution echoes lesbian feminist Audre Lorde's description of her body after breast cancer treatment and a mastectomy, when she found herself becoming "myriad selves."[28] For Lorde, living as "myriad selves" is both a response to the irreparable difference of life after surgical and chemical trauma to her body—a sense of internal multiplication—and a realization of her fundamental dependence on others, made more evident during her illness. "To this day," Lorde writes, "sometimes I feel like a corporate effort, the love and care and concern of so many women having been invested in me with such openheartedness."[29] Lorde's theory of the sick but cared-for body as both myriad selves (falling apart) and a corporate effort (held together) marks the fragile rewards of living in a body (sick, lesbian, Black) that her nation and its medical system have disinvested in, a body that has been pushed back to the bedroom, but that has found alternate forms of solidarity and care from the sickbed.

Shaw articulates sleepless nights as the time she most intensely experiences menopause as a disabling dissolution into myriad selves: "I fall to pieces in the night. / I'm just thousands of parts of other people mashed into one body. / I am not an original person" (84). Instead, she has to hold on to the pieces "before they get swept under the bed" and use the pieces to "manufacture" herself (84). Although Shaw is describing her body fragmenting, a constant process of physical and personal reconstruction, onstage she looks fully put together, still sharp in her pinstripe suit after twenty minutes of lying on benches and acting like a tiger. She lets the audience in on something we cannot see, a menopause symptom more fundamental and existential than the sweat she regularly wipes from her brow. While the self Shaw has manufactured onstage cites midcentury masculinity, Shaw reveals that her sense of herself as a corporate effort is not tied to the movie-star heartthrobs her gender presentation expertly echoes. "When I'm saying I fall to pieces," Shaw clarifies, "I'm saying Marlon Brando was not there for me" (84). As the instrumental background of Frank Sinatra's "My Way" begins to play, Shaw turns her attention fully on the audience, making it clear that she was not seduced by the look of men like Brando, Sinatra, and James Dean but that her self-manufacturing is a mutual process of seduction between herself and her audience: "Just pick the piece you want / and when I pull myself back together again / . . . I'll think of you and who you want me to be" (85). Shaw strides into the audience, kissing hands, kneeling before spectators to deliver lines directly to them, and getting one woman to take her arm off her partner's shoulder so that Shaw can shake her hand as she speaks Sinatra's lyrics.

While Shaw tries to put herself together as a corporate effort with her audience, she continues to dissolve into multiplicity, losing parts of herself, when she actually tries to sleep through a hot flash. Here is a straightforward celebration of a kind of antirelationality that is more commonly associated with theorists of gay male sex than with lesbians like Shaw or Lorde. Along with shedding droplets of sweat throughout the performance, Shaw marks the dissolution of her eggs. Her celebration of a loss of potential future motherhood, her triumph in no longer being on the hook for future reproduction and care of others, is tied up in a shattering of her sense of self through a physical, bodied experience. As she dissolves into droplets of sweat, she simultaneously shimmies free of a social role (motherhood, or, more broadly, womanhood) defined through care for others. Shaw's exclamatory arrival at the loss of her eggs—"I DID IT!"—sounds like what gay polemicist Leo Bersani calls a "self-shattering and solipsistic *jouissance* that drives [people] apart."[30] The circumstances of Shaw's self-shattering in menopause are obviously different from the circumstances of sex between men that Bersani describes. Bersani is distinctly uninterested in lesbian sexuality or queer feminist politics; menopausal women do not seem to have entered the consciousness of gay theorists as potential practitioners of antinormative sexuality. But Shaw finds an antirelational sexual achievement in menopause. Shaw's complete emptying of her ovaries is an intriguing parallel with the nonreproductive emission of sperm suggested by Bersani's moment of jouissance, on a very different timescale.

And Shaw is not the only woman who describes menopause as an experience of "antinurturing" subjectivity, in Bersani's terms: In a survey of postmenopausal women conducted by the authors of *Our Bodies, Ourselves,* 90 percent of older women expressed positive feelings about putting their "childbearing" years behind them.[31] What an unexpected—perhaps unwanted—alignment menopause brings between a theorist of antinurturing sexuality and a cohort of women who spent decades of their lives nurturing children. Given that *Our Bodies, Ourselves* was first published in the United States before abortion was temporarily legalized nationwide, and that Shaw herself was born twenty-nine years before *Roe v. Wade,* perhaps it should not be so surprising that women were happy to have passed beyond the threat of forced motherhood. It is another miraculous survival. Shaw cannot sleep at night, but at least she no longer has to worry about someone else's sleep. She does not have to reproduce herself, to get enough sleep and pull herself together, in order to take care of others. She can pursue sleep for the solitary pleasures of it.

In contrast to this antirelational strain in *Menopausal Gentleman*, the majority of Shaw's performances are oriented toward relationality. These include examinations of Shaw's relationships with her parents (*You're Just Like My Father*), her grandson (*To My Chagrin*), and her artistic partner Weaver (*Lust Gasp*). But here Shaw just gets to celebrate the miracle of her own survival. Survival is not a given in Shaw's family history, which includes unusually high rates of childhood mortality. Of Shaw's ten siblings, four died at birth, another at age fifteen. In an interview about *Menopausal Gentleman*, Shaw recounted her mother having "11 nervous breakdowns and 11 shock treatments," accounting for the pain of childbearing and childhood death within her family of origin.[32] Shaw's sleep performance—both fragilely dependent on the corporate effort of others and triumphantly selfish—is an opportunity for a queer, disabled woman to be antirelational after spending so much of her life caring for others. Shaw dramatizes reproducing herself within the context of a dissolute body and the context of solo performance. Her attempts to reproduce herself through sleep show us the self as both fiercely defended and tenderly held together.

Roommates

Despite her aversion to representing rape or femicide onstage, Shaw does not make a sleep performance that is only about an idealized, nonconfrontational, and gentle form of care. To protect her own fragile ability to fall asleep, Shaw enacts violence toward another creature, in an act that literalizes the "shattering" Bersani describes. Shaw recalls waking up in the middle of the night to the sound of pigeons outside her window. Abruptly, the stage lights come up, the music cuts, and Shaw turns on her bench to face downstage, bracing a leg and an arm on the bench in a stylized storytelling pose. Her voice snaps out of wistful memory and into the tough-guy posture of the show's opening. She says she realized that the sounds were coming from a nesting pigeon—a "mother," in Shaw's telling—and predicted that the hatched chicks would be "ugly" and "squealing." To get rid of this pigeon mother and terminate future disruptions of her fragile sleep, Shaw relates, she "took chopsticks and pushed the freshly laid eggs down the shaftway" (90). The eggs, we can imagine, shattered on the concrete several stories below. Shaw is not courageous about this killing; although she sounds tough in the retelling, she is confessing to cowardice, not even able to touch the eggs with her own hands. Moreover, Shaw failed to win a quiet night's sleep. The mother pigeon just got louder, cooing accusatorially outside Shaw's window, mourning her lost offspring. Shaw commiserates bleakly: "not that I don't know what it's like to lose eggs" (90).

This is what Shaw does to wake her audience up at the forty-minute mark. She does not have "rape . . . or a woman killed" as part of her solo performance's dramatic structure, but she has this moment of honesty about the risks of life as a corporate effort. The pigeon's eggs, external and exposed, create an interspecies interdependence between Shaw and the pigeon made visible when Shaw easily kills off a nestful. Shaw puts herself in the pigeon's shoes: She says that she too has lost eggs in her lifetime. Does the pigeon mother's loss of a nest of eggs more closely resemble Shaw's own menopause or Shaw's mother's postpartum episodes of mental illness? Is Shaw's destruction of the pigeon eggs "violence against women"?

In her reading of Shaw's 1993 performance *You're Just Like My Father,* theater scholar Elin Diamond describes Shaw's yoking together of an unlikely "female community" as "deliberately comic," a strategy that asks us to reconsider what feminist solidarity gets from looking for sameness between women in different social positions, historical eras, or fictional worlds.[33] Shaw makes a similar, perhaps even more overtly absurd, move here, pointing toward a possible likeness among Shaw, her mother, and a pigeon "mother" in their experiences of loss and grief in reproduction. Diamond reads these moments of comically exaggerated solidarity as "explor[ing] relatedness while refusing the easy assumption of analogues or common reference points."[34] When Shaw says she knows what it is like to lose eggs, she laughs bleakly at the idea that what women share is a biological reproductive capacity and a sense of mourning when it is lost. Instead, in *Menopausal Gentleman,* Shaw connects their experiences through the violence that their capacity for reproducing offspring provokes in others.

In Shaw's sleep dramaturgy, the audience and Shaw do not need to meet up in a shared experience of violence against women that marks the climax of the plot. Shaw has said that when she initially wrote *Menopausal Gentleman,* she expected it to be a tragedy because she found menopause to be sad and scary, but in rehearsals and performances she continued to provoke laughter from her audience.[35] Sleep gives Shaw a vehicle for a performance of nonaligned relation between audience and performer. Shaw's audience is laughing while Shaw performs her fear and sadness. The pigeon wanted (as much as pigeons can want) to hatch her chicks while Shaw wanted to sleep. Shaw recounts the nonalignment of spending the night with a lover: "I asked you if you would spend the night with me / and you made me promise not to go to sleep" (89). Shaw complies, "surprised that my longing didn't wake you" but patiently counting her lover's breaths instead of going to sleep herself (90). The distance between how one feels in one's own body and how other people feel in theirs cannot be bridged perfectly. If there is anything to learn from our cultural fascination with sleep as solipsism, it is that perhaps we can never truly understand exactly what it feels like to sleep in—to be in—another body.

Menopausal Gentleman tracks a series of conflicts between what Shaw's body needs and what other bodies need, and Shaw closes her performance with one more story about going to sleep alone. Although the entire performance has been about Shaw, in this story, another woman chooses to sleep alone, setting sleep against the possibility of sexual violence now represented by Shaw herself. Shaw tells a story about working a weekly gig dressing up as a man (in a suit much like the one Shaw is wearing onstage) and escorting a wealthy older woman who wants to go out dancing. Each week, the encounter ends the same way, in a performance of gentlemanliness that forecloses the possibility of spending the night together, as Shaw tells the woman that a deep sense of respect prevents Shaw from acting on any attraction to the woman Shaw might feel. The woman "puts the door between us," and Shaw departs (96). The lights fade to black. Here, I depart from my main interlocutors for this chapter: Shaw's image of the door between her and the woman with whom she will not spend the night feels small and sterile, too marked by boundaries and propriety compared to either Bersani's shattering sexual jouissance or Lorde's corporate effort. To "put the door between us" is to signal you want to end the date, and to arm yourself against physical advances. *Menopausal Gentleman* ends not with Shaw but with another woman reproducing herself—pursuing pleasure, avoiding violence, maintaining a fragile relationality with the world on her own terms, and getting her sleep.

The struggle for queer and disabled survival has often been a struggle to break out of the bedroom, to put the hidden body, with its sex and its sickness, into public space. This strategy is in Lorde's publication of her cancer journals and her vision of one-breasted women descending on Congress like Amazon warriors; in Bersani's defense of unassimilated and unredemptive gay sex; in ACT UP's kiss-ins and political funerals; in ADAPT's crawl up the steps of the U.S. Capitol; in Queer Nation's "We're here! We're queer! Get used to it!" Alongside publication and direct action, sleep performances like *Menopausal Gentleman* invite audiences into bedrooms, using the stage as a third space between the private and the public where the rejected body can assert its own reproduction as a source of power.

Let's follow Shaw beyond the crisis of menopause to a later performance, one that imagines Shaw's sleep alongside the untimely deaths of her queer, trans, and sick friends. This scene is, again, about sleeping alone and incommensurate bodily experiences. In 2011, Shaw had a stroke, and an online crowdfunding campaign for the "Peggy Shaw Pension Fund" raised more than fifteen thousand dollars to care for "our grand-butch-elder" in her illness and retirement.[36] The need for such fundraising to bankroll health care and retirement is evidence of the highly uneven distribution of health and rest along class lines. Yet this was also a moment when Shaw's many friends, including fellow artists and devoted audience members, came together to care for Shaw in a material way, attempting to create a world in which a poor, queer, anarchist, lifelong artist could take a break from work and rely on a pension.

Shaw responded to her stroke in the solo performance *Ruff*, created with Weaver.[37] *Ruff* is a much more overtly interdependent performance than *Menopausal Gentleman*. Shaw asks audience members to do things for her and uses teleprompter screens to reference her lines. In the final moments of *Ruff*, Shaw narrates another sleep scene, a "wild dream." In the dream, Shaw floats down from New York City's George Washington Bridge, landing in a "spirit-world" of "oh so gay" fish at the bottom of the Hudson River. It is an ambiguous opening. Shaw says the dream opens not just with falling but with "being pushed" from the bridge, and at the bottom of the river, she first recognizes Marsha P. Johnson, a Black drag queen and gay liberation activist, and a performer with Hot Peaches. Johnson's body was found in the Hudson River in 1992, and her cause of death remains undetermined.

At the bottom of the Hudson, the dreaming-dead Shaw finds herself among other miraculous queer survivors who still died untimely deaths. Along with Johnson, Shaw's spirit world of oh-so-gay fish includes Wilhelmina Ross (who introduced Shaw to Hot Peaches), James Neale-Kennerley (the director of Shaw's first solo performance, *You're Just Like My Father,* and the dedicatee of *Menopausal Gentleman*), Charles Ludlam (founder of downtown New York's Ridiculous Theatrical Company), and performance scholar and queer utopian José Esteban Muñoz. Their too-early deaths haunt Shaw's dream. As at the beginning of *Menopausal Gentleman,* Shaw again invites her audience into her experience of sleep. "Help me," she asks *Ruff*'s audience, as she describes the gay spirit fish who sustain her. "Help me remember their names."

In this sleep scene, Shaw again examines her own survival in the context of so many friends who have died—who have died of violence, of state neglect, of a health care system for whom they were not a priority. After her stroke, Shaw's own survival seems even more miraculous. In *Ruff*'s closing dream, Shaw achieves the fruits of her self-reproduction: not a hot flash but a cool river, not a tiger but a school of fish, not alone but with friendly gay spirits, in front of a friendly audience. Shaw and her spirit fish friends continue to have incommensurate bodily experiences—Shaw is alive and her friends are dead. But through the magically clear (and not at all polluted) dream Hudson River, they can see each other.

And Shaw likes to be seen. In *Menopausal Gentleman* she asks "to be loved in fluorescent light . . . naked in that kinda blue, flickering, kinda ugly exposed feeling of that cheap hallway light" (91). As a performer, Shaw reproduces herself by continuing to put herself onstage, by examining herself—her body, her beliefs, her history—under stage lighting that is as bright (if not as ugly) as fluorescents. In *Menopausal Gentleman,* sleep gets the fluorescent treatment. Although sleep might seem to offer little of interest to a theater audience, Shaw finds the difficult project of reproducing herself, of getting herself to sleep each night while battling insomnia and other symptoms of menopause, to be a source of dramatic action. In inviting audiences into her nightly drama of self-reproduction, Shaw also intervenes in theater's habitual reproduction of violence against women, in the form of plots about rape and murder, and in the cultural and medical prioritization of childbirth as women's most important reproductive work. By turning our attention to sleep performance, we can turn our attention toward bodies whose reproduction—whose continued, miraculous survival—has not been invested in. We can recognize a role for performance that uses its capacity to reproduce the world onstage to focus its bright lighting on the bedroom as a site of queer and disabled life.

Part Two
At Home

Three
Insomniac Housewives
Sleepless Domestic Dramas of Caryl Churchill

The documentary *Nightcleaners* captures the conditions of working-class women's sleep in 1970s Britain.[1] A multiracial group of women office cleaners is trying to unionize. They spend their days caring for their children and maintaining their own homes, and they spend their nights cleaning up after white-collar office employees. Although workingmen had strong unions in the United Kingdom for decades leading up to the 1970s, the postwar Keynesian welfare state depended on the exclusion of women and immigrants from outposts of the (former) British Empire from these secure, well-paid jobs.[2] But by the 1970s, even the "family wage" paid to male breadwinners was diminishing in buying power, and more women were raising children as single mothers; night shifts in low-paying, nonunion jobs are the only work that the women in *Nightcleaners* can do and still care for their children during the day. When do these night cleaners sleep? "Between one and three [in the afternoon] . . . if the baby goes to sleep," one answers. "From half past ten till twelve [noon]," says another. "But if the children was grown up and off of our hands we could get a day job for about twelve pound, couldn't you, and have your night's sleep." Seventeen years before American sociologist Arlie Hochschild would popularize the term "second shift," the work these women were doing in their households and outside them expanded to fill twenty or more hours of the day.[3]

Feminists in the 1960s and 1970s, exercising political acumen built in the civil rights, antiwar, and organized labor movements, attacked this unlivable situation. They campaigned for changes in how household work was compensated, so that women could have access to money of their own, and they analyzed the origins of the sexual division of labor at the crux of capitalism and patriarchy.[4] Feminists organizing against capitalism and for economic justice—often called Marxist, socialist, or materialist feminists—fought off welfare cuts in wealthy nations well into the neoliberal era and continue the fight, energetically, in many nations today. Alongside the unionization campaign documented in *Nightcleaners,* feminist campaigns for compensating household labor have other origin stories in disturbed sleep. One is the story of Johnnie Tillmon-Blackston, the first chair of the National Welfare Rights Organization and a Black single mother in 1960s Los Angeles. Tillmon-Blackston began organizing for dignified access to welfare in the United States after suffering a series of midnight raids in which welfare inspectors invaded her home looking for money, a man, or some other evidence she was cheating the system.[5] In the 1970s, Tillmon-Blackston and the NWRO intersected with a related movement, the Wages for Housework Campaign, which was started in the United Kingdom by white European and American women and became an international coalition.[6] Today, we can recognize the pervasive effects of Marxist feminist interventions in our widespread understanding of such concepts as the second shift, domestic labor, and women's struggle to "have it all." Despite rumors that Marxist feminism was short-lived, Marxist feminist analysis has become a part of our daily lives.

Across her long career, British playwright Caryl Churchill has deeply and imaginatively demonstrated the expansive possibilities born of Marxist feminist analysis. Since her first professionally produced play, *Owners* (1972), Churchill has been dramatizing the distance between what her characters want from their lives and what they experience in the trenches of the sexual division of labor. Churchill is part of a cohort of British playwrights whose formally innovative dramas for educated audiences have found success in major independent theaters like London's Royal Court, where she was the first female playwright in residence. Among Royal Court regulars like Harold Pinter, Michael Frayn, and Tom Stoppard, Churchill is uniquely concerned with women's political lives, on both an intimate and a global scale. Churchill's characters—whether a thirteenth-century Japanese concubine, a 1980s British farmworker, or a grandmother surviving a future planetary catastrophe—are inquisitive and frustrated; their actions onstage hack away at the distance between the lives they want and the lives they have. They are very often women who feel trapped at home—and are trapped onstage, in confining beds or claustrophobic domestic scenic designs.[7]

The trapped housewife is an archetypal figure of domestic drama, but Churchill handles this archetype in a new way. While domestic dramas are conventionally staged stories about households that address bourgeois themes in naturalist writing, Churchill's housewives compel a new generic ending that upends both character and audience expectations for domestic drama.[8] Although Churchill puts sleep onstage in her plays with some regularity, this chapter specifically examines plays in which a housewife character suffers from insomnia that knows no bounds. In parallel to the physiological effects of insomnia, which prevent Churchill's characters from resolving their exhaustion in sleep, the plays themselves become unable to reproduce the endings appropriate to the familiar stage genre of domestic drama. First, extreme insomnia manifests for the unhappy housewife Margaret in *Three More Sleepless Nights* (1980), disrupting the play's resolution in the formation of a new household. Insomnia also derails the resolution of a domestic drama in *Fen* (1983), but, surrounded by a reluctant community of other exhausted women, the protagonist housewife Val sees a shared nightmare come to life and participates in a shared dream of resisting the structural, material sources of her suffering—a dream that housewives in the audience might also participate in. By 2000, Churchill had moved into an increasingly eco-conscious and less overtly feminist mode of writing, but her short play *Far Away* returned to the sleepless housewife in the character Harper. No longer tied to the conditions of working-class British life, Harper instead strives to keep her family together through a planetary war.

Churchill's sleepless housewife characters—Margaret in *Three More Sleepless Nights,* Val in *Fen,* and Harper in *Far Away*—dilate on the critique of the housewife as a foundational economic figure put forth by Marxist feminists in the 1970s.[9] Foregrounded in the writing of Wages for Housework cofounders Selma James and Mariarosa Dalla Costa, *housewife* as a category yokes domestic labor to the type of person who performs it by historical default. The housewife, James and Dalla Costa argue, performs essential but uncompensated labor previously overlooked by a Marxist focus on commodity production. She does the work of social reproduction, not only reproducing and caring for future generations of workers (her children) but also keeping the current generation (her husband and herself) fed, clothed, and clean. The term reminds us that people and property need continual maintenance and that, in many historical circumstances, this work has been uncompensated, diminished, unevenly distributed, and heaped on top of other (paying) work. Describing working-class women in the middle of the twentieth century, James and Dalla Costa call the housewife "indispensable to capitalist production" and "the determinant for the position of all other women."[10] As worker in and maintainer of the home she lives in, a housewife experiences working conditions that are also her living—and sleeping—conditions, and she does not escape the job site when she goes to bed.

Three More Sleepless Nights, *Fen*, and *Far Away* push the demands of social reproduction on housewives to supernatural ends, creating housewife characters who are so taxed by domestic labor that their bodies can no longer perform the basic biological task of self-reproduction through sleep. Despite their best efforts to change their lives in ways that they imagine would make their reproductive labor sustainable—by pursuing different romantic partners, asking for help with childcare, or seeking new jobs—the exhausted housewives in *Three More Sleepless Nights* and *Fen* remain unable to sleep. In *Far Away*, this insomnia radiates outward, making the condition of 1980s housewives from Churchill's earlier plays into a planetary state of unsustainable, exhausting warfare. While the category of housewife often drops out of feminist analysis starting in the 1990s, the persistence of the sleepless housewife figure signals that the gendered labor of social reproduction remains, hauntingly, at the center of Churchill's vision of apocalypse at the beginning of the twenty-first century. In *Far Away*, the housewife's insomnia becomes the state of the world.

Three More Sleepless Nights

Churchill's 1980 short play *Three More Sleepless Nights* lists only one set piece: a double bed (247).[11] Reviewer Milton Shulman described this bed as "more deadly than the battlefield" and found that, onstage, "the mattress arouses a desire for almost everything except copulation."[12] *Three More Sleepless Nights* is a comic sketch with three scenes, each of which depicts a different squabbling couple battling in the same double bed—the characters neither physically escape its confines nor psychologically escape into slumber. The bed becomes a claustrophobic miniature stage on which women pursue romance narratives they hope will change their lives, only to see these imagined futures founder and burn out. The small differences in the three couples' distinct squabbles are swamped by the sameness of the scenes: As Churchill's title forecasts, no one in the bed gets any sleep.

My reading of *Three More Sleepless Nights* focuses on Margaret, a housewife character similar to others in Churchill's 1970s and 1980s plays. Margaret is unhappily married to Frank, with whom she shares children. They are working-class and worried about money; while Margaret is interested in working outside the home, they cannot afford paid childcare. References to popular films from the spring and summer of 1979 set *Three More Sleepless Nights* in the same historical moment as Margaret Thatcher's election on May 3, 1979, and very close in time to the play's premiere in 1980. (Margaret the housewife might draw our attention to the prime minister who shares her name.) Margaret the housewife begins the play unable to sleep. She pursues a resolution to this problem, and the larger problem of her marriage, by leaving Frank and forming a relationship with a new man, Pete, who is more vocally committed to equal partnership. Yet the play's central problem, Margaret and her partners' inability to fall asleep, persists through the end of the play, leaving Margaret without the emotional and material resolution she expects for successfully attracting a more desirable, possibly more feminist, partner. She remains trapped in a static experience of simultaneous exhaustion and sleeplessness.

Margaret's complaints about Frank in the opening scene indicate she is well aware of the endless "women's work" of social reproduction that is exhausting her. On the first of the titular three nights, Margaret hectors her husband about his infidelity, drinking, and wasteful spending. Margaret has "cleaned [his] sick off the floor," she hopes he can "get a hot dinner . . . and [his] socks washed" by his mistress instead of her, she has had sex with him when she "didn't enjoy it," and she has "carried the whole lot" of groceries up the stairs when the building elevator broke. If she were not caring for Frank's children full-time, Margaret claims, she "could have been a model, could have been a hairdresser, could have been a shorthand typist . . . could have took the pill" (249–50, 254–55). If she had not become a wife and mother, Margaret thinks, she could have accessed some of the opportunities, including employment and contraception, opened up to women by earlier feminist activism, but in her current role, she views these opportunities as beyond her reach. Margaret's incessant complaints protest the sexual division of labor in her marriage by putting Frank through the same exhaustion she already endures. While Frank is able to escape the house by going to work during the day and to the pub or his mistress's house in the evenings, Margaret refuses to let him escape into sleep at home—although this also means keeping herself awake.

By depicting Margaret at night, when she is done with her work but still unable to sleep, Churchill foregrounds not just this housewife's labor but also her attempts to make sense of labor conditions that she recognizes as exhausting and unfair, but that she cannot succeed in changing either through recruiting her partner's help or getting herself into paying work outside the house. This short, often funny scene is packed with the problems faced by women trying to claim freedom in social circumstances that depend on their unpaid domestic labor. In an audio recording of a staged reading, Margaret and Frank sound like a sitcom couple arguing, and the audience laughs frequently.[13] A couple arguing about an unfair distribution of domestic labor has become a trope of televised and onstage domestic drama, and even in the play's 1979 setting, Margaret's complaints do not seem revelatory—they are not the feminist awakenings of a woman who has just attended her first consciousness-raising circle. Instead, Margaret's extreme insomnia is born of the painful contradiction between imagining a feminist world and being unable to realize it, and she drags every other character in the play into this insomnia with her.

On the second sleepless night, a new unhappy couple is in the bed: Pete and Dawn. Pete is a film aficionado who presents an educated, aesthete contrast to Frank's stereotypical masculinity. And, as we might expect of a domestic narrative that starts off sounding like a sitcom, the third night (or third act) seems to bring about a resolution to Margaret's problem, with Pete and Margaret now together in bed. Margaret has left Frank for a man who claims to be invested in her autonomy and happiness. Yet, instead of happiness, they find only more insomnia, and both spend another frustrating night "very wide awake" with worry, cast into sleeplessness (270). Margaret and Pete repeatedly assert that their new relationship together is a meaningful change in their lives. "I've changed," Margaret says, "I was just his wife before. I had no life. . . . I've changed myself," but the sameness of the bed belies this claim (266). The unchanging bed is a scenic structure external to any particular staged partnership that metonymically stands in for the gender and class structures forestalling Margaret's attempts to change her life. In production photographs of the third scene in director Les Waters's original staging, Pete holds a mug of coffee while Margaret smokes; the stimulants indicate that neither expects to fall asleep anytime soon.[14] "You don't have to make a martyr of yourself with the housework," Pete says, but as only Pete can get a job outside the home, Margaret continues caring for their house and her children (268). Margaret reasons that she should be able to resolve the problems in her life that keep her up at night—her unfaithful husband, financial dependence, and responsibility for childcare—but her attempts at change always fall flat.

Attending critically to insomnia in Churchill's play foregrounds the tension between the change Margaret pursues and the stasis she experiences, still trapped in the double bed. Pete heightens this stasis by analyzing aloud what he calls "nightmare" scenes from popular movies. In the midst of Margaret's scene 3 complaints about how little her new relationship with Pete has changed her own financial worries, childcare responsibilities, and floundering job search, Pete invokes nightmare to describe a climactic, chaotic sequence in the 1979 film *Apocalypse Now*: "They kill a girl and rescue a puppy and the black kid on the boat gets killed and it's a real nightmare and he goes on up the river to find the colonel" (273). Pete stops in the middle of this "real nightmare" scene, his parataxis enumerating event after event, without describing the film's ending. I suggest that Churchill's use of nightmare here is a small-scale experiment with the staged dream form that she later expanded, in different ways, in *Fen* and in her adaptation of August Strindberg's surrealist *Dream Play.*[15] Pete's decision to end his retelling in chaotic medias res contrasts starkly with Margaret's feelings of burned-out stasis.

By setting Margaret's anxieties about who cares for the children, who earns the money, and who does the housework only in the bed, Churchill roots the claustrophobic stasis the characters are experiencing in the most private setting for the sexual division of labor within a partnership. In both his narration of *Apocalypse Now* and his scene 2 retelling of the final moments of the 1979 film *Alien,* Pete describes the transformation of a container—the boat in *Apocalypse Now* and the space pod in *Alien*—into a means of escape. The bed onstage serves as a container for each of the three couples in *Three More Sleepless Nights,* but it leads neither to the "good night's sleep" Pete describes as the ending of *Alien* nor to the dynamic climax of *Apocalypse Now*'s nightmare. Like Nagg and Nell's trash cans in Samuel Beckett's *Endgame,* the bed immobilizes the sleepless characters to an absurd extent, so they cannot even remedy their disordered sleep by leaving the room. All they could do to punctuate their arguments in Waters's staging was flick the bedside light on and off.[16] By setting familiar quarrels written in naturalist dialogue in an absurdly inescapable bed, Churchill stages the social structures that depend on Margaret remaining in her role as working-class housewife, trapping her in a frustrating stasis every time she tries to make a logical change to improve her life. "You keep being unhappy," Margaret complains, as much about herself as about Pete (271). Margaret's perpetual insomnia—and its attendant unhappiness, frustration, and anxiety—defies dramatic resolution in the form of the successful new household she pursues, leaving the characters onstage exhausted and the audience frustrated.

By frustration, I mean that *Three More Sleepless Nights* offers the appearance of a happy ending for Margaret but none of its affect: Reviewing the original production, critic Eric Shorter noted that the play "lack[ed] the punch which its form implies, and the dramatic intensity of its Strindbergian echoes."[17] I take Shorter's desire for dramatic intensity as a lament for Strindberg's naturalist dramas of sexual warfare, in the vein of *Miss Julie,* which amplify heterosexual squabbles like Margaret and Frank's in scene 1 until they reach violent ends. But marriage never ends in *Three More Sleepless Nights*; its participants merely swap partners. The play's three sleepless nights might extend to four, or forty, or a lifetime's worth.

Margaret's own frustration might even extend to the play's audience, as represented by Shorter. Shorter criticizes Churchill's departure from familiar dramatic forms, but this lack of intensity and resolution is Churchill's intervention in the conventions of domestic drama. Churchill replaces the positive emotions that Margaret expects to accompany her successful creation of a new relationship and new household with static, dull dissatisfaction. Further, Shorter's review suggests that spectators come to crave nightmare-like scenes: The "dramatic intensity" Shorter ascribes to Strindberg is analogous to the "real nightmare" Pete revels in while describing *Apocalypse Now. Three More Sleepless Nights* resists theater's tendency to find dramatic value in sleep onstage through the interpretive richness of staged dreams and instead exploits the fact that watching someone try to sleep—especially watching them try to sleep three times over—is a bit boring for spectators who are accustomed to more dynamic action. In dramatizing the problems faced by a working-class British housewife character circa 1980 as extreme insomnia, Churchill begins her experiments with the relationship between insomnia and new theatrical forms for representing domestic life.

Fen

In *Fen* Churchill reprises and expands her experiment with insomnia as a dramaturgical strategy for changing the narrative arc of domestic drama via a full-length play devised through a collaborative research process in the rural British Fens. *Fen* is a documentary of impoverished rural life haunted by ghosts, ghoulish stories, and a final nightmare scene that breaks open each housewife's individual anguish into a communal, transhistorical experience. Among the "folklore, history, and sociology" that Churchill and her collaborators brought to the play through their research, reviewer

Laurie Stone noted how the "scenes of private life . . . resemble dream fragments—the dirt-floor set with its smoky vapors is a dream environment."[18] In *Fen,* Churchill develops a kind of haunted documentary. She interweaves realist restagings of daily life in the Fens drawn from her research with ghosts, dreams, and songs that transcend realism, filtering these moments from the 1980s through hundreds of years of disenfranchisement and drudgery that have never really been left behind. *Fen* unpacks the limited opportunities available to working-class women in rural England in the 1980s while using these techniques of haunting to present those limited opportunities not as a foregone narrative conclusion but, instead, as born of specific historical circumstances that could be changed or resisted.

Fen uses an ensemble cast of five women and one man to play twenty-two characters, both agricultural laborers in the 1980s and ghosts of workers from centuries past. Designer Annie Smart's original set placed the walls and household objects of a cottage on the dirt floor of a potato field; the complete overlap of these two worlds onstage established an inescapable cycle of housework and farmwork for the play's working women.[19] Among a handful of interconnected storylines, *Fen*'s twenty-one episodic vignettes track the domestic drama of Val and Frank. Although the dramatic form of *Fen* differs from that of *Three More Sleepless Nights,* Churchill recycles the same foundational figure of an exhausted working-class housewife who can access some of the gains of feminism—divorce, sexual freedoms—but cannot make a new romance coalesce with her existing children and low-paying job into a successful household. Val and Frank, both married to other people, have fallen in love and have decided to leave their families to live together. Yet Frank refuses to give up his job to move to London, and Val finds that, even with Frank, she cannot feel happy stuck in the Fens. While all the women in the play are overworked, pulling double shifts of field labor and childcare, Val becomes entirely unable to sleep and, tortured by this extreme insomnia, asks Frank to kill her.

Churchill collaborated with the theatrical collective Joint Stock to create the text of *Fen* through a research and workshop process, during which she spent time in a Fens village and read an early feminist oral history of Fens life.[20] Joint Stock's process of devising

Fen included finding theatrical equivalents for the exhaustion of extreme insomnia through multiple casting and a draining physical performance vocabulary. Joint Stock's workshop to devise the text and staging of *Fen* built physical exhaustion into the actors' performances. Stage directions describe fifty-year-old working grandmother Shirley simultaneously "*ironing, mending, preparing dinner, minding a baby . . . [she] never stops moving*" (167).[21] The Joint Stock actors developed Shirley's actions in their workshops through an exercise requiring them to "iron a shirt, peel potatoes, sweep the floor, fold a sheet, feed a baby, settle a miserable child, and give a man his tea. All in ten minutes."[22] Joint Stock ultimately distinguished Shirley's physical performance by demanding that the actor playing Shirley accomplish more work in less time than seemed possible. Onstage, Shirley rationalizes why she works at such a rapid pace: She carries on with her "work work work" at home and in the fields so that she does not end up with "too much time on [her] hands" (168). Although she claims she would not work if she did not need money, the actor's physical performance belies her ability to stop. *Fen* pushes this behavior toward a level of exhaustion that tests the capacities of a living human body.

Fen also deploys multiple casting as a visible strategy for overworking the ensemble cast, limiting the actors' time to rest during a performance by continually sending them onstage to play new roles. In *Fen*'s original casting, used at London's Almeida and Royal Court Theatres, all but one actor played four roles apiece, extending the strategic double casting that Churchill used for *Cloud Nine* and *Top Girls* to create constant work for every actor throughout the play. One reviewer commented, "We are used to doubling and trebling[;] we are not used to such rapid changes in a production so involved as this."[23] Quadruple casting was an innovative strategy not only for making economical use of a small ensemble but also for incorporating the actors into the staged environment of ceaseless labor through their "rapid changes"—requiring three backstage dressers—and continual reappearances onstage.[24] By creating a play that strategically and visibly overworked its actors, Churchill and Joint Stock developed a pervasive environment of exhaustion that contextualizes Val's own insomnia and ultimately breaks down the typically individual phenomenon of staged nightmare into a full-cast performance of disturbed sleep as shared experience.

Val's chronic sleeplessness emerges both from the devised performance conditions of *Fen,* which demand overwork from the entire acting ensemble, and from the ecology of the Fens' exhausted land, which is no longer farmed in a way that can sustainably feed its own inhabitants. Like her fellow Fen dwellers, Val is aware that her working conditions are poor and exploitative and that she might be happier elsewhere. Stooped over a potato field, she insists, "I've got to leave now. . . . I'm going. . . . Sorry, I can't help it. . . . I've got to go. I've gone. Never mind. . . . I've got to go now." The design of the scene already suggests Val may not have much of an escape; although she says she will just "go back home," the potato field onstage is inside the cottage used as every worker's house in the play (148–49). Val finds nowhere else to go. Unable to convince Frank to run away to London with her, she ends up in the same house, having left her husband and taken her children to their grandmother's. She refuses everything that categorizes her as working-class housewife—potato picking, childcare, and housework—and lingers in limbo, still stuck in the field/house but with no work to determine her social role in either. She feels "like thick nothing. I can't get on. Makes my arms and legs heavy." Val grows ill and eventually becomes unable to do anything, even sleep. By scene 17, Val tells Frank she "can't sleep" and had "better die" (172, 178–79).

Fen stages a parallel between Val's flattened, exhausted emotional state and the flatness of the Fens land, deprived of its former natural resources and continuously cultivated. Through this parallel, Churchill expands the critique of the role of the working-class housewife from *Three More Sleepless Nights* to yoke the exhaustion of environmental resources to the exhaustion of workers and women. The Fens themselves have entered into a sleepless cycle of production, no longer allowed to lie fallow at times but always being worked over, perfected for higher yields. Overwork overrides older cycles of seasonal change and daily rest. In the opening scene, a multinational corporate executive describes the Fens as "very efficient, flat land, plough right up to the edge, no waste." Before the Fens were drained and developed, Fen dwellers would "walk on stilts" across the swampy ground. They adapted their behavior to the ecosystem, keeping the land underwater and living off the "fishes and eels" that shared their environment without depleting the food source (147). When the Fens were drained, the work demanded of the land itself intensified. The land was expected not merely to sustain local inhabitants but also to produce surplus livestock and crops that could be sold for profit beyond the Fens. Yet neither the Fens land nor Val is allowed to stop working. The environmental exhaustion extends into the deep history of the Fens, for even long-dead laborers cannot rest but reappear in the play as ghosts.

With the particular specter of a nineteenth-century mother identified only as "Ghost," *Fen* pushes past the stasis that characterizes both Margaret's insomnia in *Three More Sleepless Nights* and Val's in *Fen,* uncovering a potential for resistance in a form of solidarity Fens residents can access only when they have crossed beyond conscious waking life. The ghosts of farmworkers historicize overwork and land resale in the 1980s in the context of hundreds of years of worker and land exploitation. Yet they also demonstrate the power of a body disciplined by what Shirley calls "work work work": More than a century after their deaths, the ghosts of *Fen* continue to show up to their work in the fields. Denied sleep for so long in life, they seem not to need it in death. The actor who plays Val is double cast as Ghost, and, in this role, she is not merely exhausted and sleepless but supernaturally restless, unable to find respite long after her physical body has stopped working. Unlike the living farmworkers, who are cowed by threats of reduced hours and lost pay, Ghost fears nothing. She confronts a farm owner who has sold out to a larger corporation, using the plural first-person voice to assert a claim to solidarity with her fellow workers: "We are starving, we will not stand this no longer. Rather than starve we are torment to set you on fire. . . . I been working in this field a hundred and fifty years. . . . My baby died starving" (163). Ghost has not stopped her work for "a hundred and fifty years," yet while overwork fades Val into incapacitation, Ghost grows stronger. When insomnia crosses the line into death, sleeplessness becomes a supernatural source of social power and a means of connecting that transcends Val's experience of isolated poverty, bringing workers throughout the history of the Fens into solidarity with one another.

Understanding how the disparate, competitive workers in *Fen* become able to find an unexpected, tenuous form of solidarity with one another depends first on this counterintuitive interpretation of staged sleeplessness as a social experience. Val's storyline establishes the conventions of a domestic tragedy, a narrative of a failed love affair that ends in the death of one or both partners, much as critic Eric Shorter seemed to wish for when he compared *Three More Sleepless Nights* unfavorably with Strindberg's punchier marital dramas. Val becomes so desperate for rest that she asks Frank to kill her. Rather than using the knife Val offers him, Frank kills Val with his axe and hides her body in the wardrobe. Val's death, if a suicide, reflects her isolation after refusing the social roles of worker and housewife, yet if we read it as a homicide, it reflects the continuity of her social role: Wives are more likely to be murdered by their husbands than by anyone else. The ambiguity of this tragic death scene feeds further uncertainty when Val suddenly reenters "*through the door on the other side of the stage*" (187): Is she alive, or is she a ghost? The possibilities elicited screams from the audience on *Fen*'s opening night.[25] Val's death is a misdirection that makes Frank, who took the active role in killing her, look like the protagonist of the scene. Production photographs of the staging at the Royal Court show the wardrobe placed against the stage left wall of the cottage.[26] After Frank put Val's murdered body into the wardrobe, the actor playing Val climbed out through a hole cut in the stage left wall and crossed backstage to reenter through a door in the upstage wall, all in the time it took Frank to sit down with his back against the wardrobe. While the audience watched him slump down in shock, Val made her surprising reentry, her dress still bloodstained from her death. Rather than dying conclusively to complete the arc of her romantic tragedy, Val follows the pattern of Ghost, transforming her sleeplessness into a restlessness that gives her the power to shock the audience through her immediate return after death.[27]

By refusing the rest she wanted in death, Val breaks out of the isolation of *Fen*'s working housewives and finds she has access to the thoughts and dreams of her fellow villagers, both living and dead. Val reports she can now see many ghosts from the Fens, yet she focuses on a woman whose "baby died starving"—perhaps the woman who became Ghost (163). While Val could listen to many different ghost stories, she chooses a fellow mother who has lost her child, and suddenly she can access the nightmare of a teenage girl called Becky about her abusive stepmother, as well. More and more women join the scene. Val's sleeplessness prevents *Fen* from merely documenting women who are structurally condemned to unhappy, limited lives as poor, working wives and mothers in rural England. Val's decision to reject this limited life by pursuing romance does not ultimately bring her happiness, but when Val then chooses to listen to the other Fens women after her death, she opens the play to a shared nightmare scene in which these women rehearse their own alternate responses to their exhausting lives.

This scene transforms the women's apprehensions and anxieties into a nightmare that is very different from what we have been taught to expect by psychoanalytic traditions of dream analysis.[28] Rather than expressing repressed desires, the housewives onstage attempt to fight back against the material conditions that exhaust them. Each woman's alternate response performs what utopian theorist Ernst Bloch calls a "rehearsal on the model," a theatrical performance that tests options for political or social action.[29] Bloch reads nightmares as expressions of material anxieties and sees in daydreams the utopian potential for simultaneously refusing work, through idleness, and imagining militant resistance. In this final scene, the housewives' daytime apprehension of what is coming produces a scene that fully breaks from the earlier episodes' documentary form. The woman whose baby died starving enters the nightmare because she is afraid of losing her child and dying of malnutrition; teenager Becky's nightmare stems not from unconscious desires but from conscious fears of her stepmother's abuse. Because the nightmare scene is the only moment of cross-worker and cross-temporal solidarity in the play, staged dream becomes a unique opportunity to refract character anxieties through the lens of shared material conditions that extend far beyond what Val, or any other individual character in *Fen,* could change. Although Bloch sees theater as an opportunity to put this rehearsal on a model to the audience for critique and evaluation, Churchill creates a version of shared nightmare that allows her characters to be spectators of one another as they rehearse refusals of their social roles as women, workers, and housewives.

As each housewife tests an ending to her particular storyline that would change the exhausting conditions of her life and work, the other women grow braver. The nonconformist Nell crosses the stage on stilts, drawing on the mythology of the "Fen tigers," indigenous premodern Fen dwellers who hunted the swamps, elevated above the muck. "The sun spoke to me," she announces. "It said, 'Turn back, turn back.' I said, 'I won't turn back for you or anyone'" (189). Nell exits, determined in her opposition. Among these fantasies of refusal, Shirley carries on with her "work work work," now ironing the dirt of the potato field. As she tries to finish the laundry, she further soils her own clothing with the stage floor's dirt. Her nightmare is the same endless work that she earlier claimed to like. Now she articulates the emotions she has been holding at bay through constant work: "I'd forgotten what it was like to be unhappy. I don't want to" (189). While Becky defies her stepmother and Nell defies the sun, Shirley tries to defy her own habit of exhausting herself into feeling nothing. She does not want to forget how to feel—even how to feel unhappy—again. Shirley tests out the refusal of the entrepreneurial work ethic that can always find more work, dirtying her clothes just as she tries to clean them in a deliberate undoing of her own labor. The disordered sleep in this shared nightmare scene intervenes in the genre of domestic drama by transforming Val's sleeplessness into a ghostly restlessness that allows her to defy the tragic conventions of a murder/suicide ending and return after death. Rather than ending with the dissolution of a household, the play ends by forming a new social configuration in the women's shared dream.

Does this new social configuration extend from the characters onstage to the primarily middle- and upper-class spectators seeing the play in London and New York? Perhaps the shared nightmare scene models a form of feminist spectatorship across difference, inviting women in the audience who have experienced some of the same gendered concerns as the characters onstage—domestic violence, pregnancy loss, the exhaustions of housework and childcare—to consider a structural connection between their lives and the lives of the working-class Fens women who informed Churchill's play. One actor felt that audiences in New York watched "with the knowledge that they were going to have to work a bit. . . . They were open about it and listened hard."[30] A theater critic recounted speaking with "members of the audience or theatre staff . . . vividly reminded of somebody's sister in Philadelphia or grandfather in Virginia who never wore shoes."[31] While I see these audience reactions to *Fen* as suggestive of a spectatorial desire for cross-class solidarity, it is a brief and provisional alliance. This is a limitation of feminist sleep performances produced in venues that cater to and attract relatively homogeneous audiences, and I will return to this distance between performance and audience in the next chapter. But Churchill continued to use the widely shared experience of family life, in the form of domestic drama, as a starting point for plays examining political concerns that more overtly include any audience member—as we see in *Far Away*.

Far Away

On the opening night of *Far Away*, again at the Royal Court, the curtain lifted to reveal Harper, a middle-aged woman, slumped in a chair, half awake and mumbling a lullaby.[32] A child named Joan entered, clicked on the lamp, and announced, "I can't sleep" (3).[33] By 2000, when the play premiered, the demands of childcare, threatening to interrupt a woman's much-needed rest, constituted a familiar theme in Churchill's work. Yet despite the similarities between Harper and the women in Churchill's earlier plays, Harper's sleep loss quickly becomes trivial in comparison to the descriptions of genocide and global warfare that dominate *Far Away*. *Far Away* opens with a child deciding whether to call attention to the violence she has seen outside her window—or to just go back to sleep. She is persuaded to return to bed, and over the next two acts her world descends into all-consuming warfare. At first glance, the play seems to be a fable about the consequences of choosing apathy over action: if only she had stayed awake and done something!

Far Away—not typically interpreted as a specifically feminist play—shows how a Marxist feminist understanding of sleep onstage evolves when it is displaced from its origins in the 1970s and 1980s and staged at the turn of the twenty-first century. My readings of *Three More Sleepless Nights* and *Fen* describe Churchill putting sleepless housewife characters in the middle of domestic dramas, manifesting these characters' inability to sleep in the plays' inability to resolve with the formation or dissolution of a household. In *Far Away*, Churchill puts a sleepless housewife in the middle of a genocidal action that morphs into a planet-wide war zone. Rather than determining the course of the play, Harper's (and, eventually, Joan's) desire to sleep comes to seem inappropriate and out of step with the world around her—a small complaint amid mass chaos. Critics have interpreted sleep in *Far Away* as representative of political apathy, complicity in violence, or false consciousness. In their readings, sleeping onstage is a symbolic act. Sleeping signifies capitulating to harm, turning away from the violence happening just outside your door and, horrifyingly, finding that you can still rest easily. While Churchill's plays do often call on audiences to oppose violence and structural harm, the conventional reading of sleep in *Far Away* as symbol of apathetic moral failure is in tension with Churchill's earlier use of sleep onstage as a desirable experience of social and material equity—as respite from women's exhausting domestic labor. Contextualizing sleep in a Marxist feminist reading of labor in *Far Away* demonstrates that the play does not set aside the feminist analysis of the British household that Churchill developed in her earlier plays in order to take on the larger or more urgent concerns of global violence and ecological destruction. Instead, *Far Away* maintains this attention to the exhausting labor of reproduction, asking, when social reproduction has been so devalued, who will do the work of reproducing a livable version of the world?

Like *Three More Sleepless Nights, Far Away* is a three-act short play. Yet whereas *Three More Sleepless Nights* is an early-career sketch, *Far Away* is a potent distillation of political concerns from three decades of playwriting into an incisive theatrical fable. The play begins in familiar Churchill settings, the household and the workplace, before leaping from these mundane contexts into a dystopia in which the entire world is at war. In the first act, Joan wakes up Harper to say that she has seen her uncle hurting people outside her bedroom window. In the second, an adult Joan discusses labor conditions in her workplace with her colleague Todd. Halfway through the act, a parade of prisoners in elaborate hats takes over the stage. In the third act, Joan, Todd, and Harper have all become involved in a planetary war. They reunite at Harper's home to strategize their alliances in a world in which nations, animal species, and weather events all battle against one another—while Joan takes a nap.

The tension between sleep as apathy and sleep as participation in a social world emerges in act 1 as the tired Harper begins to persuade Joan to return to bed. Churchill exploits the investigatory framework of dramatic realism, which invites audiences to seek and interpret evidence for unstaged events, to do the social work of sleep theater: Interpreting the experience of sleep loss reveals the dangerous circumstances in which Joan is sleeping.[34] Putting Joan to sleep means ignoring violence, but understanding the social and material circumstances of her sleep loss means investigating this violence. At the first productions of *Far Away* in London and New York, audiences entered to find an opening curtain painted with a "bucolic vista out of a children's storybook," evoking the televised "happy cloud" paintings of Bob Ross.[35] Like the character Young Joan, the spectators are new visitors to this pastoral oasis, so when Joan asserts "I can't sleep," the play invites audience members to parse whether Joan cannot sleep merely because she is in a new place, or, alternatively, whether the cheery country scene stretched across the proscenium is covering some real danger lurking upstage.

Joan's aunt Harper faces a task familiar to many caretakers: trying to coax a restless child back to sleep, so she can get some sleep herself. When Joan admits that she not only woke up but also went outside in the middle of the night, Harper tries to ascertain why. In response to repeated questions, Joan offers a series of excuses: First she heard "a noise," then "a shriek," then "a person screaming" (6). Harper tells her the sound was probably just an owl. Joan persists in revealing material evidence that increasingly suggests a real past event as the cause of her insomnia, encouraging audience members to read sleeplessness in this scene as a mystery that can be solved. Just as Harper has explained to Joan that the shriek—not an owl—was actually the sound of her uncle having friends over for a party, Joan introduces a new piece of evidence: "If it's a party, why was there so much blood?" (9). The blood is visible on Joan's bare foot. Harper says that the blood came from their dog, who was recently killed in an accident; Joan counters, "Why was uncle hitting them? . . . He was hitting a man with a stick" (13). Each time Harper explains away Joan's evidence, Joan produces a new clue for the audience to interpret, and these clues increasingly suggest that Joan saw her uncle beat people who were smuggled to his home in a truck. Harper explains this away, too: Joan's uncle is secretly helping to rescue the people from the truck, and the man he hit was a traitor threatening to expose them. The growing gap between the evidence Joan offers for violence and the likelihood of the truth of Harper's explanations gives audiences the space to recognize the violence that Harper is trying to explain away. In the end, Harper succeeds in convincing Joan that her uncle is on the side of the good. Joan volunteers to help, and Harper offers her the task of cleaning up in the morning, inscribing her into both the reproduction of the household and the erasure of violence. The scene, which begins with Joan's "I can't sleep," ends with Harper successfully sending Joan to bed. Joan's reversal from sleeplessness to sleep might mark her ideological shift from concern with violence to acceptance of it, and the sleep that the audience may once have seen as desirable for this little girl might now symbolize apathy in the face of harm. Critics have read this scene as Joan's failure of a crucial test of political conscience.[36]

How critics have interpreted the stakes of this scene has depended on the precise historical circumstances under which they saw the play. Those who saw it before the autumn of 2001 found it of a piece with the British political theater of the previous two decades, including Churchill's earlier plays. Making comparisons to Pinter's *Mountain Language* (1988) and Sarah Kane's *Blasted* (1995), reviewers of the Royal Court premiere and subsequent West End transfer understood the play as yet another attempt to wrest middle-class Britain from its complacency about distant conflicts (like the Bosnian War) and environmental catastrophes (like global warming). Reviewers responded favorably but suggested they could do with a bit less "thesis-mongering" from Churchill.[37] Yet critics who saw *Far Away* after September 11, 2001, lauded it as, in Simon Stephens's words, "the best play about 9/11" although it was written a full year before that event.[38] They received the play's opening scene of disordered sleep as "partak[ing] hauntingly of . . . the bedtime story" in order to give audiences a "wake-up slap to the face" before they "sleepwalk" into the "nightmare future" that awaits them.[39] The body of criticism produced in response to *Far Away* powerfully illustrates the work that stagings of disordered sleep can perform when read as meaningfully embedded in a historical and political context. For post-9/11 critics, Joan's insomnia prompted entire readings of the play as an urgent, prescient cautionary tale, calling on audiences to wake up to the horrors that keep Joan from falling asleep. Post-9/11 productions of *Far Away* separated Churchill from her fellow playwriting Cassandras of the late twentieth century and distinguished her as a prophet of a world fighting a "war on terror."

Yet by reading *Far Away* in the context of Churchill's other plays about disordered sleep, especially sleepless housewives in bad marriages, we might allow a feminist understanding of the value of sleep at the level of everyday life to hinder our moral condemnation of Joan. Churchill's realist deployment of evidence onstage, praised as "a model of dramatic writing," tests Joan, and she fails, believing her aunt's words over the evidentiary value of the blood right there on her own foot.[40] But even as this scene uses dramatic writing in the realist mode, it asks if audiences can resist the thrall of realism and hold other possible outcomes in mind against the skill of Churchill's realist dialogue. In Bloch's words, it puts audiences to the test. Is asserting the complicity of a sleepy child in violence really a moral victory? What are Harper's options in resisting a husband who "hit one of the children" with a metal stick (14)?[41] Audiences might recognize the "bucolic vista" painted on the drop curtain not just as a cheerful cover over hidden violence but as a realist facade that, in its evocation of banal televised landscape painting, betrays its own realism as an artful construction.

In other words, the "wake-up slap to the face" that critics were thrilled to accept from Churchill as a rebuke for the political apathy of the late twentieth century is not so clearly positioned as the project of theater in *Far Away*. By revealing that theatrical labor has just as much potential for harm as for good, *Far Away*'s second act undercuts the moral authority that paints Joan's return to bed as a failure of conscience. In act 2, the play shifts focus from the family to the workplace as it leaps forward in time to find the adult Joan at her job of making hats, alongside her colleague Todd. Act 2 includes a sudden change in dramatic form, from small-scale realist dialogue to massive spectacle: Todd and Joan witness "*a procession of ragged, beaten, chained prisoners, each wearing a hat, on their way to execution. The finished hats are . . . enormous and preposterous*" (24). Todd justifies the hats as "a metaphor for something or other. . . . You make beauty and it disappears" (25). Todd and Joan cannot identify a tenor for the metaphor other than "life," but of course it should be *theater.* The ephemeral, beautiful, disappearing hats are a pointed metaphor for theater, which suggests, disturbingly, that theater is pointless, and even possibly destructive, artifice.

At the same time the hat parade functions as a metaphor for the ideological problems of the theater, it raises a material problem of theater: Where can a production find enough actors to stage a successfully disturbing parade? Churchill's opening stage directions specify that "*five is too few and twenty better than ten*" for the number of hat models. "*A hundred?*" she proposes (2). The parade scene not only interrupts the realist conventions of *Far Away* but also disrupts its potential for low-budget stagings. While the rest of the play needs only three or four actors and minimal scenic design, this one scene requires dozens of actors and an equal number of hats, which have dramatic value only if each is unique, elaborate, unusual, and, therefore, handmade. Given Churchill's attention to production expenses in plays like *Fen,* whose multiple casting allows it to be performed by a company with a small budget, this break with the economy of *Far Away* demands a revaluation of theater. Rather than writing a play that is inexpensive to stage, Churchill writes a play that is mostly inexpensive with the exception of one very costly scene. The high production values demanded for the success of the hat parade invest the ephemeral nature of that performance with labor and capital. Producers of *Far Away* are asked to pour the most money into the scene that most pointedly asks whether the labor of theater works toward destructive ends. Churchill stakes the value of her play on the scene that asks what we are all doing at the theater.

In act 3, the adult Joan is again asleep in Harper's bedroom, having walked away from "the middle of a war" to "regroup" at Harper's home, which Joan considers "a place of safety" even though "everyone thinks it's just a house" (29). In opposition to the obvious theatricality of the parade, Joan's sleep is nontheatrical, an offstage act referenced only in passing. While Joan sleeps, Harper and Todd discuss a situation of total warfare that is even more a "real nightmare" than the scene in *Apocalypse Now* that Pete describes in *Three More Sleepless Nights.* In a tragic mirror image of a creation myth, they name an endless list of creatures who must be destroyed: from wasps to Portuguese car salesmen, from the weather to gravity. The war is characterized by constant, inescapable activity. The violence against humans that Joan saw in the middle of the night in the first act has metastasized, burning out patterns of waking and resting among animals and other nonhuman entities. The entire planet is engaged in a war that seems destined to exhaust its every natural resource. Adult Joan, desensitized to death by her time at the hat factory, thinks only about killing and sleeping: She "killed two cats and a child under five" on her way to Harper's house to rest (37). When she wakes up, she wonders, "Who's going to mobilize darkness and silence?" (37). Who is going to mobilize the conditions of sleep against her?

If the play is just interested in condemning Joan, however, it hardly needs a second and third act. Instead, these acts put sleep and theater in tension with one another. Sleep is passively complicit in harm: It allows Joan to avoid violence and to restore her own body to full fighting capacity. In contrast, theater activates audience reflection and critique in response to this violence—but the play's most violent scene is also its most theatrically captivating, celebrating the capacities of a large cast and well-crafted costuming. *Far Away* leaves its audiences in the midst of this tension. The play ends with Joan describing a river whose allegiance she is not sure of. "I didn't know whose side the river was on," she says, because "when you've just stepped in you can't tell what's going to happen" (38). *Far Away* is less the call to action, to awake from the nightmare and do something, than critics immediately after 9/11 thought it to be. It asks, instead, for audiences to sit with uncertainty and discomfort, to hold the horrific, interpolating violence of the world in tension with their desire—everyone's desire—to escape it.

In my readings of *Three More Sleepless Nights* and *Fen,* insomnia is a burden of housewives that emerges as a block to the generic conventions of domestic drama. Neither play ends with the formation or dissolution of a household. Both instead conclude with "real nightmares": Margaret listening to another endless description of a movie and Val listening to her fellow housewives' attempts at refusing their own burdens. In this lineage of housewives who cannot sleep, Harper is the only one who may have escaped her husband, Joan's uncle. He is never mentioned in *Far Away*'s third act, which is not clear evidence that he is gone—but which suggests that the particular domestic situation that kept Harper up at night may have ended. Does this mean that Harper and Joan might now be fighting on the side of the good, having escaped the original source of the play's violence? Can there be a "good" side to the all-consuming war of *Far Away*? Are husbands the real problem in Churchill's plays?

Rather than answering these questions, Churchill's sleepless housewife plays suggest a new political value for sleep, as it is desperately needed by these women in direct response to the overwork demanded of and internalized in the political category of housewife, and thereby also suggest a new theatrical value for sleep. They do not accept sleep as a boring act to put onstage (and a sign of boredom among the audience) that must be accessed and given narrative value through the more exciting world of dream. Instead, they use sleep and sleeplessness to keep theater attentive to the everyday lives of the women in *Three More Sleepless Nights* and *Fen*, to wrest the theatrical genre that most often produces and then kills off housewives onstage—domestic drama—from its usual outcomes. By the end of *Far Away*, sleeplessness has extended from the housewives out to all of nature, which is no longer engaged in cycles of production and dormancy but is instead burning out the planet through total war.

Reading Churchill for her trajectory of sleepless characters suggests that the condition of housewives might indeed be the determinant condition of all our social lives. What Marxist feminists of the 1970s called the foundation of a capitalist, patriarchal political economy, Churchill takes as the foundation for and portent of an overworked ecology, one that will be exhausted into crisis through overproduction. This reading further proposes that the "wake-up slap" that post-9/11 critics saw in *Far Away* might have limited efficacy as a political response. The sense of constant crisis keeping everyone up at night can do little to respond sustainably to the problem, and the burdens of this wakefulness will fall more heavily on some people than on others. The global crisis that *Far Away* predicts does not replace the local household politics of feminism but instead remains a deeply feminist problem, a question of how to live in the world without either reproducing its inequities or exhausting one's own capacities. For Churchill, this question originates in the household, and her characters—even as ghosts or battle-hardened warriors—continue to rely on the domestic labor that makes the household a safe place to sleep.

Four

Bedtime Across the Border

Regina José Galindo's Maternal Power Play

In many feminist dramas of housewife life, the family is a prison for women. In Caryl Churchill's sleepless housewife plays, the labor of caring for children, maintaining the home, working outside the house for wages to meet basic needs, and surviving intimate or global violence falls to housewives, leaving them unable to get enough sleep to sustain themselves. Churchill's housewife characters find the family supernaturally imprisoning: They remain forever trapped in their households, working to meet the needs of husbands and children. The historically specific social formation of the family is a rich site of analysis for many strands of feminism. Marxist, trans/queer, and Indigenous feminists have critiqued the family as the ultimate, sometimes violent, enforcer of the sexual division of labor underpinning industrial capitalism and the ideology of heterosexuality organizing normative sex-gender roles in Europe and the territories of its former colonial empires, including the United States.[1] Since the 1970s, the family has also become the cost-free and morally untouchable replacement for state-organized welfare as neoliberal governments have hacked away at any form of social safety net. But the family can also be a refuge, for sleep and for feminist struggle. Many of us sleep most soundly around our closest loved ones; many feminists have written about the family—including chosen kin—as a refuge for people surviving difficult times and for activists dreaming up different ways of working and loving. Black feminists, for example, have complicated the critique of the family by positioning the family as a potential haven, often hard-won, sheltering its members from racism and other structures of violence from which white women often benefit.[2] Majority-world feminists have articulated how global capitalism tears families apart as much as it traps them together, as women from poorer nations migrate to work as caregivers for families in other countries, freeing wealthier women from domestic labor while these migrant working women and their own kin make do with long-distance love.[3]

Guatemalan performance artist Regina José Galindo has described the importance of her own family as a haven for sleep in an unsafe world. "I wake up and kiss my partner, I kiss my daughter, and I feel happy," she said in a 2009 interview. "I cling to the wonderful idea of waking up and finding the two people I love right there before me. During the day, I gradually wake up and once again I find myself with real nightmares—that's when my anxiety begins."[4] Galindo's "real nightmares" echo Churchill's characters' descriptions of the threats and violence they encounter in the world, but Galindo is sustained nightly, sleeping and waking alongside her partner and her daughter. Galindo roots her ability to go out in the world and make her politically confrontational art in these mornings spent waking up alongside her family. The family—in theory and also in daily life—exists in this contradiction between prison and refuge, trapping women as unpaid workers and frequent victims of violence while simultaneously sheltering restorative intimate relations against a bleak larger world.

The intertwined concerns of gender, labor, migration, and colonization are central to Galindo's performances, which make her own body publicly vulnerable to the violence of these systems. Galindo's endurance performances work like punches to the gut, giving spectators temporary, surprising, strongly felt insight into harms they might otherwise regard with intellectual distance. Galindo often performs alone, but this chapter examines a rare performance she made with her own family. Galindo sometimes performs endurance in a state of extreme, unconscious vulnerability—immobilized or anesthetized on a bed—but here I read a performance that includes a more everyday kind of sleep. In this atypical Galindo artwork, Galindo performs the role of mother at bedtime: In this new kind of endurance art, she revises the trope of maternity as a politically activating link between performer and woman spectator. I call this trope the *maternal power play* and compare Galindo's deployment of maternity with the work of German Marxist playwright Bertolt Brecht and his collaborators. Both place a mother and her family in the midst of war, with the mother finding herself responsible for strangers' sleep on the opposite side of a border.

Galindo's 2008 performance *America's Family Prison* exposes the contradiction of family as refuge and family as prison, putting Galindo and her own family simultaneously in the shared family bed she describes above and in a family-size jail cell near the U.S.-Mexico border. This chapter picks up where we left the New York City audience of *Far Away* in 2001: with feminists, sleep, and the family in the globalized post-9/11 world—where spectators in the United States are newly awake to the threat of terrorism. In the name of the security of U.S. Americans, families both within the United States and outside it were trapped in place or torn apart by a profiteering War on Terror that reshaped the U.S. approach to immigration and incarceration the world over. In 2005, the U.S. secretary of homeland security ended the policy of "catch and release" in response to undocumented immigrants entering the United States. In its place, immigration police were authorized to incarcerate whole families while they awaited trial.[5] Historian Brianna Nofil frames post-9/11 changes to immigration policy in terms of beds. In 2004, as part of efforts toward terrorism prevention, Congress set an annual minimum of eight thousand new beds across immigrant detention facilities nationwide; by 2009, a "national bed quota" was implemented to ensure that immigrants could be jailed rather than paroled.[6]

America's Family Prison explores what sleep in those jail beds looks like for immigrant families cast as threats to the idealized U.S. citizen family, a family we see celebrated in the "family values" discourse of U.S. presidential administrations. After 9/11, the federal government mobilized a raft of national securitization measures, including increased immigrant detention, alongside domestic legislation to safeguard the family as the foundational unit of good (implicitly white, Christian, non-welfare-using) American life. The ambiguous title of Galindo's performance yokes these two families together: Is this prison for incarcerating "America's family" or for protecting "America" from families who should be in prison? And is Galindo's Guatemalan family a different kind of American family from the families of U.S. citizens? Abolition feminists have analyzed how, under the cover of post-9/11 securitization, the United States expanded on two decades of family values policy that had already been putting domestic threats to the safety of the family—often identified as drug dealers and gang members and disproportionately nonwhite, trans/queer, and poor—in prison in high numbers since the 1980s.[7] Abolition feminists have also critiqued feminist support for state violence, sometimes called carceral feminism, in the form of policing, prisons, and war. The location of *America's Family Prison* within driving distance of the U.S.–Mexico border foregrounds the close relationship between domestic family policing and immigrant family detention; it asks whether "America's families" are imagined as in need of protection from families like Galindo's.

In *America's Family Prison,* sleep performance is simultaneously endurance art and maternal power play. As endurance art, Galindo and her family's incarceration for one night confronts spectators with suffering, asking them to witness the often unseen ways in which incarceration both traps and tears apart families the state sees as a threat. Jails are an especially bad place to sleep, and prolonged poor sleep contributes to the manifold physical and mental health problems caused by incarceration. Sleep deprivation, moreover, is not merely a side effect of incarceration; it became a goal of the U.S. prison-industrial complex post-9/11, as it expanded into a global network of "black sites" where sleep deprivation was employed as a common interrogation technique.[8] In *America's Family Prison,* Galindo's immigrant Guatemalan family gets pitted against the safe sleep of the vulnerable citizen family as the late twentieth-century legacy of domestic incarceration meets the post-9/11 project of homeland security. As maternal power play, *America's Family Prison* casts Galindo in the role of mother—a figure often deployed to activate political engagement among women spectators, both onstage and in protests and other performances of political organizing. Read alongside the Brecht Collective play *Mother Courage and Her Children,* Galindo's performance of motherhood at bedtime redeploys the conservative ideal of the family in opposition to the U.S. War on Terror.[9] *America's Family Prison* participates in abolition feminist critique both by directly protesting a specific family immigrant detention facility and by bringing the vulnerability of the "bad" (incarcerated as a threat) family and the "good" (protected from threats) family into contact. To spectators whose families the United States has invested in protecting—those from "good" families—*America's Family Prison* poses the question of whether their claim to safe sleep must depend on another family's nightly suffering.

A Crib Jammed Between the Bunkbeds and the Cell Door

Galindo, born in Guatemala City in 1974, is a performance artist who often enacts feats of bodily endurance that involve more extreme suffering or exposure than we typically associate with sleep.[10] When Galindo began making art in her home country, without formal artistic training, she had only "ideas, rage, my body, and public spaces." In contrast to works she later created in wealthier, more privatized countries like the United States, for her works in Guatemala Galindo could "seize" public spaces as freely available performance venues.[11] Many of the artworks she created with these tools fall into the overlapping categories of body art and endurance art, meaning that Galindo puts her body through some sort of ordeal witnessed by, or documented for, an audience. *America's Family Prison* emerged out of Galindo's practice as an endurance artist. This twenty-four-hour performance asks what kind of endurance is required to sleep in a jail cell with a baby for one night, and how our sense of this endurance changes when it is contextualized in the social relations of families and prisons in the United States in the 2000s—conditions that feminists have both critiqued and helped to create.

Galindo often stages her endurance performances on beds, where this endurance art publicizes the frequency of rape and femicide in her birth country. These performances probe the limits of women's endurance of violence. In one of Galindo's first documented performances, *El dolor en un pañuelo* (The pain in a handkerchief) (1999), Galindo propped a bed up vertically and had herself restrained, nude and blindfolded, against the bed's white sheets. Guatemalan newspaper headlines—including "Thirty Rapes in Only Two Months"—were projected onto Galindo's torso, lighting the space from her collarbone to her genitals. Performances like this one, positioned on a bed and in direct conversation with sexual violence and death, locate the site of women's sleep as simultaneously an inescapable site of potential harm. In *Reconocimiento de un cuerpo* (Recognition of a body) (2008), performed in the same year as *America's Family Prison,* Galindo was again nude on a bed. For this performance, she was anesthetized and covered by a white sheet; spectators chose whether to raise the sheet in order to "recognize" or "identify" her body. *Reconocimiento* can also mean examination, exploration, or inspection—as in the English word *reconnaissance*—and *cuerpo* can also mean corpse, suggesting medical and military exercises of power as sites that demand women's bodily endurance. The exposed, immobilized body, vulnerable to sexual violation, is a common feature of Galindo's performances. In many of these performances, then, a woman in a sleeping position is a woman who is enduring a nightly exposure to potential rape or murder.

Scholars of bodily endurance art like Galindo's foreground the intense relationship it creates between performer and audience. Rebecca Schneider describes the body in feminist explicit body art, including nude performance, as a "stage, canvas, or screen" for the artist to display the "historical, political, cultural, and economic issues" that have constituted her body.[12] This use of the body as screen is a literal one in *El dolor en un pañuelo,* where Galindo uses her nude body on the white bed like a screen for a slide projector. But in Schneider's reading of explicit body art, the gaze at the screen is not unidirectional; the screen—the artist herself—gazes back, raising questions of "who-gets-to-see-what-where."[13] Karen Gonzalez Rice asserts that endurance art is similarly intersubjective. Rice describes performances of suffering by artists as establishing "open-ended, ethically charged encounters" with their viewers.[14] Both explicit body art and endurance art intensify the interaction between performance and audience without necessarily being interactive. In fact, it is particularly the case of endurance art that audiences cannot save the performer from suffering but instead must decide what to do with their experience of witnessing pain without being able to intercede.

Lilian Mengesha describes Galindo's effects on her audience as a "model for hard feelings," an experience of "shock" and "confusion" that might prompt audiences to bear witness to suffering in meaningful solidarity with the performer.[15] Yet performances like *Reconocimiento,* in which a spectator who raises the sheet both exposes more of Galindo's anesthetized body and perhaps witnesses her performance more fully, confront spectators with extremes of exposure and endurance that can seem impossible to respond to appropriately—let alone with meaningful solidarity.

Careful readers will note, however, that neither being tied to a bed (*El dolor*) nor being anesthetized on a bed (*Reconocimiento*) is precisely sleep, nor even the struggle to fall asleep. In *America's Family Prison,* a more quotidian practice of sleep provokes similar open-ended ethical challenges to Galindo's potential audiences without putting Galindo in extreme positions of exposure, endurance, or suffering. Sleep performance accomplishes the intersubjective, ethically charged activation of spectators that critics identify in more punishing or vulnerable endurance art without making such physical demands on the artist, potentially rebalancing the scales between the performer's suffering and the audience's response. Sleep performance here also resists reproducing a spectacular carceral legacy, in which punishments for prisoners simultaneously entertain and discipline free spectators.[16] Through sleep performance, Galindo invites her own spectators to consider their role in incarcerating immigrant families without reproducing a spectacle of immigrant suffering for a citizen audience.

America's Family Prison instead reproduces the living conditions of families within a particular immigrant family detention center operating in Texas in 2008 as a by-product of the post-9/11 War on Terror. Before 2001, the number of private prisons in Texas had already increased significantly under George W. Bush's governorship, during which time the FBI was called in to investigate violent attacks by private prison guards on incarcerated people.[17] After the Department of Homeland Security began detaining undocumented immigrants awaiting their immigration trials, the T. Don Hutto Residential Center, a medium-security private prison in the rural community of Taylor, was transformed into one of two family detention centers in the United States. While the immigrants detained in this facility came from all over the world, many were from Galindo's part of the world, the Northern Triangle of Central America, which encompasses Honduras, El Salvador, and Guatemala. *America's Family Prison* thus extends Galindo's central artistic concern with "relations based on extraction": the extraction of land and labor from people in colonized countries by nations like the United States, and the way that extraction can siphon the health and life force from the bodies of the colonized.[18] To re-create the living conditions of incarcerated families, Galindo "rent[ed] a family-sized cell" for eight thousand dollars from the company that supplied the T. Don Hutto facility in Taylor, to "adapt it and live in it with [her] daughter and husband for 24 hours." Galindo installed *America's Family Prison* in a gallery of the contemporary art residency program Artpace San Antonio, 120 miles southwest of Taylor.[19] (As further evidence of the realistic conditions of this cell, the manufacturers were able to show it to potential buyers in the private prison industry while it was on display in San Antonio.)[20] The cell would remain in Artpace for two months after the performance, when the lease ended.

Galindo learned the details of incarceration in T. Don Hutto through conversations with journalists and activists, but the addition of her daughter and partner to the performance was initially a matter of practicality. When she received an offer of a residency at Artpace, she had recently had a baby and "couldn't imagine leaving [her] for two months."[21] So, like many artists who are also working mothers, Galindo incorporated her entire family into the performance. In photographs and stills from video recorded during Galindo's performance, the immediate impression is that it indeed looks like a jail cell. Galindo's design of her performance space was informed by a photograph of a cell in the T. Don Hutto facility with a cradle crammed inside. Inside Galindo's cell, then, a wooden crib and a narrow set of metal bunkbeds cover one long wall, while the other wall has a counter with one or two small stools and an exposed combination toilet and sink. The door has one narrow vertical window, like a medieval arrow slit, and the shorter back wall has two similar windows. Galindo's daughter looks like an older baby or young toddler; she can stand up and still uses a pacifier. The only concession to making the cell "family-size" seems to be the crib, which is jammed awkwardly between the bunkbeds and the cell door, making the sleeping child the first thing anyone entering the cell will encounter. While the narrow metal bunkbeds and small metal sink-toilet look familiar from other photographs of real U.S. carceral facilities, the crib looks larger and is made of wood, suggesting that it had to be purchased from beyond the prison-industrial complex, which still only rarely incarcerates babies.

In *America's Family Prison,* prison intensifies the crucible of the family by incapacitating family members together in one small place over an extended period of time. By bringing her young child with her, Galindo invites spectators to think about not what Galindo the accomplished body artist could *endure* but what it means for a family to persist through one night, or many nights, in a jail. *America's Family Prison* is implicitly a sleep performance: Immigrant detention facilities like T. Don Hutto have held adults and children for months at a time.[22] Even at the basic level of lying down for rest—in beds, in darkness—the prison cell has priorities other than sleep. The bunkbeds will separate Galindo from her partner, forcing them to sleep one above the other rather than side by side, and make it difficult or possibly unsafe for Galindo's daughter to curl up to sleep next to one of her parents if she gets scared in an unfamiliar setting. Photographs show minimal bedding—sheets and two pillows, what might be a pink baby blanket—so it is hard to know what resources the family has if it gets cold overnight. And the lights are bright, institutional fluorescents; if the jail functions like most institutionalized environments, it is unlikely the cell is ever fully dark.[23] The architecture of the family-size cell breaks the sleeping family down into atomized units of surveillance: three people in three beds under bright lighting. The minimal metal bunkbeds and wooden-slatted crib are like shelves and a crate that Galindo, her husband, and her child can be stored in overnight, making the bed quotas that the United States sets for its immigration jails tangible in the physical design of Galindo's performance. The conditions of performance in *America's Family Prison* contradict both medical recommendations for and commonsense understandings of conditions for healthy sleep, especially sleep alongside a young child. The bodily discipline of the cell architecture makes sleep not a time for bodily relaxation—unclenching muscles, sprawling postures—but a time for reinforced stillness and supervision.

This constraint reflects the real practices, and in particular the bedtime and nighttime policies, of the T. Don Hutto detention facility. Journalist Margaret Talbot's 2008 investigative reporting documents the contradictions of togetherness and estrangement encapsulated by the term "family prison" in Taylor and the harm these practices caused, especially around children's experience of nighttime and sleep. Husbands and wives lived in separate cells; young children stayed with their mothers while older children might be in a cell alone. At night, alarms sounded if anyone left or entered a cell, making bedtime—already tough for young children in their own homes—a particularly harrowing nightly challenge. Children could not keep stuffed animals with them in their cells, they were woken in the night by guards' flashlights, and, when they did wake and call out for a parent, only guards were allowed to respond. If a parent entered a child's cell anyway, child and parent were threatened with the prospect of long-term separation, leaving one child to tell Talbot that he feared, "I can never see my parents again, and I will get stepparents and they will hurt me or maybe they will kill me."[24] By gathering her family within a small cell, Galindo lets her spectators see the extremes of incapacitation that shape incarcerated immigrants' daily lives—and that, paradoxically, interfere with their sleep.[25]

At the same time that children in the T. Don Hutto facility were traumatized by separation from their parents at night, both mothers and their children were harmed by the expectation that women care for their children twenty-four hours a day while incarcerated. (The detention facility, Talbot writes, assumed "detainees would constantly supervise their children" and so never had to qualify for licensing as a childcare facility.)[26] By demanding constant care labor of incarcerated parents—ostensibly in the name of keeping immigrant families together—T. Don Hutto slipped through the regulatory cracks, leaving childcare within the facility unmonitored until local advocates realized what was happening and began protesting. Children were required to stay with their mothers during meetings with lawyers, overhearing their mothers testify to their experiences of "torture, rape, or domestic abuse." The repeated assault of one incarcerated woman by a guard during sleep hours after 11:30 at night—when no one could leave their cells without a guard's permission—happened in the cell she slept in with her child.[27] Whether family members are in separate cells or the same cell, sleep in a family prison becomes a period of nightly, intensified suffering for children and parents. While stories of family imprisonment or family separation at the U.S. southern border have become troublingly common in the twenty-first century, Nofil reminds us that the United States has long detained migrant children, from a Chinese boy incarcerated as an adult in Boston in 1910 to a Guantánamo Bay detention camp for Haitian children in the 1990s.[28]

Galindo's role as the only named performer and professional artist in *America's Family Prison* invites us to consider how women—and women's sleep—are affected when the family comes into contact with the prison. As *America's Family Prison* demonstrates, women do not escape the social demands of maternity when they or their family members enter the carceral system, even as they lose access to the rewards of family life as they chose to live it. While we may be most familiar with the harms caused when incarceration tears families apart, the U.S. carceral system also relocates families, forces family members together, and disciplines them into particular forms of domestic life. Although men are incarcerated at higher rates than women in the United States, incarcerated women (and people the carceral system treats as women) experience distinct harms tied to the expectation that they will perform socially reproductive labor. Angela Davis argues that, at least since the era of U.S. enslavement, women's punishment and imprisonment have been tied to conceptions of women as unpaid reproducers of the family—their own families but also the families of others—especially Black women and, later, poor and immigrant women. And across the history of U.S. imprisonment, versions of the intimate violence that originates in families have found incarcerated people again in prison.[29] Carceral systems reinforce regimes of gender and sexuality in violent ways, putting trans and nonbinary people in dangerous situations leading to high fatality rates, putting all incarcerated people at high risk of sexual violence, and disproportionately punishing Black women for defending themselves against intimate partner violence.

As in *America's Family Prison,* the pressure on women to do the labor of social reproduction in families does not disappear in carceral contexts, whether those women are kept with their families, are incarcerated separately from their families outside, or are themselves outside and advocating for family members within jails or prisons. Women on the outside, often under the rubric of motherhood, spearhead care and advocacy work for partners and adult children inside. Inside women's prisons, incarcerated people organize to offer one another the care that the state has denied them.[30] Incarceration, geographer Ruth Wilson Gilmore argues, causes "households [to] stretch from neighborhood to visiting room to courtroom," such that "prisons wear out places by wearing out people."[31] Motherhood as a gendered biological relation is less important here than a given person's decision to care for someone inside, to do the work of mothering across carceral boundaries and across great distances. Galindo and her husband's care for their daughter and for one another and Galindo's decision to stage her antidetention performance from within a jail cell make visible the care and organizing happening within women's and family detention.

Galindo's performance art often examines how to offer such care across great distances and in the face of U.S. foreign and economic policies that also produce family incapacitation and separation. In the wake of CIA interventions and United Fruit Company lobbying that instigated a coup followed by a military dictatorship in 1954, many Guatemalans immigrated or attempted to immigrate to the United States.[32] Galindo's 2007 performance *Curso de supervivencia para hombres y mujeres que viajarán de manera ilegal a los Estados Unidos* (Survival course for men and women who will travel to the United States in an illegal manner) was a training course for ten people in Guatemala who planned to cross the U.S. border without documentation. Galindo organized a form of care for people who had been neglected or harmed by their home country and were facing the prospect of further violence as they moved north. In photographs of the performance, the participants construct a shelter out of a tarp and start a fire with paper for kindling; they learn skills for sleeping exposed, outdoors, as they attempt to travel through dangerous terrain and cross the U.S. border. In *America's Family Prison*, U.S. domestic incarceration practices and U.S. foreign immigration policies meet to immobilize Galindo with her family and deprive them of sleep, suggesting that incarceration and immigration—in and through a country deeply invested in prisons as problem-solver—are two sides of the same coin. Both involve logics of incapacitation, trapping families either too far apart or in the wrong place.

The harms of incapacitation have sometimes been perpetrated at the behest of feminists—even as others argue that incarceration ultimately diminishes the possibilities of a feminist world. Political theorist Iris Marion Young implicates U.S. feminists in diminishing their own freedoms, and pursuing wars that harmed other women, in the months and years following 9/11.[33] Young argues that the United States after 9/11 put all its citizens in the position of women in a patriarchal household, promising increased safety in exchange for lost freedom. At the same time, Young continues, proponents of the War on Terror spotlighted the patriarchal regime of the Taliban, using the plight of Afghan women to attract U.S. feminists to supporting the war. This pursuit of safety over freedom via state violence emerged from carceral feminist logics of the 1980s and 1990s. Government-declared wars on drugs and gangs in the latter decades of the twentieth century warned American families that their homes were on the front lines of battle while comforting them with harsh sentencing laws that claimed to keep women and children safe from gang leaders, drug dealers, and sexual perpetrators. In practice, this often meant protecting white, wealthier families from poorer Black and Latino men—and, increasingly, women. After 9/11, the War on Terror justified increased securitization of the U.S. borders to protect good American families from new foreign dangers, adding Muslim and Arab people to the list of racialized threats. The specter of bad families, from the single Black mothers of the Moynihan Report to twenty-first century images of Afghan women in burqas and Central American immigrants impinging on the border, became evidence of an ever-renewing danger to U.S. family life.

The presence of Galindo's very young daughter in *America's Family Prison* evokes a particular trope of the threatening immigrant family: the anchor baby. In this anti-immigrant fantasy, these infants born on U.S. soil to noncitizen parents, children's need for care, and the significant vulnerabilities that migrant families with young children face become a power that noncitizen mothers wield. These children, like the children of Black American single mothers, are interpreted as a ploy for gaining access to U.S.

welfare provisions. The fantasy of the anchor baby reverses the logic of imperial extraction that Galindo lays bare in many of her performances: In the story of the anchor baby, it is not wealthy countries extracting resources from poorer nations but the citizens of poorer nations extracting welfare from wealthy countries via the exercise of birthright citizenship. Like sleeper cells of terrorists living in your neighborhoods and waiting for the right time to strike (a Cold War fear of sleeper agents repurposed for the post-9/11 era), immigrant women are imagined as executing a long-term plan of infiltration, strategically gestating anchor babies so that they can be happily incapacitated by the childcare needs of an infant with a claim to a U.S. passport.[34] This immigrant-phobic fantasy projects a remarkable capacity for family planning onto women arriving in a country that offers limited access to high-quality obstetric health care, especially for poor people. In photographs of *America's Family Prison*, Galindo's daughter is a different kind of anchor baby. Her growing toddler body seems to weigh down her mother, anchoring Galindo in place as her daughter sprawls across her lap. The photographs of the inside of the cell during the performance nearly all show Galindo or her partner actively caring for their daughter: entertaining her with toys, sitting on the floor with her as she toddles around, or holding her on top of their own bodies. She looks like both a weight and a comfort. *America's Family Prison* packs the contradictions of familial care tightly into this small cell: Within these twenty-four hours in this small space, care is a refuge and care is inescapable labor.

In August 2009, the work of advocates to raise awareness that this private, unregulated, largely unknown family prison in rural Texas was incarcerating children pushed the United States to announce an end to the practice of family detention.[35] By 2016, "significant public pressure" caused Williamson County, home to the T. Don Hutto facility, to end its contract with Immigration and Customs Enforcement. The county commissioner is reported to have said, "The federal government made their bed with its policies, so let them sleep in it."[36] Through *America's Family Prison*, Galindo participated in this years-long campaign of public pressure, using her commission from Artpace to build a replica family-size cell and then leaving it in the art space in San Antonio, a two-hour drive from the real prison in Taylor. *America's Family*

Prison used the particular cultural force of maternal endurance to hold the state accountable for its simultaneous reliance on family caretaking by incarcerated women and the harm it caused to the migrant families it imprisoned.

A Family on the Other Side of the War

As a performance about a family enduring a night in a jail cell, *America's Family Prison* dramatizes how different carceral life is from the daily life of the free U.S. families such incarceration claims to protect. But as a performance about a family, *America's Family Prison* also raises the possibility of spectatorial identification through the similarities between Galindo's family—and particularly her role as mother—and the families of Galindo's spectators. A small number of spectators will have seen parts of Galindo's original twenty-four-hour performance, and more could encounter the cell in San Antonio's Artpace gallery or the photographs on Galindo's professional website or the online archives of New York's Museum of Modern Art. In one video still from the performance showing the outside of the cell, five people are gathered on a narrow strip of the flatbed trailer that holds the cell.[37] Two wait their turn to look inside. The remaining three—what appears to be a man, a woman, and a child, the child mostly obscured except for visible legs—look in through the narrow window in the door. This grouping of spectators, two adults and a child, mirrors the family inside. In clustering around the narrow viewing area, they are briefly just as confined as Galindo's family, fitting themselves to the physical limits of the trailer and the cell window in order to bear witness to Galindo and her family's incapacitation. This section compares that particular photograph of Galindo's spectators with other performances that create a dichotomy between two kinds of families: a U.S. presidential speech announcing the Promoting Safe and Stable Families Program and the Brecht Collective play *Mother Courage and Her Children*.

The image of a potential family of spectators mirroring the family inside the performance offers a provocation to read *America's Family Prison* as a maternal power play. By *maternal power play,* I mean an intentional public demonstration or identification of motherhood with the goal of politically activating mothers in an audience. In national and cultural contexts that claim to revere the family, maternal power plays aim to translate social reverence for mothers into genuine public authority for women who might otherwise not wield much political power. A maternal power play can be part of a staged drama or other artistic performance, or it can be used in political activism, at protests, or in community organizing. Maternal power plays are deployed across the political spectrum: By evoking motherhood as a transcendent moral ideal, maternal power plays can elevate a particular campaign above petty partisan differences and naturalize that campaign as an obvious moral good. If moms are for it, who can be against it? On the ground, shared experiences of maternity can serve as a recruitment tactic for spectators of these performance-protests, inviting women to transfer their skills in caring for a family and networking with other women into skills in organizing for social change. Among feminist performance scholars, Las Madres de la Plaza de Mayo, originating in Buenos Aires in 1977, is a paradigmatic example of women who organized and performed under the banner of mother, calling the Argentinian government to account for the forced disappearance of thirty thousand people. The protest strategies used by Las Madres have been reperformed by self-identified mothers and grandmothers in myriad other national contexts.[38] On the right, Moms for Liberty emerged in Florida in 2021 as a strategic performance by "just a group of angry moms" who have effectively targeted trans people, teachers' unions, and abortion rights.[39] In a maternal power play, a group of visible, emotionally demonstrative mothers—whether grieving or angry, whether left- or right-wing—makes a spectacle out of a claim to a social role as morally unimpeachable protectors who have been wronged.

Identification with maternity can therefore be mobilized by many disparate political projects to protect an ideal of the family against perceived threats—including the threat of other families. The remarks made by George W. Bush at the 2002 signing of the bipartisan legislation that created the Promoting Safe and Stable Families Program perform this sort of maternal power play, calling on the average U.S. American to join an "armies of compassion initiative" to organize mentoring for children with incarcerated parents.[40] In a bizarre twist on the Vietnam protest call to "bring the war home," as U.S. troops and private contractors claimed to spread American-style democracy to Afghanistan, the speech is aimed at recruiting a parallel army of volunteer mentors to spread American-style family values to the children of incarcerated parents. These remarks construct the family as the foundation of U.S. strength: The word *strong* appears ten times in the 1,100-word speech, or more than once per minute. (*Secure* appears twice.) The speech disavows the capacity of the state to provide direct services to families ("government cannot love a child") and instead mobilizes the rhetoric of military recruitment, calling on "parents and family members and neighbors, and caring adults who have heard the call" to invoke the volunteer "armies" who will step up to care for children whose parents are incarcerated. While the United States securitized and sent troops overseas in the months following 9/11, this rhetorical performance of parallel domestic spending (promising to request millions in federal funding in future budgets but committing to only thousands of dollars in vouchers provided by state governments) yokes the American family to the project of the post-9/11 privatized military-industrial complex.

Comparison of these different activist organizations and policies—all framed around family care—reveals that maternal power does not have a particular political affiliation. This makes a maternal power play a risky but potentially potent strategy for engaging an audience in a performance piece like *America's Family Prison*. The Promoting Safe and Stable Families Program attempts to perform one version of conscripting mothers—conscripting any U.S. American who might contribute to family stability—into a political project. *America's Family Prison* performs another. While the U.S. president is a hypervisible figure speaking to his fellow (U.S.) Americans, Galindo is largely hidden within the family jail cell, performing for an audience of free people whose family living conditions are, fundamentally, different from her family's for that twenty-four-hour period. Quiet and largely unseen, *America's Family Prison* has many of the characteristics of sleep performance more broadly: Within its own performance conditions, it cannot aim to rhetorically conscript its audience as a presidential speech does, nor can it create an attention-grabbing spectacle. Seeing the external family peering in to watch Galindo's performance through one tiny window raises the question of how this performance can reach an audience and what effect it might have.

The possible chasm between Galindo and her audience in Texas reflects a perennial challenge facing feminist organizing: Can shared identification with a gendered role prompt coalition building across significant differences in structural power and daily life? How can a Guatemalan performance artist reenacting the experience of immigrants from impoverished countries meaningfully prompt a response from the comparatively wealthy U.S. audiences who are likely to visit the Artpace gallery? In her atypical choice to perform alongside her daughter in *America's Family Prison,* Galindo foregrounds her own social role as a mother as a little-used strategy in her political performance repertoire.

In the history of twentieth-century political theater, perhaps no theater-maker has been more optimistic about motherhood as a politically activating connection between characters onstage and viewers in the audience than Bertolt Brecht—a fascination that has troubled many feminist critics. Acknowledging the ambiguities of collaborative authorship in Brecht's oeuvre, I refer to the creators of *Mother Courage and Her Children* as the Brecht Collective. The logic of the maternal power play onstage, deployed with particular frequency in the Brecht Collective's theater, pursues the engagement of mothers (and sometimes women more broadly) as a distinct audience sector under the implicit assumption that mothers are more likely to be politically activated by performances of familiar scenes of maternity. Brecht Collective plays like *The Mother* and *Caucasian Chalk Circle* sidestep the politics *within* family life and instead repeatedly dramatize the separation of mother from child as an opportunity for maternal political activation.[41]

The question of how spectatorial mothers should view a sleeping family that is not their own is raised directly in *Mother Courage and Her Children,* first performed in Zurich in 1941. Mother Courage is a woman who follows the progress of the Thirty Years' War accompanied by her three adult children, living off small trade with members of the military. The seventeenth-century setting historicizes the decisions facing Europeans during the rise of Nazism, putting spectators at an intentional distance from the characters' experience so that they might think more critically about the decisions made onstage. Mother Courage does not take a side in the war, preserving her life and her family rather than joining the battle, but her two older sons are killed anyway, leaving only

Courage and her mute daughter, Kattrin. In the play's climactic episode, Kattrin learns that the nearby town of Halle is about to be attacked by the army while the townspeople sleep. A peasant woman attests that her mother and her four young grandchildren will be killed if the town is left undefended. Persuaded by this appeal to protect a distant family in danger, Kattrin climbs onto a roof and beats a drum to wake the town. She is shot by the attacking army, but alarm bells ring out, signaling that she has succeeded in rousing the townspeople to defend themselves.[42]

Since the 1970s, feminist critics have debated how to read Kattrin, even as feminist theater scholars and artists have also deployed and expanded Brechtian dramaturgical techniques in order to denaturalize gender.[43] While Courage is the play's titular mother, Kattrin is desperate to become a mother and seems to save Halle out of a maternal concern for its sleeping children. Sara Lennox reads Kattrin as emblematic of Brecht's "child-woman" characters, whose admirable behavior in moments of distress is impressive only "because Brecht is playing on female stereotypes" that cast these characters as "young, innocent, stupid, and virginal"—as unlikely heroes whose forays into successful political action are the results of emotional instinct, not the considered decision-making that Brecht advocates.[44] Iris Smith argues that feminist spectators are not activated but blocked by the mother figures in plays like *Mother Courage,* in which a predictable "mother/whore dichotomy" among the female characters limits the possibilities for feminist spectatorial pleasure.[45] Kim Solga, however, offers a more redemptive reading of Kattrin as a figure who exposes "Western patriarchy's sacred, self-sacrificing mother" as the "function of abjection" she always already is.[46] Critics at the Zurich premiere of *Mother Courage* indeed seemed primed to read women characters as self-sacrificing mothers, rather than political actors. Reviewers described *Mother Courage* as a "Niobe tragedy" demonstrating "the overwhelming strength of the mother animal," leading Brecht to revise the play for later performances, in the hope of presenting Courage's acts as decisions rather than mammalian maternal instincts.[47] In Solga's reading, Kattrin's death to save the children of Halle further demonstrates how mothers are always expected to serve a sacrificial function, thereby exposing the limited political options available to women.

But Solga concludes that her reading might ask more of the play than it can offer. This *Mother Courage* might only come to pass if Kattrin were portrayed by a "feminist performance artist."[48]

Kattrin and Mother Courage face a choice that can help us understand the implied choice facing the audience of *America's Family Prison*. Mother Courage chooses to try to preserve her own family at all costs, while Kattrin risks her life to save not only the peasants' family but also an entire sleeping town. Kattrin succeeds in this plan but dies; Mother Courage survives but has lost all her children. She is alone, calling out to the next regiment, "Take me with you!"[49] Without reading Kattrin as a hero in opposition to Mother Courage's tragic failure, this scene of the sleeping town, on the verge of an ambush, lets us see two modes of spectatorship toward a sleeping family of strangers—a family on the opposing side of the war. The spectator can try to protect her own family, or she can try to reach out, in some way, to the sleeping family she does not know. Galindo's performance in *America's Family Prison,* then, might help us understand a question raised by *Mother Courage* and countless other plays about mothers: How can a mother work, in performance, to activate feminist viewers to fight for other people's families, rather than reinforcing the role of mother as instinctive protector of her own family haven against external threats? While Solga reads Kattrin as a mother figure without children of her own, when I imagine Kattrin as a viewer of a sleeping family like Galindo's, I read her as a nonmother who is still activated by her understanding that vulnerable people are in danger—and who sacrifices her own sleep, and by extension her safety, to raise the alarm. Against the Brecht Collective's tendency to see maternal instinct (for their own children or others') as the primary motivator of women's political action, I read Kattrin's political activation—as a character who cannot speak—as a recognition of the silent or silenced position of the sleeping town of Halle.

Solga's evocation of the power a feminist performance artist would have in the role of Kattrin points me back to *America's Family Prison* and the contribution of feminist performance artist Galindo to defending families in detention in Texas. Galindo's performance in *America's Family Prison* provokes her spectators to watch her sleeping family like Kattrin looks to the sleeping town of Halle. In other words, it is not Galindo herself but Galindo's spectators who take on a role analogous to Kattrin's. Like Kattrin, they are at a distance: Unlike in many of Galindo's more body-based performances, where audience members might touch her hair or even purchase a vial of her blood, here Galindo is separated from her audience by the cell walls.[50] But like Kattrin, Galindo's spectators can see the vulnerability of Galindo and her sleeping family—and can then imagine an extended vulnerability for real detained people, sleeping night after night under similarly extenuating conditions. They might be prompted to bang a drum. Media scholar Caroline Rodrigues notes that, upon observing her audience, Galindo realized that it was a "major surprise" to her spectators that families were being imprisoned under these conditions in Texas. Rodrigues credits Galindo with contributing to the efforts to pressure ICE to close the T. Don Hutto facility.[51] Rather than asking her spectators to witness her suffering physical exposure and pain, Galindo in *America's Family Prison* instead prompts her viewers to see how isolated and endangered detained families are, and to bang a drum for them from a distance.

Galindo's sleeping family in *America's Family Prison* is an alternative to the specter of the endangered family invoked in U.S. family values rhetoric like that of the Promoting Safe and Stable Families Program. That projected family needs constant bolstering to maintain maximum strength, so it can be a bulwark against attacks from external terrorism. Galindo's family represents one of these potential, if unlikely, external threats, in the form of a migrant family who, under newly securitized borders, must be detained. The spectatorial family in the photograph offers a third version of the family that complicates this binary. While this family seems to be a potential representative of the safe and stable families the United States wants to protect—white, possibly nuclear, possibly Texan—its members might choose to reject the idea that they are in such danger that they cannot do anything to help a more obviously endangered family like that represented by Galindo and her partner and child. They might set aside, in some way, commitments to their own family as safe haven to raise the alarm about the family detention facility in Taylor.

Galindo's *America's Family Prison* makes visible the power dynamics not within the family but between families. The photograph of the family outside the jail cell peering through the window at the family sleeping within—with the two families separated by the cell wall—makes visible how the policies and discourse of the U.S. War on Terror position families as tiny states that are placed into implicit war against one another. U.S. American families who want to sleep safely amid new terrorist threats must pit themselves against enemies domestic and foreign—against the bad families within the United States who are raising children as criminals and against the bad families at the border who are trying to sneak into the country. But it is clear in this photograph of *America's Family Prison* that Galindo's family is the one under threat: that families like Galindo's, in real immigration detention facilities, are sleeping in appalling conditions, under immense threats.

America's Family Prison, then, does not critique the intrafamilial sexual division of labor but makes visible how spectatorial citizen families in Texas have been covertly conscripted as miniature military units in a War on Terror that extends not just to families in Afghanistan and Iraq but also to the treatment of migrant families at the border as potential enemy combatants. Sociologist Loïc Wacquant, building on Young's post-9/11 theory of patriarchal protection, has described this as the work of the "daddy state," a "remasculiniz[ed]" state that responds to the successes of feminism in previous decades by stripping away welfare provisions and amping up wars against poverty, drugs, and crime at home—and, we could add, foreign threats at the border.[52] The vulnerability of sleep is a powerful reminder of our need for daddy's protection, as reflected in the U.S. military's obsession with manipulating sleep, from torturing prisoners with sleep deprivation to developing drugs that would allow soldiers to stay continuously awake. Sleep makes vulnerability inherent to human experience and requires us to depend on the care of others. While Young and Wacquant describe the state in the early 2000s as behaving more like a patriarchal family, the spectatorial family viewing *America's Family Prison* is at risk of becoming more like a state at war, secured by the walls of the jail cell inside which Galindo and her own family are trapped. Like Mother Courage when she chooses to sacrifice the sleeping town of Halle, the spectatorial family who does nothing in response to *America's Family Prison* reproduces the state's estimation that security for particular subjects must come at the cost of extreme vulnerability—quite often incarceration—for others.

After the horrors of migrant family separation during the first Trump presidency—and the harrowing images of incarcerated children crying out in the night for their parents—any encounter with *America's Family Prison* and its enforced familial togetherness is further haunted by the knowledge that parents have also been torn away from their young children at the border. Galindo notes that at least five Guatemalan children have died under these conditions of border incarceration, as of 2021.[53] Again, immigrant detention practices mirror domestic family policing practices of removing children from poor families and families of color and placing them in foster care and incarcerating children and adolescents of color at high rates. With her Artpace commission, Galindo—who sees her own family as a haven, who loves to wake up alongside her husband and young child—chose to make a beloved part of her family life visible and vulnerable in order to raise the alarm about families who are incarcerated beyond view.

In this way, Galindo's sleep performance does not offer an opportunity for her women viewers to identify with the maternity of incarcerated immigrant women across differences of race, nationality, and/or class. Instead, *America's Family Prison* holds out an unusually explicit opportunity to choose political action for viewers whose families are (against their will) positioned as in need of security, at the expense of other families. When read within the genre of sleep performance, *America's Family Prison* combats the ideology of the safe and stable American family that needs protecting from families threatening its borders, offering sleep as a nightly experience of vulnerability that stretches between families in very different material circumstances.

Part Three

Among Friends

Five
Dreams from the Sickbed
Queer Care and White Death in María Irene Fornés's AIDS Play

Caryl Churchill once wrote a fifteen-line poem dedicated to her fellow playwright María Irene Fornés. "When I feel sick of / Plays," begins the first stanza, "I / Sometimes think of yours / And get a flicker / Of what it is / I like." The second stanza swoops us into a hotel room, from the abstract flickers of thought and feeling to a concrete encounter between the two playwrights: "And I liked meeting / You and your mother . . . She was a hundred / Asleep on the bed." The final line gives thanks for Fornés's plays and Fornés's mother, "for both."[1] This short poem sketches a three-person scene of sleep and friendship. Two lions of twentieth-century experimental theater meet briefly to bolster one another's spirits while an older woman dozes on a bed in the background. The poem captures how a good work of art, a good piece of theater, can revive us when we feel emotionally or physically sick, can flicker the flame back on when we are burning out. It captures a transatlantic meeting of great artists taking place at the same time as an act of everyday rest. It captures the necessity of friendship to feminist work.

Finally, it marks a turn in this book from performances that take up the household and the family as familiar, socially revered sites of sleep to performances that place sleep amid the precarious social relations outside these institutions. These performances imagine the ways friends struggle to care for one another through serious illness and social rejection; they foreground the scarcity of material resources and theoretical models for this precarious care amid the austerity and aggressive individualism of the 1990s. These performances probe the shadows and limitations of feminist imagination, resisting straightforward political readings. They deploy sleep as a thematic focus and a dramaturgical tool in nonrealist staged experiments with the intractable problem of our dependence on one another.

Three-person scenes of mixed sleeping and waking, like those in Churchill's poem for Fornés, are the foundational structure of Fornés's 1993 play *Enter THE NIGHT.* In this infrequently produced play, three friends who are coping with chronic and terminal illness gather for a long weekend together. They take turns sleeping and caring for one another. *Enter THE NIGHT* is a synthetic, episodic drama with its own rich intertextual culture built on camp reenactments of classic films and insider references to New York's queer downtown theater scene. The title *Enter THE NIGHT,* with its unconventional capitalization, functions as both a command and a stage direction, as if THE NIGHT were a character in the play. When THE NIGHT enters, sleep amplifies and expands the ways in which the three friends already feel fragmented by illness. Fornés stages the loss of bodily control that sleep allows as both terrifying and liberating. Scenes of mixed sleeping and waking allow for nonrealist shifts in identities and relationships onstage. In these sleep/wake scenes, a sleeping character's dreams merge with scenes from other performances—from films and plays that make up the three friends' shared private culture. These sleep/wake scenes are opportunities for characters to shimmy loose from their day-to-day roles as sick people and caregivers, reimagining themselves into new genders, racial identities, and relationships with one another. Among friends and through sleep/wake scenes, the three characters in *Enter THE NIGHT* reach toward kinds of care that they cannot find in their families or from other institutions, and toward relationships not defined by categories like sick or healthy, man or woman, straight or queer.

Fornés, a lodestar for generations of lesbian and Latinx playwrights, often resisted pressures to identify publicly with a particular sexual or ethnic affiliation.[2] Born in Havana in 1930, Fornés immigrated to New York with her mother and sister and became a wildly innovative writer and director in off-off-Broadway theater from the 1960s through the late 1990s.[3] Like Laurie Anderson and Peggy Shaw, Fornés was a creature of the downtown New York performance scene of the late twentieth century, although *Enter THE NIGHT* premiered at Seattle's Theater Zero. And like Churchill, Fornés experimented with new theatrical forms at a rapid pace throughout her career. Many of her plays explore intimate relationships between women and imagine whole theatrical worlds populated only by women, as in the groundbreaking *Fefu and Her Friends* (1977).[4] As a playwriting teacher, Fornés guided new generations of Hispanophone writers into production via the INTAR Hispanic Playwrights-in-Residence Laboratory while also supporting the writers materially by paying them for their workshop time, as they would be paid at a job. As a managing director, she ran New York Theatre Strategy, an off-off-Broadway collective that gave playwrights more control over how their work was produced. In this role, and when she directed productions of her own plays, Fornés worked tirelessly on everything from finding a performance space to foraging for costumes in thrift stores. A New York Theatre Strategy colleague has described entering her apartment before opening night "to find her sound asleep under her writing table . . . [having] fallen where she worked."[5] Fornés's decades of work as a playwright, director, producer, and teacher made concrete, material, and far-reaching contributions to the artistic opportunities available to women and to Spanish-speaking writers and actors in American theater—not only in the vibrant off-off-Broadway theater ecology but also in the many feminist and regional theaters across the country that staged her plays.

Fornés's plays slip fluidly between realism and nonrealism and display a modernist eagerness to separate the possibilities of dramatic character from the limitations of the human body—including the expectation that bodies have consistent races, genders, or sexualities.[6] In *Enter THE NIGHT,* sleep is the onstage act that frees characters from their bodies and identities as they dream themselves out of the strictures of sickness and the conventions of caretaking relationships. The playful slipperiness of bodies and identities, particularly gendered and sexual identities, brings Fornés's modernist dramaturgy into contact with a camp sensibility, described by Fornés's former partner Susan Sontag as

"Being-as-Playing-a-Role." A camp sensibility, Sontag posits, "sees everything in quotation marks. It's not a lamp, but a 'lamp'; not a woman, but a 'woman.'"[7] We pursue camp to flee boredom; camp transforms the stifling or moralizing into the fantastic. And the characters in Fornés's plays, although not always of the bourgeois class Sontag associates with camp, are often fleeing boredom, including the boredom of living with chronic illness and the incessant care (both caretaking and carefulness) it demands. The antiboredom, antimoralist attitude of camp anticipates theories of illness that suggest illness defamiliarizes the presumed connection between the body and the roles one can play, as in Sontag's later "Illness as Metaphor" and Eve Kosofsky Sedgwick's writing on breast cancer. In *Enter THE NIGHT,* sleeping characters dream they are someone else, and waking characters in sleep/wake scenes are freed to pretend to be other people, knowing that the sleeper cannot witness them transgressing the boundaries of their own gender, sexuality, or race. These shifting identities then shift the relationship between caregiver and care recipient. When a woman pretends to be a man caring for a sleeping girl, and an adult man pretends to be the girl, the typical gendered dynamics of caretaking labor mutate. Within these sleep/wake scenes, biopolitical categories become less determinative of leisure and labor and less predictive of what characters will do onstage.

In the background of these theories of modernism, camp, and chronic illness lingers the question of how the slippery relationship between the body and gender in performance compares to the relationship between the body and race. In Fornés's 1983 play *Mud,* the impoverished, overworked character Mae imagines shimmying free from the limitations of the human body entirely, as she reads aloud descriptions of invertebrate, potentially genderless sea creatures. Mae, like many Fornés characters, is not assigned a racial or ethnic identity in the play text. Yet at the same time that Mae reads herself toward a complete freedom from the human body, José Esteban Muñoz (like Fornés, a Cuban New Yorker) describes Mae as "lost in a brownness" that both is and is not tethered to human racial identity. Although Muñoz specifies that the brownness of the play is not based in Fornés's race, he points to Mae's desire to die "the good life of a white death"—in a hospital, rather than in the mud where she has always lived—as evidence that Mae feels brown.[8] Feeling brown, here, means dreaming of being cared for like a white person is cared for. Mae's feelings of brownness emerge not from her spoken or performed identification with a racial category but from her isolation, from a care relationship that she has been denied. The dream of receiving good care surfaces, for Muñoz, an affect not determined by the unspecified racial identity of the character or of the actor playing her.

Race shapes material conditions of care in the late twentieth-century context of *Enter THE NIGHT*. The year before *Enter THE NIGHT* debuted, Evelyn Nakano Glenn published her groundbreaking genealogy of the "racial division of reproductive labor" as "key to the distinct exploitation of women of color" in the United States.[9] This division of labor, shaped by racial and gendered hierarchies emerging from histories of enslavement and immigration, slotted women of color into low-ranking medical caretaking jobs like nursing aide and home health care aide. An increasingly globalized labor market, Lisa Lowe notes, led to the "proletarianization of Asian and Latina immigrant women" alongside Black women already doing this work in the 1980s and 1990s.[10] As the characters in *Enter THE NIGHT* struggle to dream up a version of care not based in heterosexual family dynamics, they reenact scenes from films that cast nonwhite non-Americans in the role of caretakers to characters who seem to be white U.S. citizens. In the play's sleep/wake scenes, the friends intervene in the reproduction of typical caring relationships by using theatrical tools to actively change their own identities in performance. When Fornés's characters fall asleep, they fantasize a richer experience of care by reenacting the film roles of ardent Latin lovers and gentle Asian caretakers in yellowface. Their inexact restagings of cinematic scenes produce new relationships of care and rest. This difficult play—whose most critically lauded dream of intimate care relations is also its most troubling scene—offers insights into the imaginative failures of feminist sleep performance, failures that are not unique to Fornés's play. *Enter THE NIGHT* reveals the racist fantasy and racializing stage techniques that haunt its characters' dreams of new forms of care as they live through the austere era of the AIDS crisis.

A False Mustache, Glasses, a Nose, and a Gold Tooth

In *Enter THE NIGHT,* sleep is both an opportunity to loosen or evade typical hierarchies of care labor and, still, an experience of depending on the care of others. The play begins at six o'clock in the morning and tracks a series of interactions among three old friends who have gathered to spend one day and night together. Tressa enters first, returning from working an overnight shift as a nurse. She reads aloud her notes on a dying patient's sleep; he is "raising green phlegm" and "incontinent of large amount of formed soft yellow BM" (124).[11] Tressa has two close friends who also need care. Paula is on the verge of losing her job because of her chronic heart condition and needs emergency intravenous injections to correct her fibrillations, and Jack believes he is HIV-positive because his partner has recently died of AIDS. (Tressa and Paula remain unconvinced by Jack's self-diagnosis.) Throughout the play, sleep/wake scenes punctuate the friends' time together: Paula asleep and dreaming of Jack, Jack asleep while Tressa cares for him, and Jack on the verge of sleep at the play's end. During these sleep/wake scenes, the characters' minds relax control over their bodies, allowing for a variety of influences—cinematic, theatrical, and medical—to reconfigure their relationships with one another. The sleeping character dreams of themself as a different person while the waking character uses theatrical tools like costuming and makeup to materially transform themself into a different person without worries about being watched. Dreamed or unwitnessed reproductions of cinematic scenes onstage allow the characters to use theatrical tools to loosen the grip of static identity categories on their relationships.

The play's first sleep/wake scene establishes a pattern of multiply shifted identities, intertextual dreams, and hazy borders between dream and reality. Paula wakes up and tells Tressa about an experience she had while asleep, in which Jack transformed into a "Latin" lover through a theatrical reproduction of a cinematic scene. Still "*half asleep,*" Paula tells Tressa she remembers an unknown Latin man, José Luis, entering the house where Paula was sleeping to look for a tool (124). Paula and Tressa decide that whether José Luis was real or dreamed depends on the relationship he claimed to have with Paula. Paula recounts, "He said he couldn't possibly marry me," and Tressa replies, "That sounds like Jack" (126), whom they expect to have no romantic interest in a woman. But when Paula remembers José Luis asking, "Do your legs want to wrap themselves around me?" (127), both Paula and Tressa become convinced that Jack-as-José-Luis's desire for a passionate embrace with Paula means it must have been a dream. In her sleep, Paula is fantasizing about a libidinous rendezvous with her gay friend Jack, grafted onto a straight lover from a recent film.

The recent film is Catalan director Bigas Luna's "strictly heterosexual" 1992 melodrama *Jamón Jamón,* starring Spanish actors Penélope Cruz and Javier Bardem, with Jordi Mollà as José Luis. Paula, dreaming of wrapping her legs around Jack, imagines reenacting the young Cruz's ardent gesture. Film scholar Marsha Kinder describes Luna's films as tonally ambiguous, influenced by absurdism and modernism, and populated by characters with repressed sexual desires.[12] Luna's films and Fornés's plays share these characteristics. Paula's dream, set in Luna's world of hypersexualized characters whose repressed longings emerge sideways as incestuous attractions and hammy (jamón-like) aural and visual puns, seems ripe for a Freudian reading, as does dream-Jack's search for a "tool" in Paula's dream. Paula's latent repressed desire for Jack—who is sexually unavailable because of his homosexuality and uncertain HIV status—manifests itself through dream as desire for the very sexually available, heterosexual José Luis.

Yet when the real Jack enters the stage soon after this dream narrative, he appears as a low-budget José Luis in waking life. He is wearing a theatrical disguise, "*a false mustache, glasses, a nose, and a gold tooth*" made of foil chocolate wrappers, that marks him as Mollà's character. Upon Jack's entrance, Paula "*jumps on Jack and puts her legs around him*" (136), reproducing this dreamed/remembered gesture with her own now-awake body. Paula transforms from a middle-aged woman with a husband and a serious cardiac condition into a passionate starlet entangling a new lover in a full-bodied embrace. The play does not telegraph whether we are seeing Paula's dream of Jack or whether Jack appears in the flesh. There is no theatrical evidence to distinguish a dreamed Jack from a real Jack, and this lack of interpretable evidence is an early clue to spectators that *Enter THE NIGHT* is not committed to realism. Paula and Jack both employ theatrical tools—the disguise and the gesture—to reproduce the embrace scene from *Jamón Jamón* with a difference: their own bodies and identities so unlike those of film's hypersexualized Spanish-speaking stars. These shifts in language and sexuality also shift the nature of Jack and Paula's friendship, although the particular effects of restaging this romantic embrace with camp flair remain uncertain. As the three friends work together to recall and extend Paula's ephemeral sleeping intimacies with José Luis, remembered sleep becomes social. Fornés's social, theatrical use of sleep thus contrasts with Freudian dream interpretation, which roots the drama of sleep in the mind of an individual, stripped of waking inhibitions to reveal its real desires. Fornés stated that she preferred to write characters who lived before the popularization of psychoanalysis, when people "were not constantly interpreting each other or themselves."[13] In *Enter THE NIGHT,* desire expressed through sleep—desire to be with someone and to become someone—plays out in the relationships among multiple characters. In the film *Jamón Jamón,* characters tend to strip away clothing to provoke or express sexual desire, exposing testicles, breasts, chests, and legs of ham, but in *Enter THE NIGHT,* they add layers of theatrical dress-up material, in the form of Groucho Marx masks and gold-foil teeth. Against the Freudian exposure of buried latent desire through dream, *Enter THE NIGHT* builds up further layers of theatricality in its sleep/wake scenes.

This first sleep/wake scene takes place against the backdrop of Paula's heart condition, the very reason she is taking a nap. Paula and Jack's transformation into *Jamón Jamón*'s heterosexual, energetic Latin lovers is an intertextual theatrical exaggeration of disability studies' insight that identities such as able-bodied or disabled, sick or healthy, are not only discursively constructed but also shift across a person's lifetime. Health and ability are perhaps the most obviously fluid of identity categories. Any able-bodied person might "identity shift" into illness or disability. Indeed, in her writing on breast cancer, Sedgwick suggests that traversing the porous border between healthy and sick might be the first step toward a more capacious sense of shifting identity. She describes having never "felt less stability in my gender, age, and racial identities" than she did while receiving cancer treatment—"nor . . . have I ever felt more of a mind to explore and exploit every possibility."[14] Like Jack donning a false mustache and glasses to look like José Luis, Sedgwick frames this essay on identity instability around her purchase of a real pair of white-framed glasses, worn in admiring imitation of a friend who is also sick, an attractive gay man. Illness happens upon Sedgwick, but other potential shifts in gender, age, and race become her active site of exploration—of play with theatrical props.

Playing, or even playacting, with identity is a gateway out of being stuck in the role of sick person that sleep opens for *Enter THE NIGHT*'s characters. Paula never claims to permanently become an able-bodied young Spanish lover, but she experiments with the libidinous gestures she has seen such a person perform in the movies, and the audience sees her embodying this role as she wraps her legs around Jack. Paula becomes more like Jack's lover and less like the sick friend Jack is visiting; their friendship becomes less tethered to a routine of caregiving and care needing. The half-awake, half-asleep theatricalized reproduction of a cinematic scene is the site in which necessary caretaking can happen between friends without solidifying into rigid identities of caregiver and invalid.

Yellowish White Base

In a second sleep/wake scene, another intertextual reenactment—of an interracial love scene from D. W. Griffith's silent film *Broken Blossoms* (1919)—allows Tressa and Jack to transform their caretaking relationship into a sexually transgressive and aesthetically rich encounter via Tressa's use of yellowface makeup. This sleep/wake scene extends elements of camp identity transgression seen in the play's allusion to *Jamón Jamón,* but it is both more disturbing and more critically lauded than that brief early scene. This sleep/wake scene brings *Enter THE NIGHT* into contact with the aesthetic objectification of Asian femininity through the theatrical practice of racializing makeup—and into conversation with the white face paint deployed in the much-discussed concluding scene of David Henry Hwang's contemporaneous play *M. Butterfly.*

In the scene from *Broken Blossoms,* a Chinese man named Cheng Huan cares for a sleeping white character called The Girl, trying to protect her from her abusive father. (The role Fornés calls Huang is credited in *Broken Blossoms* as Cheng Huan. I use Huang to refer to the role Tressa assumes onstage and Cheng Huan to refer to the character in the film.) Griffith is an early twentieth-century American filmmaker best known for *The Birth of a Nation*, widely regarded as overtly racist. *Broken Blossoms* is a different kind of film, focused on a small domestic unit, and has had a different critical reception. Critics of *Broken Blossoms* tend to be interested in how Griffith's skill as a silent filmmaker can sweep viewers up emotionally and aesthetically while more subtly advancing ideologies of race, gender, and sexual attraction. Tressa and Jack's reenactment of a scene of care for a sleeping, injured girl from *Broken Blossoms* takes up the aesthetic magnetism of the scene while foregrounding the yellowface makeup used in the portrayal of Cheng Huan. Jack plays the role of The Girl. Tressa, as Huang, makes up and costumes Jack as Jack/The Girl sleeps, watches as The Girl is beaten by "an invisible Father," and cradles The Girl as she dies (161–62). In the scene Tressa and Jack imitate, Huang performs costuming as an act of care: "*Huang [Tressa] takes her [Jack] up to his room (downstage) and dresses her in an embroidered silk gown, lowers her to his bed, puts makeup on her face, and puts a decorative crown of flowers on her head. She [Jack] falls asleep as he [Tressa] exits*" (162). The theatricality becomes part of the caretaking, and, in applying makeup to a sleeping Girl/Jack, Tressa transforms her job as a nurse caring for dying patients into a practice of enacting and strengthening her friendship with Jack—and a practice of eroticizing their relationship.

The scene mirrors Paula's dream in the opening of act 1: A waking and a sleeping character both experience identity shifts (in race, gender, and age) as they take on prescripted cinematic roles, and these identity shifts also change the nature of their relationship to one another. The mundanity of a nurse taking care of a sick person becomes erotic, aesthetic, and maybe a bit funny. It is a classic use of camp, in Sontag's terms, to seduce and to evade boredom. (The white interpretation of Chinese performance is also a classic use of camp; Sontag cites European chinoiserie as one of the origins of camp in the United States.)[15] The Girl/Jack's aestheticized death in Huang/Tressa's arms contrasts with the slowly dying, coughing, excreting patient Tressa has just cared for at the beginning of the play, and with Jack's painful experience of the loss of his lover Joey, whose family "didn't want me to see him when he was dying" (148). When Paula walks in on Tressa and Jack's scene, she guesses—to her surprise—that they are lovers, and Tressa confirms that she is in love with Jack, but Jack is attracted to her only when she dresses as a man. Tressa needs to be dressed as a man for Jack to want her sexually, but she seems to need to be costumed and made up as a Chinese man to continue to play a caretaking role. In escaping one stereotypical caretaking identity, the sexless female nurse, Tressa adopts another, that of a gentle, sensitive Asian man, in contrast to the brutish masculinity displayed by The Girl's violent white father in Griffith's film. As Tressa flees the limitations of her own identity, she reinforces the racial stereotypes deployed in *Broken Blossoms*. At the same time, against the flattening that serious long-term caretaking can impose on a relationship, Tressa and Jack deploy cinematic knowledge and theatrical skill to make caring for a sleeping person a pleasurable act.

Although *Broken Blossoms* does not have much in common with *Jamón Jamón*, both of the films do combine heterosexual relationships with forms of socially unaccepted—thus, possibly transgressively pleasurable—sex. In *Broken Blossoms*, this includes the threat of incest between The Girl and her father (who, feminist critic Julia Lesage argues, symbolically rapes his daughter), miscegenation between The Girl and Cheng Huan (whose sexual relationship with The Girl is a topic of critical debate), and pedophilia (as The Girl is not an adult).[16] As in Tressa and Jack's ambiguous relationship, sex between characters in *Broken Blossoms* is strongly symbolized or implied but not made explicit. Aspects of the characters' identities—including their family roles, races, and ages—make sex taboo, but, as Naomi Greene argues, "Griffith's insistence on [The Girl's] purity . . . heightens [its] erotic charge."[17] While critiques of *Broken Blossoms* focus on its portrayal of taboo and/or nonconsensual sex, a caretaking relationship also spans and complicates the ambiguous interactions between The Girl and Cheng Huan. Cheng Huan rescues The Girl from her father's violence and cares for her while she is asleep or unconscious. He enshrines her in a bed and comes close to kissing her from her bedside but ultimately kisses her sleeve, rather than her lips, when she suddenly awakens. So *Broken Blossoms* eroticizes not only The Girl's sexual purity but also the caregiving relationship based around a bedbound, sleeping recipient of simultaneous caring and libidinous attentions. In their reenactment of the scene from *Broken*

Blossoms, Tressa and Jack's grasp for this eroticized care is further heightened by the sexual taboos layered on The Girl and Cheng Huan's relationship.

Indeed, Jack and Tressa seem to be seeking taboos that can be physically represented through theatrical tools to shore up the pleasures of the relationship against the threat that it will be reduced to the dull predictability of heterosexual caretaking. At the time of *Broken Blossoms*' production, during the U.S. period of Asian immigrant exclusion, Asian actors were not cast in lead roles in Hollywood films, so white actor Richard Barthelmess played the role of Cheng Huan in racializing makeup, allowing the film to suggest the taboo possibility of an interracial relationship between Cheng Huan and The Girl without casting a Chinese man as a romantic lead. Early in act 1, long before she and Jack reenact the *Broken Blossoms* scene, Tressa applies "*yellowish white base*" makeup to her face (130), telling Paula, "I like . . . the way it feels on my skin" (133). Scholars of yellowface, the theatrical and cinematic technique of making up a non-Asian (usually, but not always, white) actor to play an Asian character, argue that the white Americans creating yellowface roles experience pleasure in this creative act.[18] While Paula is skeptical of the sexual relationship between Tressa and Jack, since she and Tressa both view Jack as gay, Tressa and Jack do not face the boundaries of racial and age difference that applied in Griffith's early twentieth-century film; they have nothing to transgress. Instead, yellowface itself becomes the transgression. In using a theatrical technique widely regarded as racist—and protested by Asian Americans since the 1960s, if not earlier—Tressa paints her relationship with Jack with an overlay of taboo and transgression, made tangible in the feel of the yellowish makeup.[19]

Tressa claims the pleasure she feels is located specifically in the yellowish makeup itself, rather than in the full range of racializing makeup techniques. It is the way the makeup feels on her skin that contributes to her sensual pleasure in costuming and caring for a sleeping Jack. The relationship between skin and makeup, between flesh and ornament, is central to Anne Anlin Cheng's reading of the "alternative American racial logic" applied to Asian (American) women. Cheng argues, "Nineteenth-century Orientalism, especially condensed around the figure of Asiatic femininity, thrives in mainstream American culture today . . . because this figure energizes a specific, aesthetic, ornamentalist practice that drives our imagination about what is beyond the human."[20] The painted-on layer of yellow skin, or "supraflesh," that Tressa wears repeats and reactivates a fascination with the figure of the Asian woman hovering at the boundary of person and object, as something "beyond the human." The yellow makeup is not just a restaging of an outdated form of Hollywood racism but part of an ongoing Orientalist imagination of Asian women as not precisely human. And the characters in *Enter THE NIGHT* are desperate to escape their human bodies. They want to be less affected by their bodies' physical limitations but also to be *more* sexually objectified and, thus, more desired. In this scene, Tressa wants to be less a human woman—and therefore not attractive to Jack—and more a celluloid character, a differently gendered sexual object, a thick layer of paint-flesh. She claims she is dressing as a man to attract Jack, but her most explicit and longest-lasting material transformation is to paint herself as a yellow woman.

The ornamentalist aesthetic pleasure Tressa pursues within the story of *Enter THE NIGHT* by painting her face with yellowish-white makeup has translated to reviewers of the play as aesthetic pleasure within their own spectatorial experiences. In a review of the original production in Seattle, *Theater Journal* called this scene the "most powerful" of the play, describing The Girl as "a beautiful victim."[21] At New York's Signature Theatre in 1999, a critic found the scene to be "one of the most beautiful movements of the play," and in a Portland, Oregon, revival in 2015, it remained "quite beautiful."[22] This is the most ornamented scene in an otherwise materially austere play. A photograph from 1993 shows how closely this original production strove to match the costuming and set dressing used in the *Broken Blossoms* scene it imitated, including racializing eye makeup for Tressa that is very similar to Barthelmess's in the film. Alongside their pursuit of an increasingly eroticized relationship, Tressa and Jack execute a strong aesthetic sensibility. Tressa's skills at nursing care become translated into an aesthetic care via the figure of Huang, a film character who can care for The Girl with a kind of tenderness and beauty not shown by her white father. In both *Broken Blossoms* and this reenactment of the scene, the characters escape the limited possibilities for their caretaking relationship, possibilities fixed by white gender norms, through a Chinese character imagined as beyond human limitations, who can be both a man and caring, or both a woman and a participant in a male homosexual encounter.

While the intertextual relationship between this sleep/wake scene and *Broken Blossoms* is explicit, the interracial romance, gender play, and use of racializing makeup in the scene also implicitly echo the central concerns of David Henry Hwang's 1988 play *M. Butterfly.* Hwang, who briefly studied with Fornés, dramatizes a nineteenth-century news story about a French diplomat in China who falls in love with a performer in the Beijing opera and has a twenty-year relationship with this performer, unaware that she is actually a male Chinese spy—and that in the Beijing opera, men play female characters. At the end of the play, having been sentenced to prison for treason, the diplomat dresses himself in the opera performer's theatrical costume, wig, and makeup and stabs himself. David L. Eng points out that this makeup is white: The French diplomat ends the play "in literal whiteface." Eng argues that, for the diplomat, the sexual interaction he had with the opera performer must remain heterosexual, and he must remain white, which leaves him dressed as a woman in super-white face paint. While this white makeup was a Chinese theatrical convention for men playing women in the Beijing opera, it breaks the conventions of twentieth-century U.S. drama when the diplomat wears it, revealing the construction of whiteness, "whiteness and heterosexuality at one and the same time," at the heart of the diplomat and performer's relationship.[23] Tressa's yellow makeup follows this logic, but with different implications. Tressa's yellow makeup is also a performance convention, of yellowface film roles in the Chinese Exclusion Era, that becomes denaturalized in the new context of late twentieth-century U.S. drama. The yellow makeup shows how Tressa and Jack's fantasies of libidinous care remain trapped in the racial-sexual order of U.S. American care labor.

Because Jack is asleep, Tressa can perform in the yellowish makeup she likes without having to fully face her audience. Because *Enter THE NIGHT* cites *Broken Blossoms,* the play can delight in ornamentalist aesthetics without fully owning up to its reproduction of yellowface. This sleep/wake scene, and the positive critical responses it has received, echoes how the new ways of caring for one another that feminists have struggled to imagine have often involved trading out gendered hierarchies of caretaking for racialized ones, so that middle-class white women become enforcers of a sexual *and* racial division of caretaking labor in pursuit of social power for women of their own race and class.[24] The sleep/wake scene that liberates Jack and Tressa from their identities and shifts the nature of their caring relationship at the same time relies on Orientalist fantasies of Chinese identity in U.S. performing arts culture and reproduces the expectation that people of color and immigrants care for white Americans. Even as that sleep onstage opens the theater up to a surreal dream scene, it reveals just how exhausted the demands of care have left the play—so much so that the characters' capacity to imagine beauty and intimacy in care among friends falls back on tired tropes of racialized performance.

Water, Cups, and Kleenex

Jack and Tressa's reenactment of the sleep/wake scene from *Broken Blossoms* contrasts two models of care: Tressa's regular job caring for sleeping patients as a nurse and Tressa's elaborately theatrical staging of care for a sleeping Jack. A third model emerges in the work Jack does outside this escapist weekend away, in his day job as the assistant stage manager for a Ridiculous Theatrical Company production of Everett Quinton's 1989 play *A Tale of Two Cities.* Quinton's downtown, queer theatrical parody of Charles Dickens's novel is yet another intertext in *Enter THE NIGHT.* Whereas *Enter THE NIGHT* founders on performance tropes of racialized caretakers, in this third sleep/wake scene the play imagines a more equitable model of care using the backstage caretaking structures of theatrical performance. Amid a larger context of plays about care set during the AIDS crisis—largely written by and about white gay men—*Enter THE NIGHT* stages a queer form of caretaking that does not merely reproduce the family within a male homosexual community.

In his job as assistant stage manager, or ASM, Jack cares for the actors performing in *A Tale of Two Cities.* He ensures they have "hot water [for] the sink and shower" and "water, cups, [and] kleenex" in their dressing rooms (168). Jack and the actors will also work together to support each other during each performance, as Jack relies on the actors' correct lines for his cues, and the actors rely on Jack to hand them props at the right times. Within the world of *Enter THE NIGHT*, Jack's caring work as an ASM for this particular production of *A Tale of Two Cities* models interdependent caring loosened from the determining identities of gender, ability, sexuality, and other forms of social difference. Fornés reveals the unseen work of an ASM to *Enter THE NIGHT*'s audience when Jack rehearses his cues aloud. Because of the rapid nature of the stage directions in *A Tale of Two Cities*, Jack and the actors are closely interdependent; without time to check his notes, Jack must listen for an actor's verbal cue and respond immediately, often placing a prop directly into the actor's hands from offstage. Jack recites chunks of his running list, such as "Fork into basket—grab fork and hand off broken fork. After fork taken—close trap door" (169), from memory. The audience at *A Tale of Two Cities* would see only the actors, but Fornés reveals the work happening behind the scenes to ensure the play runs smoothly. Jack rehearses his full list of cues for act 1 and then dozes off as he sings, "O come all ye faithful . . ." (170). This Christmas carol, sung offstage, is the final sound cue before *A Tale of Two Cities*' intermission.

It is as if Jack's work as ASM cues his sleep: He reaches intermission on the running list and automatically takes a nap. The dynamics of sleep, caring friendship, and theatrical reproduction work differently in this scene than in the prior two sleep/wake scenes. Rather than being divided between one waking character (who does the caring labor and actively costumes themself in a new identity) and one sleeping character, this scene shows Jack doing some of the caring labor and then also getting to sleep. Work and rest seem to be shared more equitably. And Jack's identity does shift, though in a way that is different from the shifts in the previous sleep/wake scenes. In those scenes, characters use costuming, makeup, and other theatrical tools to change specific elements of their identities, but when Jack works as an ASM, his identity seems to be subsumed to the larger project of staging a play. Jack is not limited to the tools an actor could use (such as costuming, makeup, and gesture) to assume a fictional, intertextual identity onstage but can instead use the fuller social relations of theatrical production to enter into a larger social world less interested in his particular identities. When the play reveals that its characters are participating in the contemporaneous offstage world of queer theatrical production—a world shared with the play's audience—it opens to a more expansive use of theatrical means to liberate identities and relationships.

Thus, the type of reproduction the sleep/wake scene allows also shifts, from restaging a fictional interaction between two characters in a film to rehearsing a backstage interaction between an (unseen) actor and an ASM in a real theatrical production, one staged only a few years before *Enter THE NIGHT* was written. *Enter THE NIGHT* premiered in Seattle and is set in "an empty warehouse or barn," rather than a city, but this cue list explicitly connects Jack to the off-off-Broadway theater scene where Fornés worked throughout her theater career. The Ridiculous Theatrical Company, a drag production ensemble founded by Charles Ludlam in 1967, predates the Stonewall Rebellion and marks the earliest days of explicitly gay theater-making in Manhattan. Ridiculous Theatrical productions brought camp and queer aesthetics to downtown experimental theater, including "us[ing] drag to question, mock, and rewrite gender" and citing and parodying popular culture in their plays.[25] *A Tale of Two Cities* was the first Ridiculous Theatrical production Quinton staged after Ludlam's death. Fornés joins Ludlam and Quinton in the project of questioning, mocking, and rewriting not only gender but other forms of identity as well, making theater that skewers and shakes up the offstage world rather than merely reproducing the given conditions of living.

Enter THE NIGHT reflects the austere conditions of care for people living outside the conventional caretaking structure of the nuclear family: The characters sleep on benches rather than in beds, Paula worries about losing her job, and they have only each other as their caretakers. Friendships that had been sources of pleasure, camaraderie, and shared culture become burdened with the weight of caretaking that cannot possibly be reciprocal, as Paula's heart condition and Jack's uncertain HIV status and fresh grief demand more care from Tressa than Paula and Jack can give her in return. Each time the characters slip the bonds of their identities by taking on new roles in sleep/wake scenes, they still remain in the roles of waking caregiver and sleeping care recipient. This pattern changes with Jack's rehearsal of *A Tale of Two*

Cities, which, rather than reaching back into his two friends' shared bank of cultural references, connects him outward to the contemporary world of theatrical production. Despite the harrowing effects of the AIDS epidemic on queer theater artists, the world of downtown New York theater imagined in *Enter THE NIGHT* is not austere—even in the 1990s, it is robust and ongoing.[26] It attracted and sustained Fornés after she immigrated to New York, and Fornés expanded it through her playwriting innovations and her work as a teacher, director, and producer. The caretaking work Jack performs as an ASM is not merely caretaking for survival but caretaking to create pleasure in the form of a parodic theatrical production that imagines a world not limited by the constraints of the present moment.

Jack worries, however, that a pervasive climate of illness and austere care will kill the parodic and transformative powers of theatrical reproduction. He fears a naturalist, diagnostic theater in which the pinnacle of acting is an exact, clinical reproduction of the quality of breathing of a terminal patient, a theater perhaps informed by the sort of nursing notes that Tressa read aloud at the beginning of the first act. He predicts:

> All plays will be about illness. . . . Instead of the ingenue, the romantic lead, the friend, the villain, the characters will be defined by their illness: the cancer victim, the AIDS victim, the tubercular, the diabetic. . . . The central issue of the plots will be the development of the illness. . . . The best actors will be the ones who can reproduce the particular breathing for each illness. . . . Plays will be funded by pharmaceutical laboratories. (158–59)

Illness Theater will exactly reproduce the world around it—"the leading characters will have the illnesses most common among theatergoers" (159)—and the stage will have no capacity to imagine identities and relationships that differ from the world of victims and caretakers that audiences are already inhabiting. This Illness Theater *cares too much* about illness; it is preoccupied with tracking the illness's progress, as Tressa tracks the progress of her terminal patient—and of Paula's heart condition and Jack's possible diagnosis. Care among friends had acquired a new meaning and intensity by 1993, more than a decade after the beginning of the

AIDS crisis yet still before any effective treatment was available. In New York, and in many other places marked by AIDS, the unexpected illness and untimely death of so many people created new needs for care and exposed the limitations of both conventional, heteronuclear family caretaking and the U.S. medical system. In the place of these unreliable caretaking institutions, friends cared for one another through illness and death, filling the gaps left by unwilling or unavailable family and unwilling or unaffordable medical services.

Well-known plays about the gay male community set during the AIDS crisis model this alternate structure for interpersonal caretaking relationships, claiming largely white cis gay men's vulnerability to illness and violence as a new kind of strength. Plays like Larry Kramer's *The Normal Heart* (1985), Tony Kushner's *Angels in America* (1993), and later Matthew Lopez's *The Inheritance* (2018) test the capacity of gay men to care for their HIV-positive friends and lovers. The plays celebrate a gay identity that persists courageously and publicly in the face of violent discrimination and mass death, asserting that it is precisely the uncloseting of intimate relationships between men that allowed them to fight for their survival without mainstream support. The heterosexual family, they demonstrate, is not the only relationship structure that can provide care and foster intergenerational legacies. Across three decades of AIDS plays and other cultural representations, gay identities and relationships have reproduced themselves, in part through plays about AIDS, expanding from the small group of men starting the Gay Men's Health Crisis in *The Normal Heart* to the teeming community of gay men onstage in *The Inheritance,* along with the substantial Broadway and West End houses all three playwrights filled in the 2010s. These plays participate in a strong narrative of AIDS as a disease affecting only (or primarily) the gay male community, and they can exemplify the Illness Theater that Jack fears. This narrative continues to obscure the role of women and nonbinary people in caring for people living with AIDS, protesting the inaction of the U.S. government and medical researchers, and making art in response to the AIDS crisis, and it neglects other constituencies with disproportionate risk of contracting HIV.

Enter THE NIGHT has, in contrast, been characterized as Fornés's "response to AIDS from a woman's point of view."[27] It may be perverse to ascribe the play's approach to AIDS dramaturgy to Fornés's gender when her work is so interested in what the lives of women can become when they are less delimited by gender—or even by species. But *Enter THE NIGHT* certainly responds to AIDS, and the new forms of care the crisis demanded, from a feminist sensibility. In *Enter THE NIGHT,* sleep/wake scenes allow Fornés's terminally ill characters and their caretakers to slip the bonds of identity, using theatrical tools like costuming and makeup to recast themselves in cinematic relationships of love and caring. By tracking these sleeping identity shifts, Fornés finds the greatest freedom to shift the rigid asymmetries of caretaking relationships in the care Jack the ASM offers to the Ridiculous Theatrical Company actors he prepares to perform with. In this relationship, caretaking is not an act of survival foisted onto friends when families and physicians have failed them; instead, it is an act of creative pleasure and industriousness.

Late in the play, Jack forcefully and finally rejects all care. He returns from an early morning walk looking as if he has been violently assaulted, with blood "*smeared*" on his bare chest (174). He recounts a series of men penetrating him without condoms. Jack, convinced that he is seropositive, is concerned for the men's safety but ecstatic when his care is rejected: "I handed them condoms and they didn't care. I've never been so happy in my life. . . . I screamed like a goat in the slaughterhouse" (176). Jack is happy when his offer of care is ignored.

Onstage, the smeared blood is theatrical makeup whose color catches the eye, echoing Tressa's yellow makeup from the *Broken Blossoms* scene. This added layer of visible makeup again marks a sexual transgression made desirable because it is taboo. But this sexual transgression does not have to hark back to an earlier era of elaborate racial coding; it is transgressive in the here and now, in a moment when unprotected sex with strangers—when contact with blood—is seen as an unconscionable risk, not only in the world of Fornés's play but also in the world of its original performance. Jack has just lost a lover to AIDS, he is working for a theater company that has just lost its founder to AIDS, and yet he delights in being allowed to be careless and un-cared-for when his condoms are rejected. He ruptures the tangible and fantastical layers of supra-flesh ornament, of makeup and costuming and cinematic allusion, that earlier cushioned the delicate interplay of care and sexual transgression he shared with Tressa. In this moment, there is no barrier between the world of the play and the world of its performance. Jack's story is equally shocking in both, and Jack is wide awake.

Jack's return, bloodied and euphoric, is the furthest thing from sleep. The sex he describes is incommensurate with the conventions of AIDS plays, in which a concrete diagnosis with HIV marks the moment of anagnorisis, the scene of recognition or discovery, and a Kaposi's sarcoma, applied with makeup to the actor's body, is the theatrical vehicle for that recognition. Because the play never provides this certainty about Jack's HIV status, *Enter THE NIGHT* never tips into being the Illness Theater Jack fears. Blood alone is not readable in this way. But the sex Jack describes also seems incommensurate with the temporary haven of care and sleep among friends that he has crafted with Tressa and Paula. That haven is not a full solution to the problems of care that the characters face. The theatrical promise of sleep—sleep as a dramaturgical opportunity for characters to slip free of their waking identities, of their diagnoses and sexual limitations and social roles—is, finally, not enough. The play's sleep/wake scenes have hypothesized new relations of care in this temporary queer respite from the family and the hospital, but they have not yet found a livable alternative.

Enter THE NIGHT ends with the three friends reconciled and speaking in harmony, reciting lines from the 1937 film *Lost Horizon*: "I see, at a great distance, a new world stirring in the ruins, stirring clumsily but in hopefulness" (178). They all know the lines by heart. As in earlier moments of allusion, the three friends rehearse and reinforce the rich shared culture of their friendship, a dense tissue of coded references they have cultivated as a haven from the mainstream world. Like *Broken Blossoms, Lost Horizon* is a white film director's fantasy, a projection of Anglo-American yearning for different ways of living onto the timeless background of East Asia. *Lost Horizon* is set in a fictional Asian utopia, the imagined Himalayan valley of Shangri-La. The film reflects a Western fascination with Shangri-La that emerged in the nineteenth century; for viewers in the 1990s, Shangri-La would also have been associated with Hollywood campaigns for a free Tibet, the nation often imagined as Shangri-La's hiding place.[28] So this "new world" at a "great distance" is simultaneously an Orientalist fantasy utopia projected onto Asia for more than a hundred years and a contemporary political fascination. Buoyed by this cinematic utopian dream, Jack again falls asleep, and by dawn Paula and Tressa are also considering slumber. Yet Jack wakes up to utter the play's final, dialectical line: "I'm tired . . . I can't go back to sleep" (179). Jack can neither fully surrender to a dreamed, fantasy world nor commit to the waking circumstances of his life. This contradiction lingers in the play's vision of a "new world," one in which the characters find respite from exhausting inequities of care, freeing themselves from their waking identities and relationships—but only by grasping for the limited view of a new world that American cinema projects onto its own creations of Asian characters and settings.

Enter THE NIGHT shares a political commitment seen in many plays about HIV/AIDS: Fornés uses the stage to imagine relational structures for caretaking that exist beyond the legally sanctioned heteronuclear family in response to a then-terminal illness and in the face of neglectful medical institutions. Yet Fornés neither follows the dramaturgical structure of better-known AIDS plays nor concludes with a strengthened sense of gay identity and the caretaking capacity of romantic relationships, queer or straight. Rather than confirming confident identities (such as HIV status or sexuality) or clearly established relationships (such as lovers or spouses), Fornés destabilizes these claims. Sleep/wake scenes free the friends to imagine different ways of relating to one another, based not in claiming a particular identity but in increasing liberation from identities they find exhausting. In scenes of mixed sleeping and waking, the three friends reenact care relationships that mine the camp pleasures of Being-as-Playing-a-Role—painting your face with makeup, donning silly glasses, putting on a show with your friends—while excavating the origins of some of these pleasures in racialized fantasies about caring Chinese men and distant Tibetan utopias. These filmic fantasies ultimately serve to protect whiteness: Cheng Huan cares for the white Girl as she sleeps, and Shangri-La, in *Lost Horizon,* is "where Buddhist monks safeguard the wisdom of the white race" through centuries of dormancy.[29]

Indeed, whiteness sleeps safely in these fantasies; whiteness is imagined as under threat but well cared for. As Muñoz suggests in his reading of brownness in *Mud,* to be white means to be cared for when your body is beyond your control, whether in the daily uncontrollability of sleep or a final loss of control in death. The characters in *Enter THE NIGHT* are not certain that they will have access to this kind of care. They are not certain that whiteness will continue to tether them to institutions of care even as their illnesses and sexualities cut them off from jobs and families. Jack has seen his lover die what seems to be a white death—cared for in a hospital and surrounded by family—but without his partner at his side. In her reading of the "yellow woman," Cheng cautions that this ornamentalist figure "stirs up a set of embattled issues that have always haunted feminism."[30] Tressa's appearance as a caretaker made up with yellowish paint shows how haunted feminist dreams of alternate forms of care remain in this play. Sleep/wake scenes in *Enter THE NIGHT* allow shifts in caretaking relationships that both reawaken erotic and aesthetic pleasures and reanimate racist performance tropes tied to fantasies of better care. At the end of the play, with Jack torn between sleeping and waking, the friends still do not know how they will be interpreted—how they will be cared for—on their deathbeds.

Six

A Dormant Trans/Queer Archive

An Intergenerational Opera by Sarah Kane and Philip Venables

Sleep is unexpectedly present in a wide range of theater and performance, but it is still true that focusing a performance on the theme of sleep and sleeplessness may limit its theatrical success. Sleep remains hard to stage. It is not what audiences expect from theater. Perhaps this is why the man sitting next to me at an opera staging of the insomniac text *4.48 Psychosis* nodded off five minutes into the performance and stayed asleep throughout. His sleep was less surprising during the opera's quiet moments, when the characters onstage were also attempting slumber. His sleep was more impressive when the singers onstage were bellowing out the line "Fuck you" at fortissimo, accompanied by percussionists sawing through lumber and banging a hammer against a pipe (215).[1] His sleep became, for me, a bonus performance of a spectator enduring an opera without having to watch it.

4.48 Psychosis is not for everyone. Like Fornés's *Enter THE NIGHT,* British playwright Sarah Kane's *4.48 Psychosis* (2000) is a late-career work that has received less critical attention than her earlier, groundbreaking plays. And, like *Enter THE NIGHT,* Kane's play interrogates care for a serious illness under austere conditions, when only friends are left to make up for the ways family and medical care abandons sick queer and trans people. *4.48 Psychosis* tries to capture the debilitating suffering of unshakable insomnia in dramatic form. The title names the mental distress caused by involuntarily waking up every morning at precisely 4:48. This untimely arousal from sleep becomes entangled with the pain of unwanted gender in such a way that medical caregivers dismiss it and suicide becomes increasingly desired. While chapter 5 notes the continuities in how productions of *Enter THE NIGHT* have staged sleep, sexuality, and illness—and, less consciously, race—this chapter focuses on how those same entangled elements reemerge in a radically new, discontinuous version of *4.48 Psychosis,* the opera restaging created sixteen years after the play's posthumous debut and seventeen years after Kane's untimely death.

Sarah Kane, born in 1971, wrote five plays and scattered other short works between 1995 and her death by suicide in 1999.[2] From the opening of her first play, *Blasted,* she was a magnet for critical vitriol, but she also became a lodestar for a generation of devotees who waited a long time to see the first adaptation of her final piece, *4.48 Psychosis,* for a new medium—in Philip Venables's 2016 operatic restaging. Fans of London's new playwriting scene in the late twentieth century will be familiar with Kane's early plays' graphic physical and sexual violence, their utter explosion of kitchen-sink realist conventions, and the extreme disgust these innovations provoked in critics. From nearly thirty years later, it is obvious that Kane's age and gender played a role in her negative reception by the London critical establishment. Although theater critics treated her early work as a shocking aberration, Kane was well educated in the history of British and European dramatic literature and participated fulsomely in the energetic world of new British playwriting that surrounded her work. Along with writing her own plays at a rapid pace, she directed Georg Büchner's *Woyzeck* and supported the next generation of playwrights through her work with new play incubator Paines Plough and the Royal Court, a noncommercial venue associated with kick-starting the careers of major British playwrights like Caryl Churchill.

When Kane died, she left a manuscript for *4.48 Psychosis,* a fragmentary, poetic text that debuted posthumously as a play at the Royal Court Jerwood Theatre Upstairs in 2000. *4.48 Psychosis* is hard to read and hard to stage. The nonconsciousness of sleep and the ambiguity of gender manifest formally in *4.48 Psychosis* as abstraction away from concrete theatrical stageability. Unlike most plays—even other avant-garde and nonrealist plays—*4.48 Psychosis* makes no attempt to represent characters. The text lists no character names, assigns no lines to specific actors, and offers almost no stage directions. We call it a play because Kane had already written four other plays (and one screenplay); without this biographical influence, *4.48 Psychosis* might be called a free verse poem. The defining formal characteristics of the play are fragmented scenes, suggesting a recursive rather than linear narrative, and narrative gaps that leave the reader or director the task of navigating an unmapped dramatic terrain. This task reflects Kane's own project in writing, trying to map the unfamiliar terrain of a mind, "the subject of these bewildered fragments" (210). This task is also continuous with Kane's penultimate play, *Crave* (1998), in which she cut back character names to single letters with no indications of embodied characteristics like gender, age, or race. The abstract form of *4.48 Psychosis* is both troubling and exciting. The text announces fragmentation as a symptom of "bewilderment"—and possibly more serious forms of mental illness—but it also continues the trajectory of formal experimentation in Kane's earlier works, reflecting a playwright whose formal control and innovation continued to grow more sophisticated.

The fragmentary text of *4.48 Psychosis* attempts to capture problems with sleep and problems with gender that have become so entangled they exceed existing syntax and vocabulary. A dense accretion of text describes how "the broken hermaphrodite who trusted hermself alone finds the room in reality teeming and begs never to wake from the nightmare" (205). The voice or voices of the play are deeply troubled by gender, as many characters in Kane's plays are. They desire to be a person of a different gender, and characters of apparently different genders meld into one person; to be forced to have a gender recognized by others is sometimes a source of physical violence and emotional suffering in Kane's work. As the anachronism "hermaphrodite" and the neologism "hermself" suggest, Kane's characters do not name this gender trouble in terms commonly used in the late twentieth century—words like *transvestite* or *trans(s)exual* (now also out of common usage) or *intersex, transgender,* or *nonbinary.* The nonconsciousness of sleep seems to authorize explorations of gender identities that do not have to be named with exactitude or claimed as permanent. As in *Enter THE NIGHT,* sleep allows for a play with identities and relationships not authorized or recognized in waking life; being forced awake is then doubly painful.

Despite what seems to be a timely textual archive for feminist readings—performances of gender trouble in the 1990s—feminist performance scholars have been unexpectedly uninterested in Kane's work. In 2007, Kim Solga noted that she and Elaine Aston seemed to be the only two who had taken Kane seriously as part of feminist theater history.[3] In the following decade, Cristina Delgado-García would argue for the explicit connection between Kane and Judith Butler's queer theory, and a handful of other scholars would publish queer and feminist readings of Kane's plays.[4] But, like the sleeping man I sat next to at the *4.48 Psychosis* opera, feminist theater scholars seem to be waiting Kane out without giving much notice to the prominence of gender and sexuality, and specifically trans and queer themes and forms, in her work. Kane does not label the figures in her late plays as queer or trans in ways we are used to recognizing, yet gender and sexuality—from "the broken hermaphrodite" to grief over the loss of variously gendered lovers—are urgent, insistent concerns in *4.48 Psychosis.*

Indeed, scholars looking to earlier historical periods have taught us to attend to diverse archives with care in search of trans/queer friends in ways that invite new readings of *4.48 Psychosis.*[5] These scholars have forged research methodologies based in reading hostile archives built by investors in white supremacy; recognizing material practices and conditions that mark sexual and gender difference amid erasures and lacunae; feeling affective connections, including love and shame, across temporal distance; and insisting that gender and sexual nonnormativity has always existed and has, in fact, constituted the narrow moving target of the normative. Among feminist scholars searching the historical archives for trans/queer friends, medievalist Carolyn Dinshaw names sleep as a figure for this cross-temporal work. "Supernatural sleep, ordinary sleep, absorption in deep thought," she proposes, "bring out life's essential asynchronicity," inviting us to see what is queer about temporally distant texts.[6] The temporal dislocation of super-sleepers like Rip van Winkle can "distance or remove the protagonist from the realm of usual, expected, or acceptable social or sexual reproduction." In other words, the time delay of sleep can "render the protagonist queer" when they wake up—and when they encounter later readers.[7]

In the spirit of Rip van Winkle (who slept for twenty years), two readings of sleep in *4.48 Psychosis* place this play in an archive of trans/queer performance and scholarship from one generation's remove. First, I read the play's use of sleep as a site of simultaneous ungendering, textual fragmentation, and emotional distress in conversation with theories of trans care—including care in response to suicide—that situate *4.48 Psychosis* in a trans/queer feminist archive. I then introduce Venables's opera restaging, which transforms the abstraction of Kane's text into expansive theatricality. Venables uses a wide range of theatrical tools, particularly ensemble casting and live and recorded sound, to go beyond anything called for in Kane's text, in order to more fully explore the range of identities and relations Kane's text evokes, even at the risk of making the performance less clear or accessible. Through Venables's 2019 New York staging of *4.48 Psychosis,* I articulate the political implications of the production's version of a queer maximalist aesthetic that is attentive to how racial injustice affects sleep and suicidality. Venables places *4.48 Psychosis* in the social context of a racist, trans-antagonistic, ableist medical system and, at the same time, in a trans/queer legacy of opera. In so doing, they mobilize *4.48 Psychosis*—specifically its simultaneous thematization of suicide and opposition to death—to intervene in the history of Black soprano deaths on the operatic stage.

To Love the Dead Is for Them to Remain with You

While feminist performance scholars have not devoted much critical attention to *4.48 Psychosis,* other scholars and directors have aimed to preserve the legacy of Kane's plays by aligning them with a masculine Euro-British playwriting canon and downplaying or avoiding their exploration of trans/queer experience. James Macdonald, who knew Kane well and directed the premieres of *Blasted, Cleansed,* and *4.48 Psychosis,* puts her in a longer tradition of British formal innovation associated with the Royal Court stage, including John Osborne's kitchen-sink dramas, Harold Pinter's menacing absurdism, and Edward Bond's explicit staged violence.[8] Scholars have grouped Kane with Samuel Beckett, with Antonin Artaud and his Theatre of Cruelty, and with her British contemporaries Mark Ravenhill and Anthony Neilson as "in-yer-face" masters of shock.[9] Identifying formal or dramaturgical qualities that Kane shares with other playwrights is a move toward legitimating her work, a response to press critics who famously called *Blasted* "a disgusting feast of filth" and responded to *4.48 Psychosis* by asking, "How do you judge a 75-minute suicide note?"—who either refused to interpret or too blithely interpreted Kane's plays.[10] Aligning Kane with European theater's provocative male avant-garde rescues her from dismissal as a minor, young, mentally ill woman writer. It is a critical move that recognizes the sexism and other antagonisms that have shaped the reception of Kane's work but also reproduces these conditions of harm—the very conditions that *4.48 Psychosis* critiques. In contrast, my critical reading of the text's insomniac drive toward suicide, in the context of trans/queer suicides and anti-trans/queer violence, aims to read the text in and as an archive of trans/queer feminist experience, from across a temporal distance.

Yet reading *4.48 Psychosis* as a trans/queer archive does not mean reducing the text to an autobiographical interpretation based in Kane's own intertwined experience of insomnia and mental illness. This textual motif does seem to have originated in Kane's life, as noted by the playwright David Greig in his introduction to Kane's collected works:

> For a period of her depression, Kane had found herself awoken, every morning, at 4.48 a.m. She took this moment, the darkest hour, just before dawn, and found in it a moment of great clarity, a moment when the confusions of psychosis seem to evaporate. The paradox in the play is that the moment of clarity in the psychotic mind is, to those outside it, the moment when delusion is at its strongest.[11]

The play's title indeed troubles this clarity with the indication that the awakening at 4:48 is a part of the psychosis, not a break from it. Yet Greig cautions readers of Kane's plays not to succumb to biographical fallacy, and particularly not to read *4.48 Psychosis* diagnostically. This is in keeping with a feminist resistance to the diagnostic position (sometimes associated with the position of the psychoanalyst) in which realist plays often place spectators, inviting them to puzzle out the etiology of a female character's particular malaise. Interpreting *4.48 Psychosis* is further hampered by Kane's absence from the rehearsal process. While Kane revised *Crave* in rehearsal, directed *Phaedra's Love,* and even acted in a few performances of *Cleansed,* her death prior to the original production of *4.48 Psychosis* means she did not get to participate in developing this text for the stage in the way that her directors and critics had grown accustomed to.

In tension with this view, some critics have argued for the important role of personal experience—of autobiography—in making feminist political performance.[12] Eric A. Stanley, a scholar of radical trans/queer movements, further asserts the critical risks of downplaying the role of suicide in trans/queer archives: "Suicide demands our attention because, left quiet, it continues to grow." In Stanley's reading of a suicide note written by a young trans person, they warn against seeing trans/queer suicide as the inevitable denouement to a "psychic drama," to the "tragedy of trans/queer existence," rather than as damning evidence that modern social life is built on anti-trans/queer violence.[13] When Stanley uses the formal language of theater—of *drama* and *tragedy*—they point to the exculpatory pull of an ancient theatrical genre. If we are allowed to read trans/queer suicide within an ahistorical tradition of tragedy, then it floats free of the particular social context in which anti-trans/queer violence is nurtured.

Within the text of *4.48 Psychosis,* the compulsion to die by suicide emerges from an existentially distressing insomnia, which appears in the text embedded in expressions of nameless gender trouble. Although Kane's text does not divide the play's lines among different characters, I refer to the mind the play most often inhabits as its protagonist (using the pronouns *they/them*) to indicate the consistent presence of a speaker suffering from serious mental distress who finds clarity only when they wake up, recurrently, at 4:48 in the morning. Many of the lines seem to cohere around one person, suffering from what they describe as "psychosis," abandoned by lovers, treated with great condescension and little care by physicians, and repeatedly expressing a plan to die. From early in the text, the protagonist characterizes this death as unavoidable: "I am charging towards my death" (207), "I have resigned myself to death this year" (208), "There's no point anyway because I'm going to die" (209). The protagonist contrasts the brief, predawn clarity of suicidal ideation with a much more pervasive experience of mental fragmentation, in which they express an inability to hold on to coherent thoughts. The protagonist's mental fragmentation establishes the formal qualities of the text, which is composed of sentence fragments and snippets of scenes without a connecting linear plot. The protagonist ties this formal fragmentation directly to their bewildering experience of mental distress, asking, "How can I return to form / now my formal thought has gone?" (213).[14] Formal changes mark changes in the protagonist's mental experience: When they are heavily medicated with psychiatric drugs, for example, the text reduces to short, one-word lines related associatively by prefix ("unpleasant / unacceptable / uninspiring"; 221) that the protagonist terms "free form" (223). Identifying a protagonist in the text (and assigning them pronouns) to some extent dismantles Kane's precise alignment of fragmentary dramatic form with mental fragmentation. But allowing a human character to emerge in readings of *4.48 Psychosis* insists that the entangled themes of disturbed sleep, hampered friendship, and suicide in this fragmentary text are deeply informed by human life, not severed from it.

Although the fragmentary form of *4.48 Psychosis* can indeed seem to float free of social context, divorced from any particular setting, the protagonist repeatedly links an aversion to their own body to the politics of the time they are living in. They describe their life as the "dreary and repugnant tale of a sense interned in an alien carcass and lumpen by the malignant spirit of the moral majority" (214), linking the suffering of being in an "alien carcass"—a body that feels unfamiliar and, uncannily, dead while still alive—to the effects of a recognizable anti-trans/queer evangelical Christian formation, the Moral Majority. The protagonist's description of themself as "a sense interned in an alien carcass" echoes the thesis that a person's bodily characteristics might not match their gender identity, which political scientist Paisley Currah glosses as "a deeply felt *sense* of oneself."[15] This understanding of gender identity, in widespread use among transgender activists by the mid-1990s, is contemporaneous with Kane's writing of *4.48 Psychosis* and offered a medical justification for policy changes to establish trans rights. The potential distance between gender identity and bodily characteristics resonates with other lines from the play, including "I dislike my genitals" (207), "I need to become who I already am" (212), and "I will drown in dysphoria" (212). The first-person speaker describes their sense of themself in the lexicon of mid-1990s trans advocacy.

Yet an *alien carcass* seems to be more than a body with characteristics that do not match its gender identity; *alien carcass* is hardly the language of medical care or legal rights discourse. An alien carcass is dislocated in both place and time, and the phrase reminds us that any potential trans/queer psychic drama in *4.48 Psychosis* (a psychic drama we might hear in first-person phrases like "I dislike," "I need," and "I will drown") does not float free of social context. *Alien* suggests something foreign or uncanny, or something alienated from the self, a body made foreign by its social context, as when a worker becomes alienated from their labor. And *carcass* again sounds uncanny—even horrifying, to feel one's self "interned" in a dead corpse rather than a living being—and at the same time suggests a temporal displacement, a feeling that the body could or should have been alive in a different time but is dead in this one. *Interned* further complicates this sense of displacement: While a dead body might be *interred* in a grave, the slightly different verb *interned* suggests incarceration rather than burial, adding to the temporal confusion between life and death in the body. When the text later asks, "Do you think it's possible for a person to be born in the wrong body?" the next line follows, "Do you think it's possible for a person to be born in the wrong era?" (215). These questions gloss *alien carcass*. It is the wrong body because it is the wrong era, because of a social context that makes this body unlivable in this moment.

4.48 Psychosis resists the trope of trans/queer suicide as individual psychic drama or inevitable tragedy through its formal fragmentation. Despite lines that describe death's inevitability, the play does not cohere into a narrative that marches inexorably toward this tragic end. In Kane's text, identity fragments in terrifying ways, leaving readers of *4.48 Psychosis* as unable to hold on to a sense of plot or genre as the protagonist is unable to hold on to a sense of self. These bewildering feelings of fragmentation are intensified by sleep. As in *Enter THE NIGHT,* sleep becomes an experience of loosening and shifting identity, but what is liberating in Fornés's play is intolerable in Kane's. During "a night in which everything was revealed to me," the protagonist sees a mind not only irreparably but revoltingly fragmented, "a mind whose floor shifts as ten thousand cockroaches . . . the cockroaches comprise a truth" (205). While "I am jealous of my lover and covet his induced unconsciousness / When he wakes he will envy my sleepless night of thought and speech unslurred by medication" (208). Feeling unslurred, the protagonist describes their mind as "a consolidated consciousness . . . as all thoughts unite in an instant of accord" (205), in contrast to their lover's medicated sleeping slurry. But the "instant of clarity" at 4:48 is a trick (206). It is a trap born of a mind so fragmented it interprets the sensation of clarity that sudden waking offers as a meaningful break in the experience of mental illness, rather than just another symptom.

The protagonist repeatedly insists that they might be able to help themself through caring relationships with friends that are different from the kinds of care they receive from medical providers. Medical providers argue with the protagonist's own understanding of their needs, asserting, "You don't need a friend, you need a doctor" (236). But doctors and medical institutions are a deeply unreliable source of care in *4.48 Psychosis.* When the hospital where the protagonist is staying runs out of beds, the "patient [is] discharged into the care of the community" (224). Although this community is never made material in the play, the hope for some form of friendship is everywhere in Kane's text. The protagonist has repeated conversations with an interlocutor about their friends. They want to care and be cared for: "to feed, help, protect, comfort, console, support, nurse or heal / to be fed, helped, protected, comforted, consoled, supported, nursed or healed" (235). These reciprocal lists of verbs, mirroring each other in their active and passive voices, imagine a care network like the networks described in Hil Malatino's study *Trans Care.* Malatino describes trans care networks as "rotating, interchangeable, and reciprocal," existing in response to forms of anti-trans/queer violence that can "make getting out of bed and getting through the day difficult."[16] Like Kane's protagonist, Malatino's care networks imagine ways of caring for one another that look very different from the inaccessible or abusive care of medical institutions and family homes.

Yet the protagonist never sees this care materialize in the text of *4.48 Psychosis*. They articulate a dream of reciprocal care among friends, but this care does not manifest to counter their early morning, insomniac conviction that suicide is the inevitable outcome awaiting someone born in the wrong body in the wrong era. Malatino locates trans care in many spaces, including archives, where "to love the dead is for them to remain with you."[17] Kane critics and directors often do feel a sense of friendship with, or love for, Kane and Kane's plays akin to Malatino's description of loving the dead in the archives. While the protagonist's symptoms might prompt a diagnostic reading of the play, the play's formal characteristics—its fragments and gaps—suggest that readers might take a friendlier position toward the play, trying to "listen and understand and when you feel contempt don't express it" in response to Kane's writing (220). I certainly feel the impulse to love the dead in the archive, to situate Kane among friends, including scholars of trans/queer life who take seriously the archive of suicide notes and the networks of trans care as a project of resisting the violence that Kane's own plays have rigorously made visible and called audiences to account for. Reading *4.48 Psychosis* in this context allows us to see the protagonist's struggle to sleep—to resist the suicidal impulses that accompany their early morning insomnia—not as an isolated and preplotted psychic drama but as a call for more, lifesaving, care.

Opera Comes at the Audience from Everywhere

Along with scholars of Kane's work, theater directors and adapters can pursue a kind of posthumous, intergenerational care in their stagings of Kane's plays. Venables's queer maximalist staging of *4.48 Psychosis* as an opera veers away from other major productions' preference for minimalist staging. This minimalism tends to avoid any social context for the protagonist's mental distress and lack of effective medical care, abdicating the play's potential feminist or trans/queer politics despite their importance for better understanding the protagonist's suicidal expressions. My reading of the production as a queer maximalist staging of Kane's work is based on the version performed in New York in 2019.[18] At the end of the chapter, I discuss a significant difference between the London and New York stagings that presses on the relationship between the typically exuberant aesthetic of queer maximalism and the persistence of racist and ableist anti-trans/queer violence.

In contrast with Venables's opera, directors often stage *4.48 Psychosis* as if it were written by Pinter or Beckett, using few actors and sparse scenic design to present an uncluttered, text-forward performance. They take the lack of theatrical cues (such as speech tags, scenic divisions, and stage directions) as a cue not to mask the serious nature of the play with theatrical tricks or frills. Macdonald's debut staging of *4.48 Psychosis* used only three actors, who delivered their lines in either a naturalistic or an artificially flattened style. With little underscoring or other sound effects, Macdonald's barely hour-long production was, like a Pinter play, full of pauses.[19] Other documented stagings have been similarly minimalist, using a solo performer or a small ensemble of actors and sparse sets.[20] These stagings have tended to exhibit the same desire for certainty in Kane's ambiguous text that the protagonist themself hopes to find in their moments of awakening at 4:48 a.m.: sharp, clear, direct access to the meaning of incoherent but suggestive fragments. Others have pushed even further in the direction of diagnosing the speaker(s) or presenting them as cisgender. One director described his choice to produce the play with a single actor as a way to focus on the individual, psychiatric nature of its depiction of mental illness and insomnia, "trying to 'personify' what psychiatrists would call, 'chemical reactions of the brain.'"[21] And a production by TR Warszawa in 2008, Delgado-García notes, "crucially omit[ted] references to intersexuality or transgender" subjectivity, including the use of the word "hermaphrodite" early in the text.[22] Although local gender politics may have prompted these omissions, this very censorship indicates the ongoingness of anti-trans/queer violence.

In contrast to these reduced or diagnostic productions of *4.48 Psychosis,* Venables's operatic composition, in Venables's own words, "come[s] at the audience from everywhere."[23] It is a maximalist chamber score, with six singers, two orchestral percussionists, projections of words, and amplified song and dialogue recordings sharing and repeating Kane's text. The singers can harmonize or unite, loudly, on a single pitch, or they can interrupt, overpower, or silence each other. They can make Kane's language two or more things—perhaps a projected textual line and a bass drumroll and a pleading facial expression—emitting from two or more places onstage, at the same time. Distributing the text of the play across many different theatrical channels allows for the fragmentation of identity that Kane's text describes and allows Venables's opera to explore the possibilities of the escape from identity that sleep seems to offer. I refer to Venables's version of *4.48 Psychosis* as an operatic restaging, rather than an adaptation, but I take up the critical proposal that adaptation and queerness can resonate with one another in performance, amplifying the performativity of gender, the potential value of negative affects, and especially the false idol of originality.[24] The friendship that Kane's protagonist hopes for is enacted by stagings like Venables's, which attends to the text with care, without reducing it to a lesson about mental wellness or a biographical footnote.

Venables is a white British opera and music theater composer whose work often combines sung lyrics with spoken dialogue. Their profane and darkly funny presentations of violence and queer desire share a sensibility with Kane's writing, as in their 2012 project *Unleashed,* exploring consensually violent sex between men.[25] Their other projects, including a commission to compose an opera based on the 1977 queer communal fantasy novel *The Faggots and Their Friends Between Revolutions,* illustrate a career-long interest in queer texts and politics across generations. London's Royal Opera commissioned *4.48 Psychosis* for a 2016 debut at the Lyric Hammersmith Theatre. Critics of the London premiere compared Venables's compositions for *4.48 Psychosis* to both those of Claudio Monteverdi, father of baroque opera, and those of twelve-tone composer Alban Berg, suggesting a kind of maximalism in Venables's musical influences along with critical enthusiasm for Venables as "one of the finest of the younger generation of composers working today."[26] In early 2019, the Prototype Festival of experimental opera and music theater brought *4.48 Psychosis* to New York City.

The queer maximalism in Venables's *4.48 Psychosis* opera takes a political project often associated with hypervisual designs and translates it to the expansive aural terrain of contemporary opera.

Queer maximalism has emerged in recent usage to describe the brightly colored, gender-expansive, never-quite-finished designs of costumer and dancer Machine Dazzle and performance artist Taylor Mac; queer maximalism names an aesthetic sensibility that is always reaching for more.[27] Queer maximalism emerges out of a critical reading of social power dynamics, producing non-realist designs that make the quiet, hidden causes and outcomes of power inequities big, loud, and over-the-top. It is socially engaged work without the aesthetics of social realism. Through theatrical spectacle, queer maximalism draws the eye to political forces we either struggle to pin down or would prefer not to notice. What I am calling queer maximalism looks very different in Venables's *4.48 Psychosis,* in which the performers wear mundane black and gray street clothes and perform on a sparse, mostly white set. Venables's *4.48 Psychosis* expands the aesthetic possibilities of queer maximalism to include a wider range of theatrical and operatic strategies—from casting practices to surtitles to classical percussion—while participating in a queer maximalist political project of making quiet, hidden power inequities big and loud. Rather than staying quiet about the anti-trans/queer violence that haunts the text of *4.48 Psychosis,* Venables's opera cares for Kane's text by making *4.48 Psychosis* a loud, expansively voiced, aurally maximalist performance.

The *4.48 Psychosis* opera further rooted the protagonist's disabling experience of sleep loss in a social context through race-conscious casting practices that establish racial prejudice as a determiner of who can access medical care and healthy sleep. Unlike Kane's original text, the opera version has named characters, including a protagonist called Gwen. Venables and director Ted Huffman established a social world for the opera in which racial difference matters by composing for six singers (three sopranos and three mezzo-sopranos) and casting Black British soprano Gweneth-Ann Rand as Gwen. The shared name between singer and role suggests that some aspects of the *4.48 Psychosis* opera were devised in collaboration with the original cast. While all six singers wore the same costume, Gwen was older and had more vocal solos—she often stood out from the ensemble. Throughout the opera, four young white women surrounded Gwen, physically restraining or harming her en masse. These stage pictures superimposed the image of one person fragmented into five or six, all costumed identically, on that of a Black woman overpowered by a mob of white antagonists. The opera used theatrical tools (here, casting) to shift the staging of *4.48 Psychosis* away from reproducing the particular life story of Kane, a white person who died at age twenty-eight, and to situate Gwen's insomnia in widespread sleep deficits shaped by racial inequities. Opera scholar Naomi André's method of engaged musicology raises the questions, "Who is in the story? Who speaks? and Who is in the audience?"[28] These questions help put the 2016 operatic restaging of *4.48 Psychosis* in conversation with the social and political context of sleep loss, including racial and gender difference.

Rooting sleep loss in a social world shaped by racial and other forms of biopolitical difference counters the habit of reading trans/queer suicide as individual psychic drama rather than, in Stanley's words, part of a world built on "anti-Black, ableist, and anti-trans/queer" violence.[29] Throughout the opera, doctor figures try to place responsibility for illness and wellness on Gwen as an individual—"It's not your fault. But you have to take responsibility for your own actions" (218)—and use psychiatric medicine as the primary method of treatment. In the opera, the older white woman Lucy often plays the role of physician or psychiatrist, with Gwen as her patient. At times, Gwen's problem is the violent racism of the world around her, as when she is surrounded and pushed to the floor by the opera's white ensemble. At other times, Gwen takes the guilt of the world's history of violence on her own shoulders. She sings, "I gassed the Jews, I killed the Kurds, I bombed the Arabs" (227). The effects of racism do more than make the environment around Gwen disabling; they pervade and further fragment her own psyche, overwhelming her ability to care for herself with a flood of problems she is not responsible for.

In response to this flood, Gwen finally agrees, "Let's shut down the higher functions of my brain and perhaps I'll be a bit more fucking capable of living" (221). Even in this moment, when Gwen accedes to individual medical intervention, Venables fragments her lines among the singer's body, projected text, and a percussion solo. The division of the lines among bodies (represented by the singers), words (projected on the upstage wall), and sounds (played by the two percussionists) resists an interpretation of this scene as a moment of waking clarity, when Gwen might fully understand and accept the identity of mentally ill or patient. Each encounter between Gwen, as the patient, and Lucy, as her doctor, aligned the two actors, sitting in chairs facing each other, with lines projected above each of their heads and percussionists standing, with lighting, above each corner of the upstage wall. Gwen, stage right, sat directly below the orchestra member playing Percussion/Patient, who struck a single timpani drum each time a new word appeared in the projection. The timpani performance took on the attitude of Gwen's lines. For example, Percussion/Patient played a drumroll for every *metaphor* when Gwen corrected her doctor's use of the term: "It's not a metaphor [drumroll], it's a simile, but even if it were, the defining feature of a metaphor [drumroll] is that it's real" (211). Gwen's literary knowledge trumped her doctor's implacable correctness in a little percussive flirtation. The orchestra member playing Percussion/Doctor, standing directly above Lucy, played various instruments to suggest the tone of an endlessly correct, uninterruptible, clinical voice: a hammer pinging against a metal pipe, a snare drum, and a saw slicing through lumber.[30] By dividing the lines among actors, instruments, and text, Venables maintains a sense of identity fragmentation even as Gwen and Lucy step into a patient-doctor relationship, as they agree to drug Gwen into slumber.

Venables and Huffman staged sleep using the full ensemble: All six actors dropped to the stage floor. Their sleep was involuntary. It was not Gwen's individual experience of medication but instead reverberated through the world of the opera. The actors lay motionless on their stomachs, their bodies crumpled in contorted positions, humped up under their dark-gray cardigans so that they, again, looked a bit like cockroaches. One by one, the women dragged themselves back into standing positions, propping hands on knees to pull themselves to their feet like very heavy marionettes. The instrumental accompaniment accelerated, and all the women but Gwen snapped into peppy, purposeful movement, pacing back and forth across the stage as they sang out the protagonist's medication regimen. The series of SSRIs, hypnotics, antipsychotics, and tricyclic antidepressants, followed by a torrent of side effects—"Sertraline, 50 mg. Insomnia worsened, severe anxiety, anorexia (weight loss 17 kgs), increase in suicidal thoughts, plans and intention" (223)—was both sung and projected. Gwen stumbled slowly among them.

At the two moments when "slept" appeared as a symptom in the text, Gwen fell immediately to the ground, instantly unconscious. The orchestra cut to silence as a percussionist plinked out a few bars of an eerie "Rock-a-Bye Baby" lullaby. *Slept,* a past-tense verb, is a grammatical oddity among the litany of noun and adjectival symptoms. *Slept* is an action rather than a condition. *Slept,* and the sound and sight of Gwen dropping hard against the stage floor, is a reminder of the human body under the fog of medical terminology.[31] The only similar verbs in this section of the text are "discontinued," referring to a change in medication (223); "discharged into the care of the community," upon a shortage of hospital beds (224); and "refused all further treatment" (225). Each past-tense verb marks a caesura in Gwen's care. The section ends with one last verbal failure of treatment: After self-medicating with a bottle of aspirin and a bottle of wine, "patient woke in a pool of vomit and said, 'Sleep with a dog and rise full of fleas'" (225). Gwen's body remains resistant, waking up even after the doctors fail to cure it and Gwen fails to kill it.

The *4.48 Psychosis* opera, then, sustains a tension throughout its stagings of sleep, insomnia, and the medical interventions that mediate between the two. Sleep remains a state of loosened identities, producing bodies that crawl like cockroaches and feelings of responsibility for all the world's violence. Yet identity also remains inescapable. While an ensemble cast and multivocal performances from singers, recorded sound, and projected text fragment the lines of a single "protagonist" across many channels of communication, Gwen was still the only Black woman onstage and still found herself restrained, attacked, drugged, and abandoned by the white ensemble surrounding her. She slept in materially vulnerable places: kicked out of the hospital, in a pool of her own vomit, uncared for. The nearly irresistible habit of reading *4.48 Psychosis* as Kane's autobiographical writing—and then staging it in ways that reinforce the clarity or singularity of that interpretation—has meant that the text's insights into the extremities of sleep loss as a failure of social care remain tethered to a specific experience of mental illness. Staging *4.48 Psychosis* this way reproduces Kane's early morning insomnia as an individual, limit-case story. The

4.48 Psychosis opera, instead, produces a version of Kane's text that uses theatrical tools to situate sleep loss in a social world shaped by everyday forces of structural racism, making chronic mental illness and the insomnia that accompanies it mutually reinforcing symptoms of social inequities.

Within this bleak context, can the *4.48 Psychosis* opera imagine any sort of "new world" in which these inequities might shift? Theater critics tend to put a lot of pressure on the final line of Kane's play, "please open the curtains" (245), as Kane's turn toward the outside world and the theater itself for hope. In Macdonald's premiere in 2000, the actors opened a window of the theater, interpolating the Royal Court building itself—where Kane's *Blasted* and *Cleansed* also debuted—into the last line of the text. The *4.48 Psychosis* opera rejects this final overture, leaving Gwen entirely alone and voiceless. The opera set, designed by Hannah Clark, had no curtains, so Gwen's closing plea seemed set up to fail. Gwen did not even sing the final line; instead, a recording played over the intercom.

Reviews indicate that Venables and Huffman staged at least two different versions of this final scene that, through only a few brief gestures, took distinct positions on suicide within the social world of the opera. In the original London staging, "pills [were] swallowed and a noose [was] strung up."[32] In the New York staging three years later, Gwen stood on a table, abandoned by the other performers and the orchestra. The stage floor remained littered with discarded bits of costuming, the other singers' shoes and cardigans, fragments of these fragments of Gwen's divided self. Here was the possibility of a friendship formed between a play text and its adapter, a generation in the future. While Gwen ended the play alone—simultaneously a Black woman abandoned by all sources of care and just another fragment among a detritus of props and costumes—she ended it alive, her story taking (perhaps) a different direction than Kane's. The opera became an anti-autobiographical interpretation. It used casting, sound design, and orchestration to maximally theatricalize the social conditions of sleep loss, in place of an individual tragedy of suffering and death. In doing so, the opera staged in New York reckoned with the theme of suicide that pervades Kane's text without reproducing death as an inevitable tragic end.

I Have No Desire for Death

Twenty-first-century opera is a friendly form for Kane's *4.48 Psychosis,* a bundle of staging conventions and opportunities through which Venables and their collaborators composed a new version of a queer maximalist aesthetic pitched against the racist, anti-trans/queer violence that is the context of the protagonist's insomniac suffering. But the *4.48 Psychosis* opera also, perhaps counterintuitively, reproduces and foregrounds the conventions of nineteenth-century opera that feminist and queer scholars have most scrutinized in the relations of death and sex the opera engenders between the performance and its spectators. Like Dinshaw's super-sleeper Rip van Winkle, awakening with his long beard and now-unfashionable clothing, these operatic conventions initially look different from those of the past, but their persistence through a period of dormancy offers further opportunities for trans/queer recognition in Kane's play. On a closer look, Venables's *4.48 Psychosis* is more conventionally operatic than it first appears.

Years before Kane or Venables staged their first performances, French feminist Catherine Clément penned a meditation on the role of women in opera that begins "Lasciatemi morir": *Let me die.* Women, Clément argues, exist in the opera to be decorative and then to expire dramatically. Onstage, female characters in opera love too much, and they are punished for it; often, they impose this punishment on themselves, flinging their bodies into fires or off of rooftops. Women in the opera audience, likewise decorative in their evening gowns, are "present for the dispatch of women like themselves" onstage.[33] Following Clément, feminist and queer opera scholarship from the late 1980s through the 1990s can be summarized in two imperative phrases sung by sopranos, centuries apart: (1) "Let me die," quoted by Clément from the libretto of a lost Monteverdi opera, and (2) "Fuck you," bellowed by the cast of *4.48 Psychosis.* Directed outward toward the audience, as opera singers' voices always must be, each lyric is, paradoxically, powerless. The singers onstage cannot make us, in the audience, kill them or be fucked (apologies) by them. But the sound of their voices, critics argue, is a queer kind of sexual contact: a "controlled shaft of air moving from a dark place out into the world" as vocalization begins, a "*secret* desire" fulfilled when a soprano and a mezzo sing simultaneously, and a physical encounter between performers and audience finally "consummated" when the audience applauds.[34] In these accounts of opera loving, the sexual contact between operatic voices and their auditors can be nongenital and arduous, shockingly lesbian, or a climactic affirmation of the future of gay sex.

Particular sexual power is accorded to harmony between two or more voices with higher ranges, whether a castrato and a soprano singing together as romantic leads (as happens often in Monteverdi) or, centuries later, a soprano and a mezzo or contralto in a trousers role duetting in Rossini or Strauss. Such a duet in Rossini's *Semiramide* reportedly sent at least one undergraduate lesbian into raptures in the 1970s; the vast possibilities of gendered and sexual antinormativity presented by castrati and women en travesti have similarly excited many a queer and feminist critic. Given the long operatic history of varying alignment between gender presentation, gender identity, and voice type, soprano and mezzo-soprano vocal ranges do not require that the singers identify as women.[35] So when the sopranos and mezzos in Venables's *4.48 Psychosis* sing out "Fuck you" to the audience, they are participating in a tradition of death and queer sex at the opera as old as the sound of a castrato voice or the score of Monteverdi's *L'Arianna*—both lost to the ages. Multiple high-range voices harmonize on an ambiguous queer imperative: Let's have sex, but also fuck you for coming to watch another soprano die onstage.

The character who nearly died—who tentatively lived on, alone—at the end of the New York production of *4.48 Psychosis* was played by the Black British soprano Rand, adding Rand to the legion of Black soprano divas who have performed suffering and death on the opera stage in front of majority-white Euro-American audiences and surrounded by majority-white co-performers. Rand, an opera lover since early childhood, identifies Black sopranos Leontyne Price and Jessye Norman as significant influences on her work. Wayne Koestenbaum notes that the famed voices of Black sopranos like Price and Norman are evidence that opera performance is simultaneously "enfranchising" and "an art of social control," as it is in his reading of opera and homosexuality.[36] The first Black singers to star on otherwise-white European opera stages portrayed Lakmé (Lillian Evanti) and Aida (Florence

Cole Talbert), two titular soprano roles that end in death by suicide.[37] In such stagings, it is not clear what separates the sexual power of the diva's voice that critics claim as queer from the colonial power over life and death that results in the diva character's demise. A long history of masculinist violence, by the state and in the home, indicates that sexual desire and desire to kill can coexist.

Opera has historically offered a venue for some of the most virtuosically voiced Black women of the twentieth century, as they reenacted spectacular deaths that dramatized the success of the European colonial project in dominating native peoples via a woman's willing sacrifice of her life for love. The opera *4.48 Psychosis* narrowly veers away from the trope of Black soprano death only at its end. In this opera, the latent surveillance of and violence toward women that Clément identified in the 1980s becomes the suffering and survival of a Black mentally ill character with a treble-clef voice. "I have no desire for death," Kane's play reads on its penultimate page, "no suicide ever had" (244). In the tradition of queer operatic sex but explicitly against the plea for death, the version of *4.48 Psychosis* in which Gwen does not die becomes an opera that stages the social context of suicide without reproducing yet another performance of Black soprano death. In contrast to minimalist dramatic stagings of Kane's work, the New York production of the *4.48 Psychosis* opera revealed the failed social relations that make Gwen's insomnia disabling while resisting the sexist and racist legacies of the operatic form.

What to make, then, of the man who slept through *4.48 Psychosis,* sitting next to me in the audience of that small theater amid a torrent of treble voices? He hardly seemed to be surveilling a performance of a woman's suffering and near death, nor did he seem to be consummating a queer relationship with the performers. A fellow spectator's sleep is, finally, uninterpretable. While queer opera scholarship does not raise the possibility of sleep, rather than sexual feeling, as a bodily response to opera, sleep is an understandable response from a spectator who finds himself in conventional opera-viewing conditions: sitting in a darkened room, listening to lyrics in a language he does not understand, feeling alone even as he is surrounded by fellow spectators, for hours at a stretch. The very spectatorial conditions that make opera feel like a private sexual encounter with pure voice can make it a perfect lullaby.

Perhaps I should leave this sleeping spectator alone and, like many a queer opera critic, interpret myself instead. Hearing six high-register operatic voices singing Kane's text did have a bodily effect on me. That sound transformed the undergraduate raptures *I* had felt long ago, when I first encountered Kane as what seemed like a singular dramatist—like nothing I had ever read before—into a strong feeling that Kane's work belongs in, and resonates with, the history of trans/queer and feminist performance. Kane's formal experimentation with staging our utter dependence on the care of others, and the ways that our structures of living fail to meet that need, belongs firmly in feminist performance history. I suspect I feel both emotionally and critically aggravated by this sleeping spectator because I know how rare and risky it is to produce a new opera like this one. Given its formal sophistication and its foregrounding of Black, trans/queer, and mentally ill experience, Venables's *4.48 Psychosis* may never be revived in New York, and that spectator may have slept through his one chance to see it.[38] Kane's own death falls halfway between the temporal nodes of Clément's critique of "lasciatemi morir" and Venables's composition for the lyric "Fuck you." After the work's twenty years of dormancy, I hope I have placed *4.48 Psychosis,* a sleepless text calling out for care, among friends.

Part Four
Out in the World

Seven
Rest in Power
Public Napping for the Future

To understand the high stakes of sleep in the world beyond the theater or art museum, let's turn to a mattress commercial. Although this book has focused on sleep performances that take up the feminist project of changing the world, the tools of performance can also make a persuasive case for sleep as a personal investment in reproducing the self as a productive worker in the world as it is. In this particular commercial, advertising the direct-to-consumer mattress brand Nectar, sitcom star and neuroscience PhD Mayim Bialik explains how sleep serves brain function. Costumed in a white lab coat, the live actor Bialik stands between a cartoon brain and a cartoon heart and addresses her audience directly. "When you sleep on a crummy mattress, your brain gets tired," Bialik cautions, and your heart, "an overemotional pump," drives your decision-making. Bialik bemoans what happens when she is too tired and her emotional heart takes over: She becomes too fatigued to do her job well, as evidenced by an ill-fated romance with a coworker and a weepy demand for her smartphone to love her. Bialik warns her audience to heed her example: "Do your brain a favor, and get yourself a Nectar." The cartoon heart makes a last plea for love and is roundly rejected: "Shut up, heart."[1]

Nectar's commercial exemplifies how sleep brands (including Buffy comforters, Casper mattresses, Brooklinen sheets, and many others) sell the value of sleep. In the commercial, Bialik physically separates a couple who are sharing a mattress, rejecting shared experience in order to assert that high-quality sleep is the key to individual productivity and success. After a good night's sleep, Bialik's cartoon brain is so supercharged it can thrive on its own, with no need for emotion, relationships, or even the body. While the contest pitting brain against body (or rational thought against reckless emotion) is a familiar locus of critique from feminist disability scholarship, the commercial works to further this divide by reclaiming *sleep* as the brain's dominion. By suggesting that the primary consequence of good sleep is rational workplace behavior, the commercial presents sleep as an investment in individual productivity, driven by a brain that is unhampered by its body and the social relations in which that body participates. Sleep brands like Nectar cannily exploit existing sleep inequities, encouraging consumers with more capital to invest in sleep products to see the future rewards of good sleep as integral to their workplace successes. More troublingly, sleep brands benefit from contemporary medical discourse on sleep by suggesting that neuroscientific sleep research (as represented by Bialik's own neuroscience training) is best aimed at the goal of individual productivity. Individuals without the resources to give their brains a good night's sleep—those sleeping on "crummy mattresses" or worse—will be stuck with the questionable fruits of their "overemotional" hearts.

This commercial awakens its audience's curiosity about how sleep affects, and is affected by, our work and our relationships. This curiosity also drives the two participatory performance artworks analyzed in this chapter, Sakiko Yamaoka's iterative performance *Best Place to Sleep/Come with Me* (2007–12) and Navild Acosta and Fannie Sosa's installation *Black Power Naps/Siestas Negras* (2018–23).[2] Each performance carefully crafts an experience of public napping for its participants. In contrast to the Nectar commercial, with its brain-focused arguments, these two artworks stage good sleep as a full-bodied experience of collective care and, in doing so, use public sleep performance to mitigate uneven access to good sleep and reclaim the space and time of sleep for those who most need it. *Best Place to Sleep* and *Black Power Naps* transform napping into a political act that reclaims time and space for unhoused people and women and nonbinary people of color, populations that sociomedical research has shown are systematically harmed by the sleep gap—that is, differential access to healthy, sustaining sleep based on race, class, and gender.[3] These performances contest the twenty-first-century wellness industry's capitalization on sleep as an individual investment, instead staging reciprocal care as fundamental to a well-rested future that can sustain feminist social justice work over the long term. Yet these performance artworks cannot be cleanly opposed to the marketing performances used by companies like Nectar to sell their sleep products. Both performance artworks and marketing performances argue for the value of sleep, and both implore their audiences to affirm the value of sleep in their own lives. *Black Power Naps* also received financial sponsorship from the sleep brand Buffy (a bedding manufacturer) for its 2019 installation at Performance Space New York. *Black Power Naps* used Buffy's sponsorship to commandeer the relationship between artists and funders, although this relationship shifted again when a later iteration of *Black Power Naps* encountered the racial-spectatorial politics of a major art institution.

Nap performances like these stage the reclamation of work time and public space for much-desired rest. In responding to the sleep gap, they participate in feminist conversations about time and social difference, acting on feminist sociologist Judy Wajcman's call for "temporal sovereignty," a freedom to decide how to spend one's own time—including when to sleep.[4] The artists muster the resources for good sleep at atypical times, inviting participants to nap in a space and time that the artists strive to protect from anti-sleep interventions, including surveillance, violence, and demands for labor or consumption. In *Best Place to Sleep,* Yamaoka napped in bank lobbies and pedestrian shopping districts; she invited participants to join her in napping in these "best places" for sleep in the companion piece *Come with Me.* In their installation *Black Power Naps,* Acosta and Sosa created a "best place" for sleep for Black Americans, who are particularly likely to experience sleep loss. Acosta and Sosa filled performance spaces in Spain and the United States with six imaginative beds and invited participants to nap in a space that had been meticulously staged for their rest. The verb *stage,* in José Esteban Muñoz's terms, refers not to a performance that happens on a stage behind a proscenium but to a performance that "suggest[s] another modality of doing and being that is in process, unfinished."[5] Napping itself might be understood as a "stage" of infancy and childhood that adults are meant to outgrow. The final section of this book examines iterative sleep performances as works in progress and explores the potential future of sleep as a feminist dramaturgical strategy and an emergent performance genre. One of the risks of sleep performance is its quiet and quotidian nature. The political interventions that these performances aim to provide for their small cohorts of participants may not reach many other viewers. The installation of *Black Power Naps* in New York's Museum of Modern Art in early 2023—which ultimately led to concerns about whether the museum was able to support an installation intended primarily for Black viewers—further complicates this conversation about how large an intervention sleep performance can make and what happens when a sleep performance moves to a mainstream arts venue.

These public napping performances might be best understood as tactics of everyday living for subjects not satisfied with their interpellation as consumers in the current matrix of wellness capitalism. In philosopher Michel de Certeau's formulation, tactics are disobedient, wandering "way[s] of operating" exercised without claims to power. Unable to lay true claim to owning a space, practitioners of tactics depend on "a clever *utilization of time,* of the opportunities it presents and also of the play that it introduces into the foundations of power."[6] Against pressures to optimize our time as workers and consumers, and even to optimize the efficacy of our political performances, the tactic of napping performance cleverly diverts public and institutional spaces into a temporary existence as communal bedrooms, without waiting for or even expecting some kind of permanent authorization of this behavior. A public nap imagines a world in which anyone feeling worn-out—from childcare, from illness, from the gig economy—could lie down and rest when they want to, unrestricted by the expectation that sleep be private and nocturnal.

By staging public naps as opportunities for collective care, *Best Place to Sleep* and *Black Power Naps* contribute to and extend a feminist philosophical tradition that identifies both material and moral value in caregiving. Caregiving is the practice of attending to the needs, safety, and comfort of (temporarily) dependent beings. Sleep is a nightly experience of dependence on individuals and social systems for safe, comfortable, and healthy sleeping conditions, even for those who otherwise see themselves as autonomous adults. Yamaoka cares for her participants by finding the "best places" for them to sleep as a form of protest without risking harm, while Acosta and Sosa create a luxurious sleep infrastructure for participants structurally at risk of regular sleep loss. Both sleep performances enact what feminist philosophers Eva Feder Kittay and Virginia Held, among others, have termed an "ethics of care": They make visible central moral values of caregiving, including "connection, attentiveness and responsiveness" and "responsibility and empathetic concern" for their collaborators.[7] *Best Place to Sleep* and *Black Power Naps* demonstrate the power of sleep—either to protest (Yamaoka) or to repair and restore (Acosta and Sosa)—when the sleeper can fully depend on the care of another.

Acosta and Sosa's writing about *Black Power Naps* theorizes the artists' caregiving practices as labor that requires compensation and frames the artists' own need to receive care as part of their reparative project.[8] Feminist organizers have long argued that dependent care is rarely recognized or compensated as the labor that it is because it is disproportionately performed by women within their own families, and by women of color as underpaid employment in the United States.[9] Among the services they provide, caregivers might ensure that their employers sleep on clean sheets, undisturbed by the nocturnal demands of child- or eldercare. As this uneven distribution of sleep shows, the timescales of sleep can act as a respite from work for some while reorganizing or increasing the work of others. Indeed, this type of caring labor demands that the caregivers adjust their own use of time, including their preferred sleep-wake cycles, to the timescales of their employers.[10] The call to recognize this caring labor as valuable, put forth in the 1960s and 1970s by campaigns like the National Welfare Rights Organization and Wages for Housework, has expanded to include a wider array of dependent care and to encompass a "global care chain" comprising caregivers who leave their own local care responsibilities in poorer nations to work as hired caregivers in wealthier ones.[11]

As feminist moral philosophers and sociologists alike have argued, any attempt to bring justice to this global care chain must include not only local changes in the gendered division of labor and a global redistribution of wealth but also a reckoning with each caregiver's own need to receive care. By demanding care and rest for the caregivers, *Black Power Naps* reconfigures the care chain into what performer and disability activist Leah Lakshmi Piepzna-Samarasinha has termed a "care web," a sustainable, interdependent network of mutual caregiving and care receiving. By sharing both the work of care and the relief of rest, Piepzna-Samarasinha proposes, participants in such care webs could resist caregiver exhaustion and burnout and transform care into "a collective responsibility that's maybe even deeply joyful . . . [a] revolutionary love without charity."[12] Acosta and Sosa extend the future possibilities of this joyful caregiving through a militant demand that art institutions and the wider, primarily white, audiences they attract change at a fundamental level. *Black Power Naps* expropriates the successful brand performance of the sleep industry to fund sleep for Black participants and reclaims space and time to repair the sleep gap. Public napping acknowledges how tired many of us really feel.

Best Place to Sleep

Best Place to Sleep reclaims space and time for sleep in little snippets—a few square feet of sidewalk here, a few minutes of rest there. In each iteration of the performance, Yamaoka and the amateur performers participating alongside her spend one to five minutes lying down together in a public space, as if they have abruptly succumbed to an urgent shared need for rest. It is surprising to watch a handful of people suddenly collapse gracefully into prone stillness in the middle of bustling lobby or walkway. Yamaoka develops their particular napping positions through collaboration with the other performers; she has called these selected positions "elegant gestures," a term that suggests an aesthetics of care in her work. The group nap iterations of *Best Place to Sleep* required Yamaoka to care for other people napping alongside her in vulnerable, public situations and at the same time attracted greater attention to the alternative world of public daytime sleep she was staging. The power of the performance lies not just in the momentary capacity of collective public napping to astonish viewers but also in the performance's long-term repetition, across at least six years and at least three continents. Any person who has participated in *Best Place to Sleep*—or even watched a video of it—could repeat the performance on their own, in their nearest bank or shopping mall. The potential for future performances inherent in *Best Place to Sleep* is evidence of the practice of collective care at work in the piece. In locating the best sites for public sleep, in developing gestures or positions that communicate sleep clearly, and in designing a performance that claims space and time for rest, Yamaoka and her fellow participants care for each other and for future weary folks, who we might imagine using Yamaoka's "best places" and "elegant gestures" to take their own naps.

Yamaoka, who trained as an oil painter in Tokyo and has worked as a performance artist since the 1990s, frequently includes amateur participants in interventions that reclaim public space through whimsy and creativity, building new social connections in urban sites. In Toronto in 2008, Yamaoka and three collaborators performed *Best Place to Sleep* in the lobby of a CIBC bank branch.[13] Video of the performance, captured by handheld camera, opens on a cluster of four people napping on the floor of the bank, directly in front of three ATMs. They wear nondescript coats and jeans and curl on their sides in the fetal position, handbags clutched to their stomachs or tucked under their heads as pillows. Off-screen, we hear the camera operator say, "You can still use the machines." A man in a blue jacket crosses in front of the camera and circles around the cluster of nappers to use an ATM. It is immediately clear that the nap cluster has interrupted the flow of people through the bank. Various patrons must circle around the nappers to enter and leave the bank lobby, and one apologizes for crossing in front of the camera en route to the bank doors. Two and a half minutes after the video begins, Yamaoka sits up from the floor, and the other three sleepers follow. Unhurriedly, they gather their bags and head toward the bank doors as the camera pans to follow them. One man smiles shyly at the camera. At the threshold of the bank, a patron asks, "So what was this about?" The camera operator responds, "Making—for art."

While Yamaoka and her co-nappers left the CIBC branch of their own accord in 2008, in other videos of *Best Place to Sleep*, a uniformed security officer eventually steps in front of the camera, rousing Yamaoka from her spot on the floor. ATM vestibules are the "best place to sleep" of Yamaoka's title, perhaps, because a global demand for constant access to cash has produced these odd, small spaces that anyone with a debit card can enter at any time. While we might expect banks to be heavily guarded, the smaller ATM rooms attached to many banks allow continuous access. *Best Place to Sleep* exploits the bank lobby's potential as a quasi-public shelter—a space that might be good for sleep. Security guards appear only when they perceive napping as a misuse of the bank. The *Best Place to Sleep* performance at the CIBC branch in fact contests the assertion, implied by interruptions from bank security in other videos, that a nap performance is a misuse of an ATM lobby. Normal bank functions continue around Yamaoka's nap-taking, but bank patrons do pause in their path to the ATMs, so that even though they are not napping, their experience of the bank slows. When the nappers interrupt patrons' path to fast cash, the pace of capitalism slackens. Therefore the bank lobby is also the *best place* for Yamaoka to sleep because napping in a bank lobby directly reclaims the space and time of capital for sleep. This sleep prompts more considerate—possibly more caring—modes of interaction between the nappers and the bank patrons.

Perhaps the CIBC performance was tolerated by bank patrons and staff because the presence of a camera suggested that the group nap had a purpose beyond mere rest. The camera operator served as a signal that the bank patrons and staff were not just observers of Yamaoka but audience to her performance. The audience at the CIBC branch was far more deferential than people often are to public sleepers who are suspected of being unhoused or otherwise inappropriately positioned. Audience members apologized, asked permission to use the ATMs near the nappers, and waited until after the nappers had arisen to ask questions. Seeing themselves, even subconsciously, as spectators made them treat the public sleepers with care. The surveillant element of the camera may have contributed to this deference, but banks are always bristling with surveillance, so seeing the camera and the nappers as parts of a performance may have caused the audience to act in ways that actually countered that surveillance. Rather than calling for a guard and asserting their right to use the bank as designed, the audience members adjusted their own behavior to care for the sleepers. By staging public sleep within the publicly accessible but not public space of the bank, Yamaoka reclaimed that space for sleep, and her nap with her collaborators took priority over her audience's planned use of the bank.

Yamaoka speaks to her ongoing interest in finding the "best" conditions for social life in her artist statement for the 2011 Vancouver Biennale. Within the "ambivalence, ambiguity and unpredictability" of performance interactions with audience and environment, Yamaoka "would like to find our varied possibilities," asking, "What was the best?"[14] Yamaoka's assertion that ATM vestibules are often the *best* place to sleep reflects the work of an artist whose performances stage small transformative interventions in everyday public spaces, bringing social interaction to sites where people often pass by one another in well-disciplined silence. In her 2013 artwork for the Bienal de Curitiba in Brazil, *High Five Gardening,* Yamaoka painted multicolored flora onto the arms and hands of volunteers, who then offered high fives to passersby. When Yamaoka and her collaborators sleep in bank lobbies, they also evoke the many other lost opportunities for public sleep throughout the city.

Best Place to Sleep may have garnered this positive reaction from its audience in part because of its similarities to the familiar public performance genre of the flash mob, first identified in 2003. *Best Place to Sleep* shares qualities with flash mobs, including in its reliance on amateur participants as performers, its multiple audiences (both in person and, later, online), and its strategic use of a bank as a politically charged, publicly accessible space. Yet *Best Place to Sleep* differs from the conventions of the flash mob in a key way: It seems never to have "gone viral," despite using both a technique (a sudden group performance surprising an unsuspecting audience) and a platform (YouTube) common to flash mobs.[15] While flash mobs designed to become viral online videos anticipate their own perpetuity in thousands or millions of online views, Yamaoka has a different goal for the future of *Best Place to Sleep,* in the form of more idiosyncratic, less trackable repetitions of the performance. By organizing public napping as a collaborative, documented performance event, Yamaoka isolates the public nap as what Diana Taylor calls a "scenario," an embodied clip of action, behavior, or practice that we can recognize and make meaning out of because of its many repetitions and reworkings.[16] *Best Place to Sleep* can evoke other scenarios of public napping: perhaps an unhoused person sleeping in another ATM vestibule, or an airline passenger dozing at her gate as she waits for a delayed flight. Public naps respond to all sorts of inequities in late capitalism's distribution of space and time. As naps exceed the space and time set aside for sleep (outside of working hours and within private property), nap performances spill over their institutional bounds. A new iteration of *Best Place to Sleep* may happen without achieving viral status or even video documentation. Participatory nap performances spill out of the containers of official art spaces and official documentation as their collaborators continue to experiment with napping.

Among the many iterations of Yamaoka's participatory public napping performances, she develops a technique she calls the "elegant gesture," which reads as an act of caregiving for her amateur collaborators. Yamaoka wants to craft performances that make her collaborators feel and look good: This care for her collaborators' comfort and confidence may allow her to stage larger group naps in riskier places. Yamaoka articulates the work of the elegant gesture in her writing about the 2007 performance of her group piece *We Are Elegant* in Bantul, Indonesia. Bantul had recently suffered a serious earthquake. In *We Are Elegant,* Yamaoka and approximately twenty participants from Bantul worked together to choose a set of gestures to perform in a local graveyard. Yamaoka asked the residents of Bantul about what *elegance* meant to them, and to "demonstrate some gestures, without using words, which they thought of as 'elegant.'"[17] From these gestures, Yamaoka developed a collaborative performance for a village responding to a recent tragedy.

One image of *We Are Elegant* shows all the participants lying among the graves on their right sides, bending their right elbows to the ground to rest their heads against their hands—a gesture similar to the napping postures Yamaoka and her collaborators employ in *Best Place to Sleep.* Yamaoka identifies this gesture in a work of political performance art as *elegant*:

> A typical gesture . . . is the raising of one's fist to the sky, meaning "Let's fight together!" "Let's assert ourselves!" Gestures were often very aggressive. And so, I would like

> to propose that the typical gesture of the 21st century becomes "elegant." There were too many fights in the 20th century, weren't there? I want to show a new form representing a fearless attitude, without giving up or becoming weak.[18]

Yamaoka's elegant gestures are pacifist but neither apathetic nor merely aesthetic. In *We Are Elegant,* the performers fearlessly confront the devastation of the recent earthquake, represented by the graveyard, from a reclined posture. Yamaoka's elegant gestures are perhaps appropriate for the twenty-first century because the twenty-first-century crises her work engages rarely have a clear enemy to battle. Who could the residents of Bantul fight to avenge the earthquake's fatalities? The combination of infrastructural problems, climate change, and natural disasters, while influenced by human action, do not cohere into a singular enemy to shake one's fist at. When Yamaoka reuses this reclined gesture in *Best Place to Sleep,* she stages a similarly fearless confrontation with the nebulous causes of twenty-first-century exhaustion, homelessness, and privatization of public space.

Yamaoka's search for a "new way of revolt" is a search for a more inclusive art practice, one that invites people who cannot or will not "fight" in the manner she associates with the twentieth century. By developing elegant gestures and performing them in public sites with her amateur collaborators, Yamaoka first opens up performance art to a greater variety of participants, and then, together, they open up public space to more expansive uses and more varied paces. A busy bank lobby and an active street corner become sites to slow down and rest. While intervening in the spaces and timescales of public life may not initially look like caregiving, Piepzna-Samarasinha asserts that collective care must redefine our uses of time and space in order to be a sustainable practice of social justice. Collective care can change pace—"people feel fine if they . . . start late because the bus broke down [or] move slower"—and, crucially, the work of caring can happen from "our sickbeds, our kid beds, our too-crazy-to-go-out-today beds."[19] Yamaoka's alternative title for *Best Place to Sleep, Come with Me,* echoes Piepzna-Samarasinha's rule of thumb for collective care, "Don't leave each other behind." The short group performances of lying down make performance art accessible to many different participants. The seeds of collective care in Yamaoka's elegant gestures facilitate many different people reclaiming pockets of time and space for rest.

Although the practice of collective care in *Best Place to Sleep* is rooted in the development of elegant gestures by Yamaoka and her collaborators, this care extends to the performance's impromptu audiences, the other people using the public space Yamaoka occupies. Later iterations of *Best Place to Sleep* reclaimed high-end commercial areas of major world cities as sites for napping. In a performance in Tokyo in 2009, Yamaoka and participants lay down on the sidewalk for brief group naps in front of a series of luxury stores, including Cartier, Chanel, Louis Vuitton, and Bulgari.[20] While Yamaoka uses *elegance* to mean nonaggressive, fearless, strong, and revolutionary, the collaborative gesture of lying down to nap in *Best Place to Sleep* also has a mathematical elegance as a revolt against the economic precarity produced by the same political economy in which Cartier thrives. Like a Brechtian gest, the group nap "allows conclusions to be drawn about social circumstances." But Brecht is of the twentieth century, a fighter who calls for his gestic theater to wake up his spectators to the world around them: Brecht's "satisfactory basic model of major theater" is a street scene of a traffic accident.[21] Yamaoka, in contrast, leads a group of collaborators into an intersection in Tokyo's Ginza district where traffic has been blocked to allow for pedestrian shopping, and they all lie down together in the middle of the intersection, performing a "street scene" that is entirely safe from traffic accidents. Against a background of LED billboards, flashing lights, and electronic advertising jingles, this iteration of *Best Place to Sleep* is elegant, a quiet pool of purposeful stillness in front of a mass of visual and aural distractions. These distractions are meant to attract pedestrians' attention, so the collective care at the heart of Yamaoka's accessible, collaborative performance becomes a form of care for the audience as well. *Best Place to Sleep* cares for its spectators by offering an opportunity to turn away from the exhausting attention economy of digital advertising and toward the nap as an alternative use of their own time in public space.

Finally, the participants and even spectators in *Best Place to Sleep* stage a form of collective care for public space itself, challenging the incursion of luxury consumption—particularly its advertising and surveillance mechanisms—into spaces for walking, socializing, and resting. Yamaoka and participants began their 2009 performance in Tokyo across the street from a Cartier store. In the video documenting the performance, they stand in a cluster near the crosswalk, blending in with the many other window-shoppers. Yamaoka arcs her way out of the cluster, standing out less for her beige parka than for the new decisiveness in her movements. She crosses the street, heading directly for the corner of the store. The camera cuts back to her collaborators, looking on, and when the shot returns to Yamaoka, she is lying down, almost camouflaged by the pale sidewalk and tan exterior walls of the Cartier building. Within a few seconds, people mass on the corner around Yamaoka: some to lie down next to her, and some to take photos or videos with their phones. Until the instant they lie down, any of Yamaoka's collaborators could be just onlookers. By performing with a larger group, Yamaoka not only attracts a bigger audience but also blurs the distinctions between participant and spectator.

Yamaoka and her collaborators form a cluster of bodies around the corner of the Cartier store: Lying on their backs or sides with their legs bent, they make bodily gestures similar to those deemed "elegant" in Bantul. Pillowing their heads on their bags becomes part of the performers' elegant gesture, contrasting the use value of the handbag for sleep with the exchange values of the designer bags on sale inside. Eventually, a black-suited guard emerges from Cartier, talks into a headset, and reenters the store. But the performers neither block the whole sidewalk nor barricade the entrance to the store—they form a puddle of people, an organic barnacle latching onto the geometric edge of Cartier's imposing storefront. Within a minute of first lying down, Yamaoka pops back up, and her collaborators walk away from the store, blending back into the crowd streaming down the street.

One minute is a short nap. *Best Place to Sleep* is an elegant gesture toward a future when people who need a nap can reclaim larger swaths of time in public space. It is, in Muñoz's words, "just a stage," a Certeauvian tactic on the way to reclaiming public space for rest and leisure that does not have to include consumption. Like napping, *Best Place to Sleep* is sustaining and can be reiterated over and over again. *Best Place to Sleep* makes incisive changes in the use of public space and time in ways that Yamaoka's collaborators could continue to do even without her presence, activated by the tactical care Yamaoka shows in testing out the best places to sleep and extending an invitation to "come with her" and try it.

Black Power Naps

Black Power Naps shares Yamaoka's project of inviting participants to reclaim time and space through napping. Instead of finding a preexisting site, however, Acosta and Sosa design their own nap infrastructure, transforming an arts venue into a sovereign land created for Black people's sleep. Through their lush, large-scale, rainbow-colored installation, Acosta and Sosa practice collective care not only by designing luxurious beds but also by inviting their participants to see and feel themselves as deserving of rest and, ultimately, by asserting the artists' own needs for care and rest as well. *Black Power Naps* resists a tendency to see sleep as a universal human experience that brings us all closer together. Against phenomenologist Jean-Luc Nancy's claim that "sleep itself knows only equality . . . all sleepers fall into the same, identical, and uniform sleep," *Black Power Naps* asserts that the material experience of sleep has been shaped by the legacies of the transatlantic slave trade, settler colonialism, and U.S. imperialism, such that sleep is decidedly not experienced as equal.[22]

When I visited the iteration of *Black Power Naps* at Performance Space New York in 2019, the work of reclaiming space for safe sleep felt intensified by recent U.S. immigration policies separating immigrant children from their parents in overnight detention. In order to claim space for vulnerable peoples to nap, the creators of *Black Power Naps* established their exhibition at PSNY as a sovereign space distinct from the United States, with its own laws for sleep. The creation of an unexpectedly sovereign world within an art gallery through elements of scenic design worked as a "worlding irritant," Rachel Hann's apt description of scenography's ability to separate politically distinct spaces.[23] An altar marked the entrance to the installation, functioning as a signpost or border marker with guidelines for the exhibition's audience. "To the beings that come into the space," it hailed attendees in neon-green

Gothic font, "here we tell you the laws of our land." Some of these laws were common to galleries and theaters, including requests that attendees "Leave everything intact," "Put your mobiles on silent," and not eat or drink. Yet other laws spoke more directly to the mixed nature of the exhibition's expected audience: both the attendees who were invited to sleep in the exhibition's many beds and those who might disturb their naps. "Continue to mind that the space is to be enjoyed without extracting or hurting," one law cautioned; another announced, "If you see a Black person resting, don't call the police! Never." By establishing "laws of our land," *Black Power Naps* declared that sleep is an issue of contested sovereignty. In order to truly relax control of the body into the vulnerability of sleep, sleepers must know they are in a protected space, in which harms from the small ("don't disturb others' dreams or rest") to the state-size ("don't call the police!") are forbidden.

These laws attest to the artwork's project of reclaiming space for "Black Rest," which Acosta and Sosa define as "the unique intersection in which circumstances line up to invoke a rare vortex of pleasure, joy, and rejuvenation" for Black Americans.[24] *Black Power Naps* invited Black spectators to experience Black Rest by napping within the installation. While each visitor chose how to interact with the installation, white audience members were explicitly asked to respect Black Rest and implicitly discouraged from taking up the bed space created for attendees of color. In order to allow for Black Rest, Acosta and Sosa reclaimed and transformed the materials of Black, Indigenous, and migrant exploitation within the history of the United States into an opportunity to nap on beds crafted to help sleepers see and know the embodied feeling of themselves at rest.

The title *Black Power Naps* is a portmanteau of Black Power, the militant movement for Black self-determination, and *power nap,* a term that psychologist James B. Maas claims to have coined in his 1998 guide *Power Sleep: The Revolutionary Program That Prepares Your Mind for Peak Performance.*[25] While Maas uses *performance* to refer to workplace productivity, taking a power nap at the office also establishes napping as a performance of power in the workplace. The power napper's job is so important that it cannot be abandoned for more than a few minutes, but the napper and his acumen are so essential to the job that the napper's brain must be at peak function whenever he is working. Power naps are not for workers en masse but for individual workplace performers. Even for those not familiar with Maas's productivity-oriented approach to sleep (further elaborated in *Sleep for Success!* and *Sleep to Win!*) "power nap" connotes a few minutes of sleep caught in the middle of the workday by someone who has a couch in their office. It frames midday sleep as empowering for a mid-level white-collar executive, while for many Black Americans, Acosta and Sosa note, midday sleep can retain "racist stigmas passed on from the days of slavery, when falling asleep during the day was a heavily punished act." The pithy title *Black Power Naps* encapsulates a foundational contradiction within the political analysis of sleep. Sleep is genuinely essential to sustainable, self-determined life, but it is also easily harnessed as a technique of productivity, one that—as power napping has taught us—can be chopped up to fit a twenty-minute break in the workday. Sleep takes a person out of the cycle of production but also prepares her to be an even better worker when she returns.

The performance *Black Power Naps* yanks the "power" at the center of its three-word title firmly in the direction of Black self-determination, dragging "naps" along with it, such that napping is transformed into a brief enactment of a world where constant productivity is not demanded of Black people. As *Black Power Naps* claimed sovereignty within the relatively small square footage of PSNY, the nap claims sovereignty in the flow of time, excising a few minutes out of the workday. Naps allow sleep to overflow its bounds in the night and steal daylight hours. Like *Best Place to Sleep, Black Power Naps* overflows the container of a single performance. This chapter focuses on the January 2019 New York installation and two issues of *Black Power Naps Magazine,* for which Acosta and Sosa served as artistic directors: The first issue was produced for their premiere at Matadero Madrid's Centro de Residencias Artísticas, and the second for PSNY. These magazines feature photographs of the installation beds in use and critical and creative writing about the exhibition; the magazines encourage audiences to take the possibilities of *Black Power Naps* home with them. Yet *Black Power Naps* still overflows the bounds of this chapter. Acosta and Sosa have performed a capsule opera, staged photo shoots, created online programming, curated a library of bedtime reading, and created further installations in Miami and in New York's Museum of Modern Art.

The audience experience of *Black Power Naps* in 2019 also overflowed the senses, extending beyond what a viewer could consciously absorb during a visit to the performance space. From any given vantage point in the large, open gallery, a spectator could catch only glimpses of the exhibition—not just of the artworks, but of anyone sleeping within them. Six titled, bed-like installations were placed throughout the large square room in a grid pattern, each identified by a plaque on the floor and an accompanying gallery map: Pelvic Floor in the far left corner, Black Power Base in the far center, Atlantic Reconciliation Station in the far right, and so on. Under low lighting, the windowless room, with dark walls and floor, became even more shadowed. Within the sovereign land of *Black Power Naps,* the rules of sleep changed, and the incredible support built up by the installation meant that the biological sustenance of sleep—and particularly the luxury and immediate gratification of daytime, public sleep—no longer demanded exposure and vulnerability in exchange. These fantastic, nourishing spaces for sleep staged what Piepzna-Samarasinha describes as the future of collective care, a "dream [of] mutual aid . . . where everyone gets access to many kinds of care—from friends and internet strangers, from disabled community centers, and from some kind of non-fucked-up non-state state."[26] *Black Power Naps* is, perhaps, a non-fucked-up non-state state, a sovereign space that provides the infrastructure for rest without admission fees and without exploitation or surveillance.

In place of external surveillance, sleepers at *Black Power Naps* are invited to watch themselves falling asleep, to see their own slumber as an aesthetic pleasure. Above the central bed, a giant tie-dyed mattress titled Polycrastination Station, a large overhead mirror offered the unusual pleasure of watching yourself fall asleep, glimpsing what you look like in a state of almost complete rest. The large mirror, described in the gallery guide as a "suspended vanity," invited self-spectatorship; the oversize mattress invited expansive rest. Learning to recognize yourself experiencing rest, *Black Power Naps* suggests, is an essential practice for achieving "a total divestment" from the performance of continual, diligent labor historically demanded of Black Americans. The term *vanity,* describing "that which is of no value or profit," echoes the practice of divesting from performing one's worth through work. Instead, the bed is a space of "polycrastination." With the replacement of "pro-" with "poly-," polycrastination loses the sense of putting off a task toward *(pro-)* a predetermined tomorrow *(cras)* and replaces it with a sense of multitude *(poly-),* of many possible tomorrows. Polycrastination further breaks down the discourse of productivity that has spawned interest in both procrastinators and power naps by joining a Greek prefix *(poly-)* with a Latin root *(cras),* creating a mixed term that transgresses etymological borders to imagine a different relationship to the future within our language.[27]

Polycrastination Station's base is a mattress tie-dyed in a rainbow palette of pastels, a color scheme that appears on many of *Black Power Naps*' beds. Like the term *polycrastination*—and like napping itself—tie-dye is overdetermined, an aesthetic that overflows any single interpretation. It has roots in many traditional textile practices; it is redolent of New Age culture and of childhood craft projects; it has become an expensive fabric that wears the cost of laborious hand-dying on its twee surface. But under designer Betsy Chester's variegated, indirect lighting, tie-dye was sublime, "counter, original, spare, strange . . . fickle, freckled . . . adazzle, dim" like Hopkins's pied beauty.[28] Photographs taken from the vantage point of the vanity show sleepy models gazing languidly up at themselves in repose, their blue-shadowed lids, sequined skirts, and rhinestone body jewels blending into the tie-dye under soft disco-ball dapples. Napping in Polycrastination Station allowed sleepers to see other futures for themselves by seeing themselves fully at rest.

Yet truly falling asleep depends on the napper's feeling safe enough to surrender the sense of sight and know their surroundings only by feel. In the second issue of *Black Power Naps Magazine,* jamilah malika's poem "Rest/Woke" guides the transition from self-spectatorship to a felt knowledge of safety and relaxation.[29] Malika repeats "notice" as an anaphora calling on her audience to attend to how they feel when they are at rest: "notice your eyes—like your tongue—can rest inside your dear head" and "notice all the parts of you that rest to any surface like the floor, chair, or bed." Good sleep is not just about accessing time and space but also about learning how rest feels in the body and which pleasures make stopping work worthwhile. "Rest/Woke" encourages nappers to make restful sleep a part of the repertoire of Black American experience, what Taylor describes as an "embodied memory" encoded and preserved by the napper's attending to how the onset of sleep feels in the eyes, breath, and limbs.[30] Malika's poem shifts the practice of self-spectatorship from a visual act of seeing your own supine body in the mirror above to a proprioceptive process, knowing the feeling of your own body at rest. When the visual perception ends—when the eyes close and sleep happens—the performance and its attendant spectatorship also end. Black Rest, even within a performance space, is, finally, not a performance.

The beds in the *Black Power Naps* installation reclaim material objects used or associated with the U.S. history of anti-Black and anti-immigrant politics. Acosta and Sosa use materials not typically associated with sleep and reconfigure them into beds, so spectators can experience them as pleasurable and restful. Black Bean Bed is composed of gold Mylar survival blankets and dried black beans, materials associated with the deprivations experienced by immigrants approaching the U.S. southern border. The beans form the mattress of the circular bed, creating a deep well "designed to soothe someone experiencing a panic attack." Writing in *Black Power Naps Magazine,* cultural critic Janine Francois describes how "the beans swallow your body while cooling your skin, enveloping you in comfort."[31] The foil blankets are familiar from photographs taken in immigration detention facilities at the U.S. border. Colloquially known as *hieleras* (iceboxes or coolers), the detention facilities are so cold that detainees need heat-reflective blankets even indoors. In the comfortable temperature at PSNY, these blankets were no longer needed for survival, so they became a beautiful canopy surrounding the bed, reflecting the dim lighting and attracting spectators who might be coaxed into a nap.

Together, the beans and blankets also create a micro-soundscape, activated by the sleeper's movements as she slides her body through the beans or brushes past the blankets. The quiet rustle of clicking beans and crinkling foil welcomes pleasurable fidgeting. The sleeper is invited not to discipline her body into silence—which is impossible, with so much noise-making material around her—but to burrow in and get cozy while creating an analog version of the "white noise" electronic static often used to facilitate sleep. Bunches of dried lavender hang above the bed; if the blanket-curtains move enough to create a small draft, the lavender also rustles, releasing its soothing scent. "Whether it's in our voices, in our toys, in our music, in the jiggle of our curves," Acosta and Sosa write, "Black pleasure is vibrational. What are 'good vibes,' if not the manifestation of Black pleasure?" Vibrations are the meeting point between what is felt and what is heard, and *Black Power Naps* thrums with subaural soundscapes that can be heard only by spectators who are close enough to touch the beds. Along with Black Bean Bed's rustles, low-frequency tones play beneath Pelvic Floor's trampoline mattress. These tones can be felt, like a low rumble of thunder, by a spectator touching the trampoline. As the sleeper's body moves with the elastic trampoline, parts of her body oscillate closer to and farther from the vibrations, every move a minute shift in a personal soundscape she cocreates with the bed itself. If the trampoline represents the "pelvic floor" of its title, the vibrations below the trampoline take on the quality of intimate pleasure writ large. A spectator resting on the trampoline can feel the pleasure of her body as its priority, as "good vibes."

But not all visitors to *Black Power Naps* are there to nap. Part of the project of creating a sovereign space that values Black Rest is building up this sleep infrastructure for spectators of color, but another part of it is managing white attendees (like myself) who are not explicitly invited into the experience of Black Rest. The "laws of the land" at the entrance altar—particularly "If you see a Black person resting, don't call the police!"—establish a baseline policy of nonintervention in Black Rest. Francois also uses her article in *Black Power Naps Magazine* to draw attention to "a recording of the artists reading science fiction texts written by Black trans women play[ing] so softly that it's inaudible."[32] Sosa explains this subliminal audio transmission as "a device that provokes hyper-empathy in white people, planting this neurological map that they don't have. They're reprogrammed to interpret reality in a different way." The work of reclaiming space for Black Rest extends right into white attendees' gray matter. Sosa lays a claim to white spectators' brains as territory (a "neurological map") to be reclaimed, not through force but through a painless, subconscious reprogramming. Francois suggests that, through *Black Power*

Naps' deployment of subaudible neural remapping, "white people, for once, become the spectacle—the ones being scrutinized by the Black gaze." If white attendees stay off the beds, they do not experience the privileges of self-spectatorship under Polycrastination Station's vanity, or withdrawal behind the curtains that enclose many of the other beds.

The inaudible recordings extend *Black Power Naps'* epistemological reorientation of the body toward knowing rest, experienced by Black attendees, through to a cognitive reorientation of white spectators toward supporting Black Rest. While Black spectators cultivate an empirical, proprioceptive knowledge of Black Rest by napping on the installation's beds, white spectators' brains are passively cultivated toward a future when Black Rest is valued. Deploying science fiction as the discourse for white neurological remapping makes a provocative, future-oriented intervention among spectators; it incrementally stages a future when no one will need to be told not to call the police on a Black person who is napping. Francois categorizes this reclamation of white thought as the work of reparations, "reminding us that reparations are not solely about money, but also time."[33] To nap, in *Black Power Naps,* is both to release the mind and body from the demands of self-spectatorship (including self-discipline, self-surveillance, and self-censorship) and to reclaim the time of the workday, the space of the gallery, and the very materials of anti-Black (and, often, anti-Indigenous and anti-immigrant) racism for one's own rest. Perhaps a blissful nap in public is what full citizenship could feel like.

Sleep After Care

Before spectators entered the sovereign space of the *Black Power Naps* installation at PSNY, they passed through an advertising display for *Black Power Naps'* sponsor Buffy. Buffy had, at the time, attracted substantial media attention among a sea of sleep products for its signature Cloud Comforter, a fluffy white duvet that indeed resembled an embraceable cumulus. The aesthetic shift between the lobby and the installation at PSNY was striking: The lobby was bright white and well lit, filled with plush piles of Cloud Comforters and social media ads glowing on wall-mounted plasma screens. In contrast, the gallery space itself was dimly lit and strewn with hammocks, waterbeds, trampolines, and air mattresses, beds that predated or exceeded contemporary sleep brands' streamlined packaging of "springs, gel, and foam."[34] Buffy's globalizing motto, "Let's make the world a more comfortable place, together," is at odds with *Black Power Naps*' project of carving out a small, sovereign place—in Hann's scenographic terms, a discrete world—that is specifically comfortable for Black and Indigenous people. *Black Power Naps*' beds are particular to their audience and their historical context; while sleep brands reduce their costs by putting forth a small number of optimized products that suggest good sleep is the same for everyone, *Black Power Naps* cares for its sleepers by considering what particular feelings, sights, smells, and sounds will best help them rest. The obvious expense of this bespoke art installation raises questions about how to meet the future costs of sleep when truly restorative rest requires such detailed care. In its spatial relationship with its sponsor Buffy, *Black Power Naps* stages both a critique of the capitalist logics underlying the twenty-first-century sleep brand and a positive alternative within the near future by extracting value from Buffy while leaving the brand out in the lobby and out of the bedroom.

Buffy's progenitor is Casper Sleep, which became an early leader in the sleep industry when it launched a direct-to-consumer mattress in 2014, proclaiming a wellness brand identity on its website: "We believe sleep is the superpower that changes everything people do. . . . It makes us friendlier, faster, smarter . . . even warmer-and-fuzzier." Casper, Buffy, and other sleep brands capitalize on feminist insights into the value that socially reproductive care labor generates for the productive labor market. Ensuring that a worker gets a good night's sleep and sustains his own labor power is essential to capitalist production. (And a "warmer-and-fuzzier" worker hardly sounds likely to file a workplace grievance or instigate a strike.) Now, however, it is not a wife or mother but the mattress itself that is responsible for this sustaining sleep. Success in the sleep-wellness industry is premised on seriously valuing care—not to *compensate* those who perform care work, or to foster a widespread ethic of care as a moral value, but to objectify and sell care in the form of aspirational products. While we may not produce or consume within capitalist markets while we sleep, *Black Power Naps* critiques the sleep industry's premises, showing that the industry's targeted approach to cultivating consumers for sleep products is part of a larger terrain of uneven investment in different populations' access to sleep. The sleep-wellness industry uses medical discoveries about the benefits of sleep made by neuroscientists to sell sleep as an investment in reproducing our own human capital. Unfortunately, anxiety is bad for sleep, so there is little chance that our investment in our own sleep will succeed to the extent that we stop pursuing better sleep through better sleep products—a good business plan for brands like Buffy.[35]

In a broadsheet headlined "Welcome to Soft-Space," available in the lobby outside *Black Power Naps,* Buffy asserts its mission as a developer of "soft goods that utilize environmentally safe materials," including eucalyptus and recycled water bottles.[36] Buffy extends its implicit claim that sleep is an investment in human capital to pitch sleep as an investment in the planet. Like *Black Power Naps,* Buffy reclaims unexpected materials for use as bedding, but Buffy's recycling produces a sleep product whose only relationship with the sleeper is that of consumer and commodity. Buffy sells the sleep its comforters invite as valuable not in and of itself but because it funds this recycling, which expiates the guilt from the guilty pleasure of rest: "The result is cruelty-free and less wasteful, sure, but it's also softer than any conventional product." Buffy's justification for the pleasures of softer bedding anticipates consumers who are skeptical about the value of sleep on its own. They must be convinced to invest in sleep not based on how it feels but based on its contribution to a kinder, gentler, "cruelty-free" capitalism. As in Bialik's Nectar mattress commercial, brands turn sleep into an intellectual project.

This version of feeling good while you sleep is not the good feeling of rest that your body knows, like the feeling of sinking into those cooling black beans and sensing your body is immersed and held. Instead, you have to be sold on feeling good about Buffy. For consumers who grew up with millennial television programming, the Buffy brand echoes Buffy the Vampire Slayer, teen television nemesis of sleepless, superpowered creatures. But Buffy's brand name also (unintentionally) evokes one of Marx's more vivid metaphors for the logic of capitalism. For Marx, the vampire *is* capital, "dead labor which, vampire-like, lives only by sucking living labor, and lives the more, the more labor it sucks."[37] The blood the vampire sucks is surplus value, extracted from the labor time of the worker. Marx's model of surplus value theorizes how workers spend their time—a theory that Buffy's marketing materials implicitly refute. If a worker produced only enough to cover the cost of her own labor and the raw materials she used, Marx argues, her boss would never turn a profit. But when a worker produces more than is needed to pay off her boss's initial costs, she generates surplus value. Therefore, "if the worker consumes [her] disposable time for [her]self, [s]he robs the capitalist," so the capitalist demands longer working hours of his employees.[38]

In *Buffy the Vampire Slayer,* as in many tales of vampires over the past two centuries, the vampires must hunt for fresh blood to satisfy their endless thirst. Marx's capital-vampire resolves this problem through the surplus labor army, the endless supply of new generations of workers—a supply often expanded through colonization—who break their backs and give up their blood in the work of industrial production. But Buffy offers another solution to capital's thirst for new blood. Good sleep makes labor a *renewable* resource, a resource well suited to Buffy's brand identity as a company that recycles plastic bottles into bedding. When a worker consumes her disposable time pursuing the best sleep she can achieve, she is not, as Marx asserts, robbing the capitalist. She actually makes an investment for the capitalist, increasing her labor power so she can work more productively the next day. If workers can be incited to invest their wages in their own sleep, capital can suck the metaphorical blood of their labor every day and send them home to rest up and regenerate on the workers' own dimes. Buffy comforters do not slay the vampire of capital but instead domesticate it, ending its need to hunt and inviting it into your home. And anyone who has watched *Buffy* knows never to invite a vampire into her home.

Buffy's stated justification of comfortable sleep as an investment in cruelty-free capitalism, and its implicit justification of good sleep as an investment in becoming a better worker, underscores the contradiction immanent in any claim to sleep's value. As soon as sleep is recognized as valuable *for the sleeper,* that value can be co-opted as an initial investment in the expropriation of surplus value from the sleeper's future labor. *Black Power Naps* resists Buffy's domestication of capital by leaving Buffy's own Cloud

Comforters out of the exhibition space and, therefore, outside the sovereign land *Black Power Naps* demarcates for Black Rest. Acosta and Sosa, moreover, reject the idea that sleep should serve to make each individual worker a self-renewing resource. They assert that sleep is a respite from labor that was historically denied to African Americans by chattel slavery, a debt that remains unpaid. And they demonstrate that only through meticulous caretaking can this respite be offered to people long disciplined not to rest—and especially not to rest in public, during the workday. Every light, sound, color, smell, word, and vibration that makes up *Black Power Naps* is crafted to care for sleep.

Finally, Acosta and Sosa disabuse us of the idea that sleep is an autonomous practice of individual self-renewal by claiming their own need for rest and care from the institutions that host their art. In an artists' statement titled "Una guía para instituciones blancas que reciben artistas racializades y a sus públicos" (A guide for white institutions that receive racialized artists and their audiences), Acosta and Sosa connect the performance of Black Rest within the installation to the production and sustenance of Black Rest at the level of the hosting institution.[39] The "Aftercare" section of the guide begins, "What is most likely, if the event is open to a wide audience, is an exhausting experience for the racialized artist. . . . White fragility (and arrogance) can dry, drain, and tire us." For Acosta and Sosa to create a sleep infrastructure in the performance space, they must also have backstage infrastructure for rest. "Aftercare" goes beyond requesting water, snacks, and phone chargers to imagining a future for the art institution as a comprehensive welfare program of "social security, vacations, retirement/pension, life insurance, financial planning/investment support, credit, [and] mortgages," not only for its full-time employees but also for the artists it commissions. This would, Acosta and Sosa acknowledge, require a complete restructuring of the institution's budget, in a commitment to "abandoning the demand for slave labor under the excuse of diversity." Much of the care that Acosta and Sosa request is, at its best, a partial foreshadowing of collective care. Social security, pensions, and life insurance ask every participant in a group to pay in some amount to ensure greater financial resources are available as members of the group become unable to work. Vacation time redistributes or pauses work so that every employee can take a rest. By reclaiming material support for rest not only within the installation but also in the art institution itself, Acosta and Sosa redistribute the responsibility for the care of the racialized artist onto the institution extracting surplus value from the artist's labor.

In early 2023, *Black Power Naps* reappeared at its wealthiest host institution to date, New York City's Museum of Modern Art. Under the title *Black Power Naps: La Biblioteca Is Open,* Acosta and Sosa's artwork was installed as an interactive piece for four months in MoMA's Creativity Lab, which hosts participatory art and art-making activities for museum visitors. Two months into the MoMA installation, Heather Agyepong, a British Ghanaian photographer and actor, was "kicked out" of the exhibition after she asked a white woman in the gallery to quiet her loud laughter in order to keep the installation focused on Black visitors' experiences. The white woman called Agyepong "aggressive," and the museum told Agyepong and another Black woman to leave. In Agyepong's own words, "Basically [MoMA] told me: You can never rest!"[40] These events at MoMA also left *Black Power Naps* itself restless and unhoused. A major arts festival scheduled to install the artwork later in 2023 canceled with little notice, leaving the creators scrambling to find and pay for storage for the large-scale installation.[41] An assemblage of full-size beds, whose scale and majesty make their own argument for the value of Black Rest, is not easy to preserve over the long term.

This story is tired and tiring. A canonical art institution casting Black women as aggressors and removing them at the behest of a white patron, amid a post-2020 effort to pursue racial justice in the museum, seems entirely predictable. These dynamics of power—white women policing so-called Black aggression, white institutions flubbing attempts at diversity—are familiar ones. Sosa and Acosta's own guide for white art institutions working with artists of color predicts the failures of care they describe experiencing as MoMA artists. As their exhibition moved into this more canonical, less community-connected venue, the artists describe trying to take on the labor of protecting their intended audience from the institution itself. Although they had requested antiracism training for the museum's employees, MoMA delayed offering it, until the adverse publicity brought about by the museum's treatment of

Agyepong. As *Black Power Naps* moved into more substantial art institutions with larger audiences and higher admission prices, it also faced a more powerful, instrumentalized extraction of the surplus value of Acosta and Sosa's artistic labor and racial identities. Showing their work in higher-profile institutions, the kind of institutions that have the means to better compensate the artists, also exhausts the artists further, demanding more labor to defend people of color—both themselves and museum visitors—from the white fragility they know will "dry, drain, and tire us."

While the fantastical beds that constitute *Black Power Naps* are stuck in the here and now of unreliable institutional and financial support and expensive storage needs, *Black Power Naps Magazine* imagines an alternative. The section title "Aftercare" in the guide for white institutions makes a granular temporal distinction between the time of the installation, when Acosta and Sosa provide care for sleeping participants, and the time after, when they request these forms of workplace care for themselves. Yet "Aftercare" also projects a more distant future *after care*—that is, after the sort of robust care that Acosta and Sosa both enact for sleepers and demand for themselves has become a given. It is the sort of care one might find in a world where bank lobbies are also bedrooms—where, as in *Best Place to Sleep*'s incisive, elegant gesture, public and semipublic spaces are completely repurposed toward care for the weary. With this sort of care, *Black Power Naps* would not need Buffy and would overhaul MoMA. In staging public naps, *Best Place to Sleep* and *Black Power Naps* share as their goal a complete institutional restructuring rooted in the forms of collective care that sleep beseeches.

Let's contrast the future that *Black Power Naps* and *Best Place to Sleep* stage with the bizarre future Bialik's commercial forecasts for Nectar mattress customers. Bialik assures her audience that Nectar has an unlimited warranty, "so even if you die and reincarnate as an animal, you can still use it!" In this etiolated account of reincarnation, the quality of your new life is determined not by metaphysical principles but by your old bedding. In this future, you must change yourself completely (into a different species), but your material world will stay the same. This commercial captures a final contradiction inherent in what appears to be a new appreciation of sleep's value within the workplace and, more broadly, within late capitalist life. While this new appreciation for sleep seems to hark back to a slower, gentler—indeed, precapitalist—existence, it in fact demands a huge amount of new, future-directed change. Change your mattress, yes, and then change your heart, change your brain, change your workplace behavior, change your relationships with other people. Change your unconscious desires, until you dream only of increased productivity. Change the very biological basis for your sleep.

Or, *Best Place to Sleep* and *Black Power Naps* urge, accept how tired you already feel. Acknowledging fatigue, exhaustion, and burnout can seem anathema to the work of feminism and its affiliate political projects: When there is still so much to do to make the future we want, asking for rest can feel like an unconscionable luxury, or an admission of defeat. Piepzna-Samarasinha encourages activists to think of organizing around the principle of collective care "as a place where building in many pauses . . . makes the movements more flexible and longer lasting."[42] Napping is a practice of pausing; *Best Place to Sleep* inserts an unexpected pause into the pace of capitalism while *Black Power Naps* invites its audience to seek out those pauses as experiences of pleasure. Both provoke us, as viewers, to be better caretakers of sleep, to pursue forms of collective care that countenance rest beyond the strictures of private property, the working day, and the wellness industry. By understanding the public nap as a political act anticipating collective care, we stage a future where rest—and its attendant pleasures—is worth more than work.

Coda
Sleep, Death, and Ways of Living

Sleep, onstage, can look like death. From the audience's perspective, sleep and death share aesthetic markers, such as recumbent forms and closed eyes. Both feigned sleep and feigned death allow a spectator to watch without being seen. For the actor onstage, sleep and death require similar embodiment. An actor performing sleep and an actor performing death might both lie motionless, making their breathing slow and shallow, willing themselves into stillness. The similar appearances of the sleeping character and the dead character onstage raise questions about what spectators to a sleep performance understand through sight, which might confuse sleep with death, and what they come to know through other ways of sensing and feeling. How do the performances we watch habitually train us in this understanding of sleep's proximity to death? William Shakespeare's problem play *Cymbeline* (circa 1611), about a fictional princess whose sleep is deathlike, and Davóne Tines's short music film *Vigil (an exercise in empathy)* (2020), about a real nighttime state-sanctioned killing, pose these questions on the terrain of gendered and racialized violence, in settings where the state claims the right to administer death. This intentionally unlikely pairing probes the limits of sleep performance as a site for working through feminist politics, asking what performance can and cannot do in the face of deeply engrained habits of seeing vulnerability as an openness—or even an enticement—to harm.

The plot of *Cymbeline* is complex, but, simply put, sleep enables the play's most consequential scenes.[1] In one of these scenes, a princess named Imogen refuses the advances of a man named Iachimo, who tries to seduce her into extramarital sex. Iachimo eventually seems to accept this refusal and asks merely to store a large chest in Imogen's bedchamber overnight. When Imogen falls asleep, Iachimo emerges from the chest, determined to gather false evidence that Imogen did have sex with him, so he can win a wager on Imogen's failed chastity. *Cymbeline* is a lesson in the likelihood of confusing sleep and death onstage. The scene of Imogen's invaded bedchamber teaches the play's audience to recognize a sleeping woman as an opportunity for both sexual violation of a living but compliant body and aesthetic appreciation of a lifeless, statue-like form that will not wake.

This scene asks the audience to see the sleeping Imogen with Iachimo's eyes, to share the spectatorial and epistemological perspective of a voyeuristic sexual predator. Iachimo decides that his mere ability to describe Imogen's bedchamber will not be enough to prove their intimacy. Instead, "some natural notes about her body" are needed to support his false claims of Imogen's adultery (2.2.31). Upon making this decision, Iachimo calls on sleep in an apostrophe: "O sleep, thou ape of death, lie dull upon her / And be her sense but as a monument / Thus in a chapel lying" (2.2.34–36). The "monument . . . in a chapel lying" refers to tombstone effigies of recumbent women and alludes to a simile in Shakespeare's own long poem *The Rape of Lucrece,* in which Lucrece also sleeps "like a virtuous monument" (2.2.n32).[2] So Iachimo's lines yoke sleep to death through their mimetic relationship—how sleep can "ape," or imitate, death. Further, Iachimo places the sleeping Imogen in a long intertextual lineage that figures a woman's sleeping body as an aesthetic object, a tombstone monument, whose deadness simultaneously makes the body art (a sculpture rather than a living woman) and available for rape (a compliant, not a struggling, woman). And sleep accedes to Iachimo's plea. Imogen remains asleep even as Iachimo repeatedly touches her body, noting a mole on her breast and yanking a "slippery" bracelet from her wrist (2.2.34). Along with the suggestion of "slippery" sexual penetration, the conflation of bracelet and genitalia can also run in the other direction, suggesting that Imogen's sleep has become true objectification, transforming her entire body into an ornament like her bracelet. The audience is invited to see Imogen's body in the way that Iachimo sees it. She is at once dead (and frozen in beauty like a tombstone effigy) for the purposes of art and asleep (and alive but compliant) for the purposes of sex.

Here I return to the gendered aesthetic-sexual gaze as directed at the sleeping beauty, the starting point for my reading of Laurie Anderson's *Institutional Dream Series*. The male gaze, as named in Laura Mulvey's essay on scopophilic pleasure, is now part of our everyday vocabulary for talking about visual culture.[3] When I assign Mulvey's essay to students of aesthetics, their intuitive understanding of Mulvey's critique is often that the male gaze is gross. Being the object of unwanted sexualized viewing or being the unwished-for objectifier of another person's body strikes them as obviously wrong. These students raise caveats to Mulvey's claims, but they arrive already convinced of her central argument.[4] This is a victory for feminist performance scholarship. Yet while any of us, like these students, may feel gross about complicity with a voyeuristic male gaze, the problem for me is not the viewers' potential gratification or guilt about what they are seeing onstage. Instead, it is the training in seeing sleep that this scene engenders. Watching Imogen sleep from Iachimo's perspective trains spectators to see sleep as the meeting point of sex and death. Sleeping Imogen is available for both aesthetic pleasure, like the lifeless effigy on a tombstone, and sexual violence, like Lucrece. A sleeping beauty can satisfy both desires.

How spectators view a woman's onstage death is also a central concern of early feminist performance scholarship, as examined in the staging of a potential suicide in the *4.48 Psychosis* opera. In 1977, two years after Mulvey's critique appeared in the British journal *Screen*, French philosopher Hélène Cixous published an equally forceful reading of gendered violence in live theater. "How, as women," she asks, "can we go to the theatre without lending our complicity to the sadism directed against women, or being asked to assume, in the patriarchal family structure that the theatre reproduces *ad infinitum*, the position of victim?"[5] Both Mulvey and Cixous raise questions about what it means to remain in the audience of mainstream performance cultures—as we all do, at least some of the time. *What are we paying to watch?* they ask. But also,

What are we being trained to desire watching? Although they critique different performance forms, both Mulvey and Cixous are furious. It is clear to them that everything must change. The sleep performances discussed in this book tend to share this feminist perspective. They explore the foundational interdependence and vulnerability of human life that is made inescapable in sleep, using their spectators' shared witnessing of this interdependence to experiment with its possibilities for feminist projects that intend to change the world. But viewing sleep in performance—particularly sleep that rubs shoulders with death—may also train us to see from Iachimo's perspective, to see the vulnerability of a sleeping character as an invitation to harm.

Death emerges as a concern of feminist sleep performance more often than might be expected. Caryl Churchill makes the housewife Val's sleeplessness so powerful and pervasive that the character will not leave the stage, even after her boyfriend kills her. Sleep is the only medium in which characters in *Enter THE NIGHT* can contest others' views of their terminal illnesses, while debilitating sleeplessness pushes the protagonist of *4.48 Psychosis* toward suicide. In Regina José Galindo's response to family incarceration and Sakiko Yamaoka's response to the Bantul earthquake, both artists organize performances against a backdrop of mass loss of life. Peggy Shaw asks her audience to help her remember the names of friends who died too early, to revive them in her dream of gay fish in the Hudson. And when Navild Acosta and Fannie Sosa instruct their viewers, "If you see a Black person resting, don't call the police!" they raise the specter of Black deaths caused by police violence.

Acosta and Sosa created *Black Power Naps* against the backdrop of a U.S. American history of punishing Black people for resting. Being unable to rest is a true existential horror, not just an exhaustion of the body's physical capacities but a destruction of any sense of sanity or safety. The daily experience of too much work and too little sleep haunts Fannie Lou Hamer's claim to being sick and tired of being sick and tired; the nightly fear of a welfare inspector's visit drove Johnnie Tillmon-Blackston to campaign for dignified welfare rights. "Police terror," anthropologist Christen A. Smith writes of anti-Black state violence, "is cumulative, lingering, time bending, and space collapsing."[6] The killing of Breonna

Taylor is one recent instance of the particular strain of police terror that intentionally strikes in the middle of the night. Like most people who learned about Taylor's death, I first encountered it as a spectator, seeing forensic reconstructions of police invading her home and video footage of vigils and protests mourning her death. As a performance scholar, I want to understand the relationship between how we come to know about Taylor's death—our epistemological entry point, as spectators—and the analysis we form from it, how or if it changes our conception of sleep, death, and the state. How does this spectatorship teach me to see a sleeping Black woman, or a sleeping person who is structurally vulnerable? Am I being trained to see with Iachimo's eyes, to understand the vulnerability of this person's sleep as inevitably close to death—as an invitation to harm that I see and lament from the audience but do not play a role in?

Among the artists who responded to Taylor's death, American opera singer Davóne Tines created the musical performance "Vigil," a vocal solo that tenderly proclaims, "Where there is darkness, we'll bring light." Tines developed "Vigil" iteratively, starting with music he had cowritten with Dutch French composer Igee Dieudonné and lyrics that emerged from an improvisation exercise. Tines created several versions of the performance, versions shaped both by a reckoning with anti-Blackness in U.S. performance cultures and by the unusual constraints placed on live performance in 2020 and after.[7] My closing reading of the creation and revision of "Vigil" parallels my reading of Tracey Emin's *Tent,* asking how artists like Emin and Tines grapple with contemporary feminist concerns as part of their examination of particular conditions of sleep. At its heart, "Vigil" is a three-to-five-minute vocal solo, sung by Tines with varying forms of instrumental accompaniment. As Tines repeats the lyric "Where there is darkness, we'll bring light," his voice leaps from his bass-baritone range into a higher register before climbing higher still to sing two slow, extended hallelujahs. The tone is steady, direct but not rushed, serious but not weeping. In September 2020, Tines revised earlier performances of "Vigil" into a short music film with the amended title *Vigil (an exercise in empathy),* which debuted on Lincoln Center's social media accounts.[8] Through this revision, *Vigil (an exercise in empathy)* refuses its audience voyeuristic access to the aftermath of Taylor's death and redirects spectators' impulse to empathy toward their own embodied knowledge of sleep. In contrasting Taylor's death with the audience's sleep, *Vigil (an exercise in empathy)* refuses spectators a cathartic visual encounter with Taylor's death and aspires to reorient them toward the unspectacular repetition of lifelong political work.

Although *Vigil (an exercise in empathy)* has the low-fi aesthetic of many video performances created in 2020, this revised version reflects a longer reckoning with what Tines has called the "majority audience" for opera. As a Black, gay American opera singer, Tines works in a repertoire of heterosexual stories written for white audiences while also developing new vocal works that aim to reach a more expansive audience. Tines has described repurposing an earlier work—a song he and Dieudonné had composed in an unexpected midnight rush of inspiration—when he was invited to contribute to a recital in early 2020. This original "Vigil" was performed in a tightly framed video that showed Tines singing (footage that was itself borrowed from another pre-2020 video piece) and, in his words, "the imagery of vigils . . . [of] different documentation that has happened around George Floyd and Breonna Taylor." After a conversation with an audience member, Tines became concerned that the imagery of vigils had been received as a kind of "trauma porn," a display of suffering that is conciliatory for audiences to witness.[9] "Porn" connotes a particular relationship between performance and audience: The performance gratifies an audience desire to watch something without participating. Tines was concerned that trauma porn allows spectators to "feel let off the hook"—the hook being the recognition that they are already participants in the racial politics of state violence, that there is no outside position from which to view the fallout of police killings.

The term *trauma porn* appropriates the moralizing force of critiques of sexual pornography, while the modifier *trauma* indicates content not intended for sexual pleasure. Although the term appears more often in popular media, some recent scholarship on racial literacy also defines trauma porn as representations or recordings of Black people in pain, made for white or racial-majority consumption.[10] While using *porn* in a negative sense may pose disturbing echoes of fundamentalist sexual conservatism, the connotations implied by the term may be better understood as stemming from feminist critiques of pornography. Recent scholarship has reconstructed the arguments of both antiporn feminists and their many feminist opponents—including Black feminist critiques of porn's typical racial dynamics—and reconsidered what feminists might do with porn in the twenty-first century.[11]

But trauma porn is also distinctly a concept from the era of free online video streaming, when the ubiquity of access to porn has changed the terms of its production, circulation, and reception. (This same video streaming infrastructure allows Tines's music films to circulate freely online.) In this medium, philosopher Amia Srinivasan argues, "porn *trains*"; the repetition of male sexual violence toward women in mainstream online porn "etches deep grooves in the psyche" of the spectator.[12] Srinivasan points out that young people viewing porn can explicitly dislike or disavow this violence and still expect that it will be part of their sexual encounters, as they struggle to imagine other kinds of intimate interaction. So trauma porn might train majority audiences in a racial politics that dislikes and disavows Black suffering without working to imagine another distribution of power. Here I am not asking whether trauma porn trains viewers to personally hurt Black women (this was certainly not the intent of the vigil footage in Tines's original video) but whether it stymies our capacity to imagine acting in pursuit of different racial politics—whether it can, perversely, satisfy an expectation of injustice in the world rather than prompt an intervention. Performance scholars have examined the politics of reproducing Black suffering for both majority-white and specifically Black audiences; below, I revisit a particular critique of reproductions that claim to evoke spectatorial empathy.[13] Trauma porn is a concern not only because the spectator who sees it might be let off the hook of taking action but because it teaches us to *be spectators* to anti-Black violence, to expect this violence in our performance cultures.

To revise "Vigil," Tines replaced the imagery documenting real vigils with what he calls an "embodiment exercise," an exercise borrowed from his own preperformance rituals as an opera singer. In the opening of the music film, tightly focused shots of Tines singing are intercut with title cards that instruct viewers to notice their bodies. They read, "Pay attention to your breath / Try to feel the weight of your body / Try to feel the surface your hand is touching." These soft imperatives ask viewers to be conscious of how their bodies feel in the present moment. They echo jamilah malika's poem "Rest/Woke" for *Black Power Naps* and Shaw's progressive relaxation exercise in *Menopausal Gentleman*—and, like Shaw's exercise, Tines's lines borrow from theater training in a way that starts to sound like a sleep meditation. Paradoxically, preparation to sleep and preparation to act can take the form of the same exercise: noticing your breath and sensing your body. Like Anderson in *Institutional Dream Series, Vigil (an exercise in empathy)* suggests that audiences might perceive Taylor's death in some way other than visual witnessing—through senses and feelings beyond sight.

Instead of giving viewers voyeuristic access to vigils, the revised music film contrasts the conditions of the viewer's sleep with the circumstances of Taylor's death. The next section of intercut text reads: "Remember how you slept last night? / Remember how the sheets felt on your skin? / Did you wake up this morning? / Breonna Taylor was shot dead in the middle of the night in her own home. She was unarmed. She was innocent." Taylor's name lingers on the screen. Between the interrogation and the information—between the questions and the fact of Taylor's murder—is the link between the viewer's sleep and her death. Counterintuitively, the written instructions and sung lyrics in this version of *Vigil* do not strike me as calling for empathy with Taylor herself. Claims of empathy trouble scholars of performance and race. A performance that aims to elicit spectatorial empathy for Black suffering might erase the social differences that underpin racist violence and invite spectators to take pleasure in imagining themselves into the experience of a Black person's pain. In her study of coerced or willfully misinterpreted "performances" by enslaved people for a white audience, literary critic Saidiya Hartman asserts that such claims of empathy indulge the white spectator's feelings and project them onto Black bodies not conceived of as equally human. "The endeavor to bring pain close exploits the spectacle of the body in pain," Hartman writes, "and oddly confirms the spectral character of suffering and the inability to witness [that] pain."[14] A claim to empathy can reproduce the negation of Black humanity that slavery depended on, that anti-Black violence still depends on.

Yet the subtitle *(an exercise in empathy)* does not function precisely to invite viewers to empathize with Taylor, or non-Black audiences to empathize with the fear or pain of people directly suffering anti-Black violence. This word *empathy,* which is never mentioned in the performance itself, may ultimately act as a misdirection, enticing audiences by promising catharsis to viewers who want to be "let off the hook" for their role in deaths like Taylor's. The written instructions in the exercise *do* focus on the feelings of spectators, a potentially controversial approach. But they call on viewers to recognize the distance between their feelings and the undepicted events of Taylor's death and her loved ones' grief—not to collapse this distance through emotional identification but to act on this distance politically, outside the frame of the performance. The written questions redirect the focus to spectators' sleep, calling on spectators to remember and reckon with their own quotidian feelings of safety, comfort, and interdependence. Asking, "Remember how you slept last night? / Remember how the sheets felt on your skin? / Did you wake up this morning?" they summon viewers to exercise their memories, to re-create the haptic effects of a nightly experience that is easily glossed over, to empathize with their own sleeping selves, the everyday version of the self that is most dependent on protection from harm. That sleeping self, when unharmed, is also a source of undervalued pleasures. "Remember how the sheets felt on your skin?" asks viewers to linger in rest past the call of the alarm clock, to feel skin contact with soft fabric. The questions in *Vigil* reckon with specific deaths by charging viewers to feel how much they value the nightly pleasures of ordinary sleep.

When I talk with students about my research for this book, sometimes I ask them to think about all the people who have watched over them as they slept. It is an exercise inspired by Emin's inclusion of her grandmother as one of the people she "slept with." I, too, remember each of my grandmothers caring for me in my sleep: one rubbing my back when I was struggling to nap, the other letting me sleep in her bed when I had nightmares. Students name parents, of course, and other family members. Students living in dorms have new experiences of roommates' sleep and sleeplessness. Some name their buildings' security guards, and we talk about social contracts of care, agreements not to do things while others are sleeping, as when construction workers shifted their working day to later hours to accommodate dorm residents' desire to sleep in. We talk about police, and we talk about homelessness. Care for sleep is unevenly distributed among us, with life-and-death consequences. Our need for care in sleep is also our exploitable weakness, making nighttime raids such an effective and dangerous form of state discipline, of biopolitical control. Sleep falls under the rubric of what Foucault calls the state's "power to *foster* life or *disallow* it to the point of death."[15]

In *Vigil,* viewers remembering how their sheets felt on their skin is the preface to their reckoning with Taylor's death and their own responsibility to "do something about it," per the written instructions that follow. If a vigil is a watch kept on an eve in anticipation of the coming day, *Vigil* asks its viewers to contemplatively, imaginatively watch themselves at nighttime, to feel as they felt when they slept, in anticipation of the following moment when they will take action. At the end of the video, after Tines's voice fades out, the imperative mood returns, now in a series of five instructions prefaced with the line "Justice hasn't been served. Do something about it." The instructions call on viewers to consider their own affective response to Taylor's death, to seek out organizations already pursuing racial justice, and to give time or money to them. The final instruction reads, "Repeat." The instructions to "search for organizations" that will let spectators act on their "emotional response to what's going on" and to then "research them, promote them, give them your time and money as *you are able*" is familiar—maybe quite familiar—from both online and in-person calls to action, exhortations to move resources to experienced activist organizations. But the single word "repeat" is distinctive. Tines's hallelujahs, gliding into the higher registers of his voice, echoing an ancient word of praise giving, hope for that possibility—that viewers might move from feeling their most vulnerable, their most in need of care, to repeated action that redistributes that care more justly. It is a precarious hope; how much can one performance do, when performance can so often go wrong? The hallelujah praises an action that might not happen, trying to perform it into the world—a fragile but laudatory prefiguring.

The call to take political action beyond the limits of the performance is not, for me, a call to treat performance as merely an instrument of politics. The time-mediated interaction between a performance and its spectators is dynamic and unpredictable. When spectators are confronted with an unexpected performed act—such as sleep—they react in their own unexpected ways. Some of these reactions are documented or witnessed, from Anderson's story of the night court judge trying to take away her friend's camera to Yamaoka's audio footage of a spectator asking about the purpose of her public nap. Some are hailed or hoped for, as when Shaw calls on her audience to help her remember the names of late friends, or Galindo reenacts a night in family incarceration to try to shut down a migrant jail. Some arise from unforeseen context, like the reaction of New York critics who interpreted Churchill's *Far Away* as a post-9/11 wake-up call. And some reactions—including that of the man who slept next to me in the *4.48 Psychosis* opera audience—remain beyond the reach of my explication. For feminist performance to differ from other, more instrumental forms of political intervention, we have to allow it to have unwanted outcomes. Feminist sleep performance might at times strive to instruct its audience, but what it more capably does is demand an encounter between what is scripted or crafted and what is as yet unimagined.

Within the recent history of American theater, feminist sleep performances pursue new tactics for political theater to engage a purportedly apathetic audience. For the past century or more, the goal of much political theater has been to awaken its audience to the crisis at hand and startle them into action. The urgency in these awakening performances has long since been co-opted by populist politicians and a twenty-four-hour news cycle, so that an ever-present performance of crisis exhausts, rather than engages, our attention and our capacity for action. The desperate appeal to audience attention, moreover, whether through immersive art exhibitions or theatricalizations of existing intellectual properties, has become a hallmark of commercial theater as it competes and colludes with more powerfully coercive forms of media. Live theater productions now cannot decide whether they should require spectators to lock their phones away in pouches, like schoolchildren, or force them to use their phones for basic theatrical logistics, like ticketing. In feminist sleep performances, theater is neither an advertisement nor a wake-up call. Sleep, onstage, relinquishes audience attention in favor of modeling practices of rest and recovery as part of political work. Sleep, as a dramatic theme, invites unpopular, sidelined, minor, and intractable political problems into shared consideration and experimentation. Sleep performance takes seriously our capacity as spectators to manage our own attention, to experience something in the leisure time of theatergoing that makes us reimagine the political potential of leisure, of rest and sleep, in the world.

Witnessing sleep in performance reminds us that we humans are slow-moving creatures, no matter what the pace of our economies or news cycles suggests. We spend one-third of our existence as a species doing nothing just to survive. And for all the deep achievements chalked up to feminism, lasting feminist change is often won at a glacial pace—despite its life-and-death stakes, despite our desire to make it happen overnight. Good sleep can be a good metaphor for feminist political practice. It is repeated and consistent, it is interdependent on others, it is unspectacular, and it is lifelong. Long after the awakening, sleep is the bedrock of both the material urgencies of repeated daily action and the expansive dreams of different ways of living in the future.

Acknowledgments

Many teachers, students, and readers contributed to this book. Thank you, all.

The first individual acknowledgments go to the members of my dissertation committee, who spent a decade thinking through this project with me: Jean E. Howard, W. B. Worthen, and Julie Stone Peters. Jean, Bill, and Julie—I could not have asked for better teachers. Debra Levine, Derek Miller, Katherine Biers, Denise Cruz, and Carrie Preston have gone above and beyond in supporting my work. Columbia University's Department of English and Comparative Literature, Institute for Research in Women's and Gender Studies, and Heyman Center for the Humanities funded my research. Thank you to Kate Daloz, Arden Hegele, and Marcella Manoharan for jobs that made me a better writer and to my siblings in GWC-UAW 2110. Student colleagues in colloquia and writing groups gave generous readings of chapters in progress; special thanks to Emily Kuntz and Kimberly Takahata for ongoing support.

My dissertation became this book during a postdoc at Boston University's Kilachand Honors College. Among all at KHC, particular thanks to Amy Fish, Talia Shalev, Chris Rominger, Stephanie Ahrens, Sravanthi Kollu, Can Evren, and Joanna Davidson. Other institutions provided readers, friends, and financial support: Thank you to many people in Theater, Dance & Media and the Theater and Performance Colloquium at Harvard University; in the Women's, Gender, and Sexuality Studies Program at Northeastern University; and in the Department of Writing, Literature, and Publishing at Emerson College. An award from Emerson's Research Hub supported the completion of this book. For timely questions and comments that prompted new thinking, I am indebted to Elin Diamond, Trent Masiki, and Glenn M. Gordon. A special thanks to my colleagues at the Isabella Stewart Gardner Museum, the Museum Teachers, for their bountiful good cheer.

Thank you to everyone who funds the arts and contributes to programs for affordable theater and museum tickets. My research was made possible by workers at the British Library, the Brookline Public Library, Columbia University Libraries, the Hemispheric Institute, Hong Kong's Asia Art Archive, Mugar Library, the New York Public Library for the Performing Arts, NYU's Fales Library and Special Collections, and the Victoria and Albert Theatre and Performance Archives—and at countless venues where I had the pleasure of watching live performance. Thank you to my editor Leah Pennywark, to Anne Carter and her coworkers at the University of Minnesota Press, and to Judy Selhorst and Martin L. White. Adair Rounthwaite and Telory D. Arendell gave insightful, invaluable comments on the manuscript.

Finally, I am grateful for the teaching and mentorship of Gwen Detlefsen, Suzanne Lottridge-Polzien, Ken Urban, Elizabeth Lyman, J. Michael Griggs, Martin Puchner, Chloe Preedy, Cameron Toman, and Marion Wrenn. Thank you to my college theater friends backstage and onstage. Tim Lundy read every word of this book and made it better; any remaining comma errors are mine. To my family—Mom and Dad, the Dreeses and the McMullins—many thanks and much love.

Notes

Introduction

1. Neal Brown, *Tracey Emin* (London: Tate, 2006), 37–49.

2. Brown, *Tracey Emin*, 40.

3. These works were, respectively, Marcus Harvey's *Myra* (1995), Marc Quinn's *Self* (1991–present), and Chris Ofili's *The Holy Virgin Mary* (1996).

4. Jack Tinker, "This Disgusting Feast of Filth," *Daily Mail*, January 19, 1995.

5. Sleep is often a vehicle for formal innovation in Emin's work, as in appliqué quilts like *Hotel International* (1993). Emin reached the peak of her notoriety with the Turner Prize–nominated installation *My Bed* (1998), her own nondescript bed made memorable through its accretion of "soiled sheets, bloodied underwear, empty vodka bottles, discarded tissues, [cigarette] ends, [and] used condoms." Mandy Merck, "Bedtime," in *The Art of Tracey Emin*, ed. Mandy Merck and Chris Townsend (London: Thames and Hudson, 2002), 119. See also Renée Vara, "Another Dimension: Tracey Emin's Interest in Mysticism," in Merck and Townsend, *Art of Tracey Emin*, 172–94; Brown, *Tracey Emin*, 83–87, 94.

6. José Esteban Muñoz, *Cruising Utopia: The Then and There of Queer Futurity* (New York: New York University Press, 2009), 65.

7. Anne Carson, "Ode to Sleep," in *Decreation: Poetry, Essays, Opera* (New York: Random House, 2005), 41.

8. Steven W. Lockley and Russell G. Foster, *Sleep: A Very Short Introduction* (Oxford: Oxford University Press, 2012), 2.

9. Jonathan Crary, *24/7: Late Capitalism and the Ends of Sleep* (London: Verso, 2014), 25.

10. Jacqueline Rose, *On Not Being Able to Sleep: Psychoanalysis and the Modern World* (Princeton, N.J.: University Press, 2003), 105–6, 110.

11. My claim that sleep is a social practice is indebted to Shannon Jackson's concept "social practice artworks." Jackson describes such works as "art events that are inter-relational, embodied, and durational," "cross-disciplinar[y]," and "gestur[ing] to the realm of the socio-political." Shannon Jackson, *Social Works: Performing Art, Supporting Publics* (New York: Routledge, 2011), 12–13. Some of the sleep performances I read here would meet these criteria (see chapters 4 and 7). Sleep itself is "inter-relational, embodied, and durational," and sleep performances often foreground these qualities of sleep—which may not always be the qualities of the artworks themselves.

12. Other studies that tie sleep practices and meanings to particular contexts include Matthew J. Wolf-Meyer, *The Slumbering Masses: Sleep, Medicine, and Modern American Life* (Minneapolis: University of Minnesota Press, 2012); Alan Derickson, *Dangerously Sleepy: Overworked Americans and the Cult of Manly Wakefulness* (Philadelphia: University of Pennsylvania Press, 2013); Sasha Handley, *Sleep in Early Modern England* (New Haven, Conn.: Yale University Press, 2016); Silvia Montiglio, *The Spell of Hypnos: Sleep and Sleeplessness in Ancient Greek Literature* (London: Bloomsbury Academic, 2016); Franny Nudelman, *Fighting Sleep: The War for the Mind and the US Military* (London: Verso, 2019); Benjamin Parris, *Vital Strife: Sleep, Insomnia, and the Early Modern Ethics of Care* (Ithaca, N.Y.: Cornell University Press, 2022).

13. Sarah Sharma, "The Biopolitical Economy of Time," *Journal of Communication Inquiry* 35, no. 4 (October 2011): 441–42. See also Michel Foucault, *The Birth of Biopolitics: Lectures at the Collège de France, 1978–1979* (New York: Picador, 2010); Ernest Mandel, *Late Capitalism* (1972; repr., London: Verso, 1999); Teresa Brennan, *Exhausting Modernity: Grounds for a New Economy* (London: Routledge, 2000).

14. Adrienne Rich, "When We Dead Awaken: Writing as Re-Vision," *College English* 34, no. 1 (1972): 18–30. Rich turns her own powers of revision on a play with a sleep metaphor in its title, Ibsen's *When We Dead Awaken*. Philosopher Catherine Clément argues for the importance of closely reading what is actually written in antifeminist texts as well (see chapter 6).

15. Anna Lowenhaupt Tsing, *The Mushroom at the End of the World: On the Possibility of Life in Capitalist Ruins* (Princeton, N.J.: Princeton University Press, 2015), 17, 21.

16. A note on names: Navild Acosta has also created work under the name niv Acosta, and Fannie Sosa sometimes uses Sosa as a mononym. During her lifetime, María Irene Fornés published under the name Maria Irene Fornes (without accents).

17. Sara M. Evans, "Women's Liberation: Seeing the Revolution Clearly," *Feminist Studies* 41, no. 1 (2015): 146, emphasis added.

18. Verónica Gago, *Feminist International: How to Change Everything*, trans. Liz Mason-Deese (London: Verso, 2020), 3, emphasis added.

19. Kemi Adeyemi, "The Practice of Slowness: Black Queer Women and the Right to the City," *GLQ: A Journal of Lesbian and Gay Studies* 25, no. 4 (2019): 545–67; Laurie Fuller and Erica R. Meiners, "Feeling Fatigued? Collectivize and Organize," *GLQ: A Journal of Lesbian and Gay Studies* 26, no. 2 (2020): 220–23; Johanna Hedva, "Sick Woman Theory," in *How to Tell When We Will Die: On Pain, Disability, and Doom* (New York: Hillman Grad Books, 2024); Tala Khanmalek and Heidi Andrea Restrepo Rhodes, "A Decolonial Feminist Epistemology of the Bed: A Compendium Incomplete of Sick and Disabled Queer Brown Femme Bodies of Knowledge," *Frontiers: A Journal of Women Studies* 41, no. 1 (2020): 35–58; Jenny Odell, *How to Do Nothing: Re-*

sisting the Attention Economy (Brooklyn, N.Y.: Melville House, 2019); Sarah Sharma, "Because the Night Belongs to Lovers: Occupying the Time of Precarity," *Communication and Critical/Cultural Studies* 11, no. 1 (2014): 5–14.

20. Along with *The Tent*, the Momart fire destroyed another of Emin's large temporary shelters, a beach hut titled *The Last Thing I Said to You was Don't Leave Me Here*. Brown, *Tracey Emin*, 94.

21. By "austerity politics," I mean cuts to public services driven by a neoliberal philosophy of governance that makes acquiring the basic necessities of daily life the responsibility of the individual, not the state or collective. Austerity politics are often justified through the demonization of poor women of color and immigrant women as benefiting from unearned state support, as we see in the specters of the "welfare queen" and the "anchor baby." My accounting of austerity and neoliberalism draws on Wendy Brown, *Undoing the Demos: Neoliberalism's Stealth Revolution* (New York: Zone Books, 2015); Naomi Klein, *The Shock Doctrine: The Rise of Disaster Capitalism* (New York: Metropolitan Books, 2010); Elizabeth A. Povinelli, *Economies of Abandonment: Social Belonging and Endurance in Late Liberalism* (Durham, N.C.: Duke University Press, 2011).

22. Hannah Proctor, *Burnout: The Emotional Experience of Political Defeat* (London: Verso, 2024), 186–98.

23. August Strindberg, *Miss Julie*, trans. Harry G. Carlson, in *The Longman Anthology of Drama and Theater: A Global Perspective*, ed. Michael L. Greenwald (London: Longman, 2001), 930. All parenthetical page citations refer to this edition.

24. August Strindberg, "Preface to *Miss Julie* (1888)," in *Theatre, Theory, Theatre: The Major Critical Texts from Aristotle and Zeami to Soyinka and Havel*, ed. Daniel Charles Gerould (New York: Applause Theatre & Cinema Books, 2000), 377.

25. Strindberg, "Preface to *Miss Julie*," 374–75.

26. Strindberg, "Preface to *Miss Julie*," 380.

27. Nicholas Ridout, *Passionate Amateurs: Theatre, Communism, and Love* (Ann Arbor: University of Michigan Press, 2013), 33–57.

28. Marjorie Garber, *Dream in Shakespeare: From Metaphor to Metamorphosis* (1974; repr., New Haven, Conn.: Yale University Press, 2013).

29. Mary Jo Lodge, "Dance Breaks and Dream Ballets: Transitional Moments in Musical Theater," in *Gestures of Music Theater: The Performativity of Song and Dance*, ed. Dominic Symonds and Millie Taylor (New York: Oxford University Press, 2014), 75–90.

30. Mary Rodgers and Marshall Barer, "Sensitivity," in *Once upon a Mattress* (1959) (New York: Chappell Music, 1995).

31. Paul Vitello, "Jane White, Actress and Singer Who Found Racial Attitudes to Be an Obstacle, Dies at 88," Arts, *New York Times*, August 8, 2011.

32. Jeanine Tesori and Lisa Kron, "Changing My Major," in *Fun Home* (New York: Samuel French, 2015).

33. Nudelman, *Fighting Sleep*, 133–34.

34. Julian Beck and the Living Theatre, "The Archaeology of Sleep," manuscript, 1984, New York Public Library for the Performing Arts. In his review of *The Archaeology of Sleep,* Frank Rich described the effects of listening to actors recount their own dreams: "The program . . . lists five sleepers whose dreams we are meant to follow—but you must add five to the theater's seating capacity to get an accurate total of the number of sleepers in the house. It's impossible to tell the official somnambulists apart in any case." Frank Rich, "The Archaeology of Sleep," Theater, *New York Times,* January 19, 1984.

35. Susan Bennett, *Theatre Audiences: A Theory of Production and Reception,* 2nd ed. (London: Routledge, 1997), 154.

36. Danielle Drees, "The Sleeping Spectator: A Sleep Cultures Critique of Punchdrunk's *Sleep No More,*" *Performance Research* 21, no. 1 (2016): 101–5.

37. Patrick Kingsley, "96 Days Later, Nonstop Church Service to Protect Refugees Finally Ends," World, *New York Times,* January 30, 2019. Sacred rituals are often cited as ur-performances. They are seen as the oldest examples we have in the archaeological record of humans gathering to enact "restored behavior," Richard Schechner's term for the human practice that is "the main characteristic of performance." Richard Schechner, *Between Theater and Anthropology* (Philadelphia: University of Pennsylvania Press, 1985), 35.

38. Rachel Aviv, "The Trauma of Facing Deportation," *New Yorker,* March 27, 2017.

39. Lockley and Foster, *Sleep,* 41.

40. Lizzie Simon, "Lying Down on the Job? It's in the Contract," *Wall Street Journal,* June 23, 2011; "Obituary of Jeanna (Janette) Belkin Klein," Joseph N. Garlick Funeral Home, accessed July 11, 2024, https://josephngarlickfuneralhome.com/tribute/details/777/Jeanna-Janette-Klein/obituary.html.

41. Fannie Lou Hamer, "'I'm Sick and Tired of Being Sick and Tired': Speech Delivered with Malcolm X at the Williams Institutional CME Church, Harlem, New York, December 20, 1964," in *The Speeches of Fannie Lou Hamer: To Tell It Like It Is,* ed. Maegan Parker Brooks and Davis W. Houck (Jackson: University Press of Mississippi, 2010), 76, 79.

42. Christina Sharpe, *In the Wake: On Blackness and Being* (Durham, N.C.: Duke University Press, 2016), 4–5, 27.

43. The editors of Hamer's collected speeches describe her as "often gravely ill, penniless, and exhausted" through fifteen years of full-time political activism, until her death at age fifty-nine in 1977. Maegan Parker Brooks and Davis W. Houck, "Showing Love and Telling It Like It Is: The Rhetorical Practices of Fannie Lou Hamer," in Brooks and Houck, *Speeches of Fannie Lou Hamer,* 15.

44. Betty Friedan, *The Feminine Mystique* (1963), excerpted in *The Essential Feminist Reader,* ed. Estelle B. Freedman (New York: Modern Library, 2007), 277, 270.

45. Shubhra Parmar, "Feminist Awakening in Rwanda," *Indian Journal of Political Science* 74, no. 4 (2013): 687–98; Leta Hong Fincher, *Betraying Big Brother: The Feminist Awakening in China* (London: Verso, 2018); Cecilia Sosa, "Mourning, Activism, and Queer Desires: Ni Una Menos and Carri's *Las hijas del fuego*," *Latin American Perspectives* 48, no. 2 (March 2021): 137–54.

46. Crary, *24/7*, 23.

47. Sara M. Evans, *Tidal Wave: How Women Changed America at Century's End* (New York: Free Press, 2003), esp. "Undertow," 98–127.

48. Mariarosa Dalla Costa and Selma James, *Women and the Subversion of the Community* (1972), in *Materialist Feminism: A Reader in Class, Difference, and Women's Lives*, ed. Rosemary Hennessy and Chrys Ingraham (New York: Routledge, 1997), 51.

1. Not a Sleeping Beauty

1. Yosano Akiko, "The Day the Mountains Move" (1911), trans. Laurel Rasplica Rodd, in Freedman, *Essential Feminist Reader*, 184. Akiko was asked to write this poem (titled "Sozorogoto" in Japanese) for the first issue of the women's magazine *Seitō*. Yukiko Tanaka argues that Akiko's poems demonstrate her identification with eleventh- and twelfth-century Japanese women court poets, including *The Pillow Book* author Sei Shōnagon, rather than her immediate predecessors in Japanese literary production. Yukiko Tanaka, *Women Writers of Meiji and Taishō Japan: Their Lives, Works, and Critical Reception, 1868–1926* (Jefferson, N.C.: McFarland, 2000), 96–98.

2. Chicago & New Haven Women's Liberation Rock Bands, "Mountain Moving Day," on *Mountain Moving Day*, LP (1972). Weisstein's widely published 1968 article on psychological constructions of women has been described as "a catalyst for [the] feminist awakening" of many of her fellow psychologists; Weisstein spent the later years of her life managing chronic fatigue syndrome while continuing her research and activism from bed. Laura C. Ball and Alexandra Rutherford, "Naomi Weisstein (1939–2015)," *American Psychologist* 71, no. 1 (January 2016): 77; Jesse Lemisch and Naomi Weisstein, "Remarks on Naomi Weisstein," Chicago Women's Liberation Union Herstory Project, 1997, https://www.cwluherstory.org; Naomi Weisstein, "Days of Celebration," *Red Wedge*, July 1, 2015, http://www.redwedgemagazine.com.

3. Laurie Anderson, quoted in Lydia Yee, *Laurie Anderson, Trisha Brown, Gordon Matta-Clark: Pioneers of the Downtown Scene, New York 1970s* (Munich: Prestel, 2011), 78.

4. Barbara Kruger, *Untitled (Your Body Is a Battleground)*, 1989, photographic silkscreen on vinyl, 112 × 112 inches, The Broad, Los Angeles.

5. Updated editions of *Our Bodies, Ourselves* were published for decades afterward. Boston Women's Health Book Collective, ed., *Our Bodies, Ourselves* (New York: Simon & Schuster, 1973). See Barbara Deck, "The

Birth of Our Bodies Ourselves: Remembering the 1969 Female Liberation Conference," Our Bodies Ourselves, accessed November 18, 2025, https://www.ourbodiesourselves.org.

6. Boston Women's Health Book Collective, *Our Bodies, Ourselves,* 83; Silvia Federici, "On Elder Care Work and the Limits of Marxism," in *Revolution at Point Zero: Housework, Reproduction, and Feminist Struggle* (Brooklyn, N.Y.: Autonomedia, 2012), 119; Audre Lorde, *"A Burst of Light" and Other Essays* (1988; repr., Mineola, N.Y.: Ixia Press, 2017), 130.

7. RoseLee Goldberg, *Laurie Anderson* (New York: Harry N. Abrams, 2000), 56, 38, 12.

8. See Sean Cubitt, "Laurie Anderson: Myth, Management and Platitude," in *Art Has No History! The Making and Unmaking of Modern Art,* ed. John Roberts (London: Verso, 1994), 278–96; Silvija Jestrovic, "From the Ice Cube Stage to Simulated Reality: Place and Displacement in Laurie Anderson's Performances," *Contemporary Theater Review* 14, no. 1 (February 2004): 25–37; Ainhoa Kaiero Claver, "Deconstructing the Singer: The Concerts of Laurie Anderson," in Symonds and Taylor, *Gestures of Music Theater,* 165–77; Eddie Paterson, "Post-Punk Monologue and the Performances of Laurie Anderson," in *The Contemporary American Monologue: Performance and Politics* (London: Bloomsbury Methuen Drama, 2015), 79–101.

9. Anderson repeatedly returns to the phrase "nerve bible," titling both a performance and a monograph *Stories from the Nerve Bible.* She explains that the phrase, to her, means "the body," and the retrospective book *Stories from the Nerve Bible* "is my way of looking for something, of frisking myself, like looking for keys." Laurie Anderson, *Stories from the Nerve Bible: A Twenty-Year Retrospective* (New York: Perennial, 1993), 6. We can understand sleep—as one of Anderson's many body-based practices—as a technology for "frisking" herself, searching her body for interpretations of her environment that do not arise in the same way in her waking brain.

10. Laurie Anderson, in brochure for *Laurie Anderson: The Weather,* multimedia exhibition, Hirshhorn Museum, Washington, D.C., 2021–22.

11. Laurie Anderson, wall text written for the section "*Institutional Dream Series,* Photographs, 1972–73," in *Laurie Anderson: The Weather* exhibition at the Hirshhorn Museum.

12. Sigmund Freud, *On Dreams* [1901], trans. James Strachey (New York: W. W. Norton, 1952), 40.

13. Quoted in Goldberg, *Laurie Anderson,* 140. In 2021, Anderson ended her first public lecture as Harvard University's Charles Eliot Norton Professor in Poetry with a Pillow Speaker performance. She also told a purportedly true story about a moment of bodily fusion with this technology: an experience when acid leaked from the speaker and the speaker "glued itself" to the roof of Anderson's mouth. She found a pharmacist who "just got a Q-tip and some alcohol and *pop* pried it out and handed it back to me. No comment." Laurie Anderson, "The River," lecture in the series

"Spending the War with You: Virtual Backgrounds," Charles Eliot Norton Lectures, Harvard University, February 10, 2021.

14. For another reading of public sleep performance in libraries, see Sarah Sharma's study of how unhoused people must "perform," or feign, alertness while attempting to sleep (against regulations) in the Vancouver Public Library. Sarah Sharma, "Conclusion: Toward a Temporal Public," in *In the Meantime: Temporality and Cultural Politics* (Durham, N.C.: Duke University Press, 2014).

15. Kleege uses "blind" to encompass a range of visual impairments. Georgina Kleege, *More Than Meets the Eye: What Blindness Brings to Art* (New York: Oxford University Press, 2017), 2–4.

16. Cubitt, "Laurie Anderson," 279.

17. Laurie Anderson, interview in *Art, Performance, Media: 31 Interviews*, ed. Nicholas Zurbrugg (Minneapolis: University of Minnesota Press, 2004), 29.

18. Anderson, *Stories from the Nerve Bible*, 11.

19. In *Night Life* (2006), Anderson drew her dreams rather than writing them down. In a short essay included in the published collection of her *Night Life* drawings, Anderson calls dreams "the secret language of the body." While we experience REM sleep, Anderson writes, "the set of neurons that sends information to the brain about the location of the head and body opens two new channels—audio and visual. . . . Along with this idling brain activity comes the invention of the shape shifting dream body, the body that can fly or float or just hang around observing the action." Laurie Anderson, *Night Life* (Paris: Edition 7L, 2006), unpaginated.

20. Michel Foucault, *Discipline and Punish: The Birth of the Prison* [1975], trans. Alan Sheridan (New York: Vintage Books, 1995).

21. Laura Mulvey, "Visual Pleasure and Narrative Cinema," *Screen* 16, no. 3 (Autumn 1975): 11.

22. Udo Kultermann's survey of sleeping women in Western art history builds on research conducted by German archaeologist Sibylle von Cles-Reden for her monograph *The Realm of the Great Goddess: The Story of the Megalith Builders* (London: Thames and Hudson, 1961). Kultermann describes a terra-cotta statue called *Sleeping Lady* found in Malta. Cles-Reden suggests the statue might depict a priestess whose dreams served an oracular and perhaps healing function. Kultermann dates the "specifically gender-oriented representation of a sleeping woman observed by a male partner" later, to ancient Rome. Udo Kultermann, "Woman Asleep and the Artist," *Artibus et Historiae* 11, no. 22 (1990): 131–34.

23. Hugh Ryan, *The Women's House of Detention: A Queer History of a Forgotten Prison* (New York: Bold Type Books, 2022), 21–27.

24. Yoko Ono, *Cut Piece*, 1965, 16 mm film (black-and-white, sound) transferred to video, Walker Art Center, New York.

25. Valie Export (also styled VALIE EXPORT), "On Work of the Late 1960s: In Conversation with Devin Fore," in *Sexuality*, ed. Amelia Jones

(London: Whitechapel Gallery, 2014), 104. Export's *Action Pants* or *Genital Panic* performances may not have happened in the live scenarios she describes; Mechtild Widrich characterizes this work as "'imaginary' performance." Mechtild Widrich, "Can Photographs Make It So? Several Outbreaks of VALIE EXPORT's Genital Panic 1969–2005," in *Photography Between Poetry and Politics: The Critical Position of the Photographic Medium in Contemporary Art,* ed. Hilde Van Gelder and Helen Westgeest (Leuven: Leuven University Press, 2008), 61.

26. Judy Chicago and Miriam Schapiro, "Female Imagery (1973)," in Jones, *Sexuality,* 73–75.

27. Danielle Shang, "Yayoi Kusama, *Narcissus Garden,*" Smarthistory: The Center for Public Art History, August 9, 2015, https://smarthistory.org.

28. Rosalyn Baxandall and Linda Gordon, "Wonder Woman," in *Dear Sisters: Dispatches from the Women's Liberation Movement,* ed. Rosalynn Baxandall and Linda Gordon (New York: Basic Books, 2000), 123; Byllye Y. Avery, "Breathing Life into Ourselves: The Evolution of the National Black Women's Health Project," in Baxandall and Gordon, *Dear Sisters,* 131–33.

29. Boston Women's Health Book Collective, *Our Bodies, Ourselves,* 14, 3.

30. Anderson added, "I realized that photography is a kind of mugging—a kind of assault." Quoted in Goldberg, *Laurie Anderson,* 41. This 1973 project has also been titled *Object/Objection/Objectivity,* echoing the language of the art "object" from feminist critiques of visual art. Laurie Anderson, *Fully Automated Nikon,* photography, 1973. Anderson's work grew more explicitly feminist in the 1980s, and she continued to interfere directly in gendered visual logics as a form of feminist protest through her work with the Women's Action Coalition in the 1990s. See Cubitt, "Laurie Anderson," 286–87; Anderson, *Stories from the Nerve Bible,* 263.

31. Anderson, quoted in "When the Sky Was the Limit," in Yee, *Laurie Anderson, Trisha Brown, Gordon Matta-Clark,* 22.

32. Nocturnal courtrooms have a long history as sites where people vulnerable to the legal system are used as free entertainment by wealthy tourists. The women's court's own publicity materials in the 1910s encouraged people to visit the court for its entertainment value, and slummers compared it to visiting Harlem or Chinatown, suggesting that racial difference contributed to their pleasure in viewing. Just over a decade after *Institutional Dream Series,* the television series *Night Court,* set in a Manhattan municipal courtroom, began its nine-season run on network television. In the 2010s, a tourism reporter from the United Kingdom, sent to check whether the Manhattan court's "guaranteed drama, character development, [and] plot twists" were all that travel guides had advertised, found his experience closer to "extreme voyeurism," more of an indictment of the U.S. legal process than a free source of live entertainment. The most dramatic event was a call for another spectator to put away their phone—echoing Anderson and Pontius's experience of being asked to stop using their camera. Ryan, *Women's House of Detention,* 24; Callum

McCulloch, "NYC's Night Court Is the Weirdest Tourist Attraction in the World," *The Tab US,* July 21, 2016.

33. Some records of *Institutional Dream Series* also include a one-sentence description of a fourth performance at the South Street Seaport, conducted between the university library and night court performances.

34. Nudelman, *Fighting Sleep,* 129–33.

35. Goldberg, *Laurie Anderson,* 15.

36. Boston Women's Health Book Collective, *Our Bodies, Ourselves,* 8.

37. Julie Lynette McGuire, "The Language of Laurie Anderson" (PhD diss., Indiana University, 2002), 29–30; Samuel Austin McBride, "Performing Laurie Anderson: The Construction of a Persona" (PhD diss., University of California, Riverside, 1997), 129–30.

38. Goldberg, *Laurie Anderson,* 38. After graduating with her MFA, during the years she was making *Institutional Dream Series,* Anderson also taught art classes around New York City. Julie McGuire argues that Anderson developed the storytelling technique she uses in many of her live performances, as well as the dream narratives in *Institutional Dream Series,* while teaching, in an attempt to better engage her students' attention. In a class Anderson renamed "Skrooples," she raised moral questions about art, including "Why do people bother to make art?" and "What purpose does it serve?" The art-making practices and political interventions that become more obvious in Anderson's later work show up in the early 1970s in smaller interventions like her public sleeping and pedagogical experiments. McGuire, "Language of Laurie Anderson," 23–24.

39. Anderson, *Stories from the Nerve Bible,* 264. In a 1991–92 interview, Anderson described pamphlets similar to *A Feminist Bestiary* as "cartoons about men, women, and power" that she distributed to passersby. Laurie Anderson, "The Speed of Change," in *The Twentieth Century Performance Reader,* ed. Michael Huxley and Noel Witts (London: Routledge, 1996), 17. Anderson has also retold the story of picketing the Playboy Club in her spoken-word piece "Listen, Honey," which she has inserted into larger performances including *Empty Places* (1989). See McGuire, "Language of Laurie Anderson," 31; Paterson, "Post-Punk Monologue," 98–100.

2. Fluorescent Bedrooms

1. Peggy Shaw, *Menopausal Gentleman,* in *A Menopausal Gentleman: The Solo Performances of Peggy Shaw,* ed. Jill Dolan (Ann Arbor: University of Michigan Press, 2011). All parenthetical page citations refer to this edition.

2. In the United States, the history of disallowing access to public spaces might be traced back to nineteenth-century "ugly laws," city statutes forbidding people with visible disabilities from using public thoroughfares. As Shaw was writing *Menopausal Gentleman* in the 1990s, new battles were being waged over public access, both for people with disabilities (under the newly minted Americans with Disabilities Act)

and for people with HIV/AIDS, due to stigma and misinformation about HIV transmission through casual contact. Today, the restroom remains a multipronged site of potential exclusion from public space: People with disabilities can be kept out by inaccessible design, nonbinary people by gendered exclusivity, and unhoused people by the lack of free public restrooms in most U.S. cities. See Susan M. Schweik, *The Ugly Laws: Disability in Public* (New York: New York University Press, 2009); Bess Williamson, *Accessible America: A History of Disability and Design* (New York: New York University Press, 2019); Gregory M. Herek, "AIDS and Stigma," *American Behavioral Scientist* 42, no. 7 (1999): 1106–16; Alison Kafer, *Feminist, Queer, Crip* (Bloomington: Indiana University Press, 2013).

3. Peggy Shaw, "How I Learned Theater," in *Cast Out: Queer Lives in Theater,* ed. Robin Bernstein (Ann Arbor: University of Michigan Press, 2006), 29. On queer solo performance as a genre that includes candid discussions of personal experience, see Holly Hughes and David Román, "*O Solo Homo*: An Introductory Conversation," in *O Solo Homo: The New Queer Performance,* ed. Holly Hughes and David Román (New York: Grove Press, 1998), 1–16.

4. Stories of people living with breast cancer, HIV/AIDS, and other illnesses being encouraged to try to look healthy—or, conversely, to stay out of public life entirely—abound. In particularly, see Audre Lorde's description of being taught how to wear a prosthetic breast and Eve Sedgwick's consideration of whether to go out in public sporting one, two, or *three* breasts. Audre Lorde, *The Cancer Journals* (1980; repr., San Francisco: Aunt Lute Books, 2006); Eve Kosofsky Sedgwick, "White Glasses," *Yale Journal of Criticism* 5, no. 3 (January 1992): 193–208. ACT UP's direct actions involving the remains of people who died of HIV/AIDS also put bodies that the U.S. government neglected or ignored into public spaces, often spaces closely related to that state neglect. Debra Levine, "How to Do Things with Dead Bodies," *emisférica* 6, no. 1 (2009), https://hemisphericinstitute.org/en.

5. Hysteria was also sometimes called neurasthenia. The theater/cabaret and the clinic/hospital, Showalter argues, became mutually reinforcing sites for diagnosing hysterical women. Elaine Showalter, *Hystories: Hysterical Epidemics and Modern Media* (New York: Columbia University Press, 1997).

6. José Esteban Muñoz outlines this debate and establishes his stake in utopianism in *Cruising Utopia,* esp. 34–35, 90–95.

7. Shaw, "How I Learned Theater," 28–29. Shaw has also expressed her commitment to not reproducing violence in her theater as "I want to produce new images, not old lies." Peggy Shaw, *You're Just Like My Father,* in Hughes and Román, *O Solo Homo,* 180.

8. Shaw, "How I Learned Theater," 28–29. Caryl Churchill's 1983 play *Fen* (see chapter 3) and Philip Venables's 2016 opera version of Sarah Kane's 2000 play *4.48 Psychosis* (see chapter 6) both experiment, in different

ways, with sidestepping the conventional dramaturgy Shaw describes here as "a rape . . . or a woman killed."

9. Along with the printed text of *Menopausal Gentleman,* my discussion of the performance draws on a recording of Shaw performing in Buffalo, New York, archived by New York University's Hemispheric Institute of Performance and Politics. Peggy Shaw, *Menopausal Gentleman,* directed by Rebecca Taichman, Hallwalls Contemporary Art Center, Buffalo, N.Y., 1998, https://hemisphericinstitute.org/en.

10. David Román, in his study of solo performances about AIDS by gay men, argues that the "dialectical relationship" between the performer in real life and the version of himself he presents onstage, especially in ostensibly autobiographical work, is heightened for the "already marked body" of a gay man. David Román, *Acts of Intervention: Performance, Gay Culture, and AIDS* (Bloomington: Indiana University Press, 1998), 135. Here, I suggest that the title *Menopausal Gentleman* and Shaw's appearance in drag do similar work to heighten the tension between multiple selves in Shaw's performance.

11. In *Menopausal Gentleman* and many other performances (particularly *Last Gasp WFH*), Shaw has discussed how her use of terms like *lesbian, butch,* and *queer* has evolved over her decades of participation in queer and trans communities. Split Britches, *Last Gasp WFH,* Zoom, La MaMa Experimental Theatre Club, New York, 2020, http://www.split-britches.com.

12. "Bawdy, adj.[2]," *OED Online,* last modified 2006, http://www.oed.com.

13. Marcia L. Ferguson, review of *Menopausal Gentleman,* by Peggy Shaw, *Theater Journal* 50, no. 3 (1998): 374–75.

14. Shaw first met Ross in 1972; three years later, seventy-three portraits of Ross, a Black trans woman, appeared without naming Ross as the subject in Andy Warhol's series *Ladies and Gentlemen.* Neil Printz and the Andy Warhol Foundation first identified Ross in these prints in 2014. Shaw, "How I Learned Theater," 25; Sotheby's, "Andy Warhol | Ladies and Gentlemen (Wilhelmina Ross) (1975)," Artsy, 2016, https://www.artsy.net; Elizabeth Hoover, "Andy Warhol's Trans Subjects Finally Get Named," *Paper,* August 24, 2018, http://www.papermag.com.

15. Quoted in Jill Dolan, "Introduction: A Certain Kind of Successful," in Dolan, *A Menopausal Gentleman,* 11. Jill Dolan argues for the foundational relationship between Shaw's working-class background and her artistic production: "The kind of work [Shaw] has produced and the venues in which she has worked have precluded a leisured, or even middle-class, life. Creating performance from scratch as Split Britches did, later devising the solo pieces . . . based on invitations from colleges and universities, touring down-at-the-heel performance spaces—all of this has required Shaw to husband her resources and curb her expectations about creature comforts. As a result, Shaw is one of the few contemporary American artists with a clear analysis about class issues." Dolan, "Introduction," 10–11.

Of the possibility of getting government funding herself, Shaw has said, "I couldn't understand why the government would give me, an anarchist queer, any money." Shaw, "How I Learned Theater," 28.

16. Peggy Shaw, interview by Craig Lucas, *BOMB Magazine,* no. 69 (Fall 1999): 36.

17. Notable examples of such scholarship are Elin Diamond, "Brechtian Theory/Feminist Theory: Toward a Gestic Feminist Criticism" (1987), in *Sourcebook on Feminist Theater and Performance: On and Beyond the Stage,* ed. Carol Martin (London: Routledge, 1996), 120–35; Kate Davy, "Reading Past the Heterosexual Impulse: Dress Suits to Hire," *TDR: The Drama Review* 33, no. 1 (1989): 153–70; Jill Dolan, *The Feminist Spectator as Critic* (Ann Arbor: University of Michigan Press, 1991); Sue-Ellen Case, ed., *Split Britches: Lesbian Practice/Feminist Performance* (London: Routledge, 1996).

18. Shaw has collaborated repeatedly with Holly Hughes, a member of the NEA Four, whose artist grants were cut in 1990. As Román notes, the National Endowment for the Arts fully eliminated its grants for "solo theater artists" in the mid-1990s. Román, *Acts of Intervention,* 124. Reflecting this lack of funding, just after she premiered *Menopausal Gentleman,* Shaw estimated her credit card debt at $15,000 to $20,000. Shaw, interview by Lucas, 2. Stephen Greer considers the ways that solo performance might be complicit in a neoliberal economic system that expects individual artists to prove their value by earning their own funding (as part of a larger rationale of "compulsive individuation") but ultimately argues that solo performance is able to leverage a "powerful critique" of the neoliberal ethos it appears to accommodate. Stephen Greer, *Queer Exceptions: Solo Performance in Neoliberal Times* (Manchester: Manchester University Press, 2019), 2.

19. Dolan, "Introduction," 11–12.

20. Sarah Schulman, *Let the Record Show: A Political History of ACT UP New York, 1987–1993* (New York: Farrar, Straus and Giroux, 2021), 633–40.

21. Sedgwick and Audre Lorde each died of breast cancer at age fifty-eight. Sedgwick describes the high suicide rates among queer youth in the opening essay of her book *Tendencies.* Eve Kosofsky Sedgwick, "Queer and Now," in *Tendencies* (Durham, N.C.: Duke University Press, 1993), 1. On lesbian deaths from breast cancer, see Mairead Sullivan, "Marked for Life: Breast Cancer and Lesbian Biopolitics," in *Lesbian Death: Desire and Danger Between Feminist and Queer* (Minneapolis: University of Minnesota Press, 2022), 49–66.

22. Jaclyn Pryor, "Peggy Shaw Pension Fund," Indiegogo, accessed January 28, 2019, https://www.indiegogo.com.

23. The differences between Shaw's performance in Buffalo and her printed text suggest that Shaw makes small improvisatory changes at any given performance. For the 1998 recording in Buffalo, her second worry was not being a bad mother but needing to get up to move the car in the morning.

24. Anne Fausto-Sterling, "Menopause: The Storm Before the Calm," in

Feminist Theory and the Body: A Reader, ed. Janet Price and Margrit Shildrick (London: Taylor & Francis, 1999), 170–71.

25. In 1993, Betty Friedan's *The Fountain of Age* was discrediting what Friedan saw as an exaggerated obsession with menopause among what now seems like a very small number of feminist writers. Elizabeth Siegel Watkins, *The Estrogen Elixir: A History of Hormone Replacement Therapy in America* (Baltimore: Johns Hopkins University Press, 2007), 227, 234–37.

26. Women's Health Initiative, "WHI Hormone Trial Findings Questions and Answers," accessed January 2, 2019, https://www.whi.org (page no longer available). Subsequent research has added nuance to the potential health outcomes of hormone therapy.

27. On feminist investigations into bodily exhaustion, see Susan Wendell, *The Rejected Body: Feminist Philosophical Reflections on Disability* (New York: Routledge, 1996); Ann Cvetkovich, *Depression: A Public Feeling* (Durham, N.C.: Duke University Press, 2012); Porochista Khakpour, *Sick: A Memoir* (New York: Harper Perennial, 2018); Emily K. Abel, *Sick and Tired: An Intimate History of Fatigue* (Chapel Hill: University of North Carolina Press, 2021); Samantha Harvey, *The Shapeless Unease: A Year of Not Sleeping* (New York: Grove Press, 2020); Emily Nagoski and Amelia Nagoski, *Burnout: The Secret to Unlocking the Stress Cycle* (New York: Ballantine Books, 2019). While several popular books prescribe more sleep to people of all genders, they tend to advocate sleep as a means toward superhuman productivity and health for the otherwise average person, rather than plumbing the thornier relationship between illness and exhaustion.

28. Lorde, *Cancer Journals,* 9.

29. Lorde, *Cancer Journals,* 29.

30. Leo Bersani, "Is the Rectum a Grave?" (1987), in *"Is the Rectum a Grave?" and Other Essays* (Chicago: University of Chicago Press, 2010), 30.

31. Bersani, "Is the Rectum a Grave?," 22; Fausto-Sterling, "Menopause," 176.

32. Shaw, interview by Lucas, 38.

33. Elin Diamond, *Unmaking Mimesis: Essays on Feminism and Theater* (London: Routledge, 1997), 159.

34. Diamond, *Unmaking Mimesis,* 181.

35. Shaw, "How I Learned Theater," 29.

36. Pryor, "Peggy Shaw Pension Fund."

37. Peggy Shaw and Lois Weaver, "Ruff," *PAJ: A Journal of Performance and Art* 40, no. 2 (2018): 108–32. All quotations from this work appear on pages 130–31.

3. Insomniac Housewives

1. Berwick Street Collective, *Nightcleaners Part 1* (London: Lux, 1975).

2. David Graeber, "The Beginning of Something Yet to Be Determined (1971–Present)," in *Debt: The First 5,000 Years* (Brooklyn, N.Y.: Melville House, 2011), 361–92.

3. Arlie Russell Hochschild, *The Second Shift* (1989; repr., New York: Avon Books, 1997).

4. *Patriarchy* is a contested term within this body of research. It can refer specifically to societies in which fathers exercise power over their female offspring or, more broadly, to societies in which men exercise more power than women. I use the term here to capture Marxist feminist discourse in the 1970s but avoid it otherwise because of this definitional fuzziness. For analyses of the sexual division of labor that emerged from this fruitful period, see Michèle Barrett, *Women's Oppression Today* (London: Verso, 1980); Angela Y. Davis, *Women, Race and Class* (New York: Vintage, 1983); Silvia Federici, *Caliban and the Witch* (London: Pluto, 2004). On the ongoing project of international materialist feminist organizing, see Cinzia Arruzza, Tithi Bhattacharya, and Nancy Fraser, *Feminism for the 99%: A Manifesto* (London: Verso, 2019); Gago, *Feminist International.*

5. These raids illustrate a racial-sexual respectability politics that treated the household maintenance and sexual behavior of single Black mothers as available for public scrutiny. Abigail Goldman, "Welfare Rights Pioneer Tillmon-Blackston Dies; Activism: In the 1960s, a Single Mother in a Watts Housing Project Helped Form a Group That Sought Better Treatment and Services for the Poor," *Los Angeles Times,* November 25, 1995.

6. Wages for Housework was an international movement that sought solidarity between working-class women in wealthy countries and women in countries impoverished by colonization. See Louise Toupin, *Wages for Housework: A History of an International Feminist Movement, 1972–77* (Vancouver: University of British Columbia Press, 2022). Amia Srinivasan has pointed to the continuity of 1970s-era feminist international campaigns in the work of Polish and Argentinian feminists involved in organizing Global Women's Strikes in the twenty-first century. Amia Srinivasan, "Who Lost the Sex Wars?," *New Yorker,* September 6, 2021.

7. Churchill, who read English literature at Oxford, married and had children in the 1960s. She has described her own early life as an upper-middle-class housewife as "claustrophobic." Sarah Lyall, "The Mysteries of Caryl Churchill," Theater, *New York Times,* December 5, 2004.

8. The role of modern naturalist drama in class struggle has been a topic of debate since the late nineteenth century, with critics such as Émile Zola, György Lukács, and Raymond Williams weighing in. Among early critics of modern drama, Emma Goldman is uniquely attentive to naturalist drama's confrontation with the problems of marriage. In a lecture on Ibsen's *A Doll's House,* Goldman asks, "Is there anything more degrading to woman than to live with a stranger and bear him children?" Emma Goldman, *The Social Significance of the Modern Drama* (1914; repr., New York: Applause Books, 2000), 12.

9. On Marxist feminist theories of the housewife and social reproduction, see also Juliet Mitchell, *Woman's Estate* (1971; repr., New York: Verso, 2015); Federici, *Revolution at Point Zero.*

10. Dalla Costa and James, *Women and the Subversion of the Community,* 40.

11. Caryl Churchill, *Three More Sleepless Nights* (1980), in *Churchill: Shorts* (London: Nick Hern Books, 1990), 245–74. All parenthetical page citations refer to this edition. *Three More Sleepless Nights* opened at the Soho Poly in London in 1980.

12. Milton Shulman, "Venom at Bedtime," *Evening Standard* (London), August 6, 1980.

13. Caryl Churchill, *Three More Sleepless Nights, Rehearsed Reading,* directed by debbie tucker green, Royal Court Jerwood Theatre Downstairs, London, 2008, audio recording, British Library Sound and Moving Image Collection.

14. Nobby Clark, production images from *Three More Sleepless Nights,* August 5, 1980, Theatre and Performance Archives, Victoria and Albert Museum.

15. Churchill developed the one-act form she used for *Three More Sleepless Nights* by writing radio plays while caring for her young children, and she used short plays to test new dramaturgical strategies for full-length plays. The interrupting dialogue in the first scene of *Three More Sleepless Nights* served as a test run for Churchill's use of this style of dialogue throughout the opening dinner scene in the first act of *Top Girls.*

16. Shulman, "Venom at Bedtime."

17. Eric Shorter, "Signs All Couples Will Recognise . . . ," *Daily Telegraph,* August 1980.

18. Laurie Stone, "Labor of Love," *Village Voice,* June 7, 1983.

19. *Fen* was first performed January 20, 1983, at the University of Essex Theatre and then transferred to London's Almeida Theatre and eventually to the Royal Court.

20. Rob Ritchie, ed., *The Joint Stock Book: The Making of a Theatre Collective* (London: Methuen, 1987); Mary Chamberlain, *Fenwomen: A Portrait of Women in an English Village* (Boston: Routledge & Kegan Paul, 1983).

21. Caryl Churchill, *Fen,* in *Plays 2* (London: Methuen Drama, 1990), 143–92. All parenthetical page citations refer to this edition.

22. Jennie Stoller, quoted in Ritchie, *Joint Stock Book,* 152.

23. J. C. Trewin, "Fen . . . at the Royal Court Theatre, London," *Birmingham Post,* August 1, 1983.

24. R. Darren Gobert, *The Theatre of Caryl Churchill* (New York: Bloomsbury, 2014), 148.

25. Ritchie, *Joint Stock Book,* 28.

26. John Haynes, Leslie McIntyre, and Martha Swope, production images from *Fen,* July 27, 1983, Theatre and Performance Archives, Victoria and Albert Museum.

27. Elin Diamond attends to the representational politics of this staging when Val walks back onstage moments after dying. This "exten[sion of] the boundaries of what can be seen or said as representation" is key,

Diamond argues, to the political success of the play, "not because a redemptive socialism is asserted but because the representation apparatus has been suggestively implicated as a tool of social oppression *and* as a means of resistance." Diamond, *Unmaking Mimesis,* 93–94.

28. Readings of *Fen*'s closing nightmare scene have illuminated anticapitalist ecological activism, Brechtian critiques of representation, tensions between realist and surrealist dramatic forms, and imaginative strategies of communication among women. See Diamond, *Unmaking Mimesis*; Sheila Rabillard, "*Fen* and the Production of a Feminist Ecotheater," *Theater* 25, no. 1 (1994): 62–71; Elaine Aston, *Caryl Churchill* (Plymouth: Northcote House in association with the British Council, 2001), 69; Siân Helen Adiseshiah, *Churchill's Socialism: Political Resistance in the Plays of Caryl Churchill* (Newcastle: Cambridge Scholars, 2009), 160.

29. Ernst Bloch, *The Principle of Hope,* vol. 1 [1954], trans. Neville Plaice, Stephen Plaice, and Paul Knight (Cambridge, Mass.: MIT Press, 1986), 413.

30. Linda Bassett, quoted in M.L., "Success Story," *What's On,* August 4, 1983.

31. Anthony Masters, "Repression and Root Crops Beneath a Rustic Harrow," *The Times* (London), July 23, 1983.

32. *Far Away* opened in December 2000 at the Royal Court Upstairs, London, and transferred to the Albery Theatre in the West End in early 2001. The first American production, at New York Theatre Workshop in 2002, maintained the original director, Stephen Daldry, and designer, Ian MacNeil, but cast American actors.

33. Caryl Churchill, *Far Away* (New York: Theatre Communications Group, 2001). All parenthetical page citations refer to this edition.

34. Harper's investigation into why Joan is awake follows a convention of realist drama, the expectation of an underlying problem or past event that might explain present-day pathological behavior—in this case, Joan's insomnia. Diamond describes this convention as a development of "Ibsenite realism," as seen in late nineteenth-century plays that "endow the fallen woman of popular melodrama with the symptoms and etiology of the hysteric" and put the audience in the role of Freudian analysts who "read and interpret" the etiology, or cause, of the hysteria. Diamond, *Unmaking Mimesis,* 4, 30.

35. Ben Brantley, "Where Trust Is Smothered by Violence," Theater, *New York Times,* November 12, 2002; David Finkle, "Far Away," *TheaterMania,* November 12, 2002.

36. In her review of the New York Theatre Workshop production, Una Chaudhuri asserted, "It is chilling to see how easily moral and political concerns can be deflected, how easily the habit of not seeing what one sees can be cultivated." Una Chaudhuri, "Different Hats," *Hunter On-Line Theater Review* (blog), January 2003, http://www.hotreview.org. When the play was staged at the Young Vic in London in 2014, Aleks Sierz read the scene along similar lines, evoking the Holocaust through his allusion to

Hannah Arendt: "When the scenes are domestic, the idea of the banality of evil—simple acts committed by ordinary people—comes across strongly." Aleks Sierz, "Far Away, Young Vic Theatre," *Arts Desk,* November 13, 2014.

37. Matt Wolf, "Far Away," *Variety,* December 10, 2000.

38. Simon Stephens, quoted in Sierz, "Far Away, Young Vic Theatre."

39. Charles Isherwood, "Far Away," *Variety,* November 11, 2002; Lyn Gardner, "Far Away," *The Guardian,* May 28, 2010.

40. Michael Billington, "Far Away," *The Guardian,* December 2, 2000.

41. On sleep deprivation as a common component of domestic violence, see Pam Lowe, Cathy Humphreys, and Simon J. Williams, "Night Terrors: Women's Experiences of (Not) Sleeping Where There Is Domestic Violence," *Violence Against Women* 13, no. 6 (June 2007): 549–61.

4. Bedtime Across the Border

1. See Kathi Weeks, "Abolition of the Family: The Most Infamous Feminist Proposal," *Feminist Theory* 24, no. 3 (2023): 433–53. My understanding of the material and ideological work of the family is also shaped here by trans/queer and Indigenous critiques, specifically Sarah Schulman, *Ties That Bind: Familial Homophobia and Its Consequences* (New York: New Press, 2009); Kim TallBear, "Identity Is a Poor Substitute for Relating: Genetic Ancestry, Critical Polyamory, Property, and Relations," in *Routledge Handbook of Critical Indigenous Studies,* ed. Brendan Hokowhitu et al. (London: Routledge, 2022).

2. Hazel V. Carby, "White Woman Listen! Black Feminism and the Boundaries of Sisterhood," in *The Empire Strikes Back: Race and Racism in 70s Britain,* ed. Centre for Contemporary Cultural Studies (London: Centre for Contemporary Cultural Studies, University of Birmingham, 1982), 212–35.

3. Barbara Ehrenreich and Arlie Russell Hochschild, eds., *Global Woman: Nannies, Maids, and Sex Workers in the New Economy* (New York: Holt, 2004); Eileen Boris and Rhacel Salazar Parreñas, eds., *Intimate Labors: Cultures, Technologies, and the Politics of Care* (Stanford, Calif.: Stanford University Press, 2010).

4. Regina José Galindo, *Regina José Galindo* (Milan: Silvana, 2011), 154–55. The interview quoted was originally published in 2009 in the newspaper *La Verdad* in Murcia, Spain, on the occasion of the Fifty-Third Venice Biennale.

5. Margaret Talbot, "The Lost Children," *New Yorker,* February 24, 2008, https://www.newyorker.com.

6. As of 2024, the minimum required number of immigrant detention beds was set at 34,000. Brianna Nofil, *The Migrant's Jail: An American History of Mass Incarceration* (Princeton, N.J.: Princeton University Press, 2024), 217–18.

7. Angela Davis locates the U.S. "prison boom" in the 1980s, alongside "the dismantling of social service programs such as Aid to Families of

Dependent Children," and notes that, while men make up the majority of incarcerated people in the United States, women began to be incarcerated in much higher numbers in this decade as well. Angela Y. Davis, *Are Prisons Obsolete?* (New York: Seven Stories Press, 2003), 65. Trans and queer people were also incarcerated as part of the 1980s War on Drugs and associated prison expansion and continue to be imprisoned at higher rates than the cis/straight population. Incarceration increased further in the 1990s, with the system often targeting the "working or workless poor." Morgan Bassichis, Alexander Lee, and Dean Spade, "Building an Abolitionist Trans and Queer Movement with Everything We've Got," in *Captive Genders: Trans Embodiment and the Prison Industrial Complex,* ed. Eric A. Stanley and Nat Smith (Edinburgh: AK Press, 2011), 15–40; Ruth Wilson Gilmore, *Golden Gulag: Prisons, Surplus, Crisis, and Opposition in Globalizing California* (Berkeley: University of California Press, 2007), 6, 15.

8. State interest in sleep as a weapon drives medical research into the effects of sleep loss. Sociologist of sleep Simon Williams compares sleep deprivation as a form of torture within prisons to the sleep deprivation experienced by women living in abusive relationships, noting that "sleep disruption may constitute both a *strategy* and an *effect* of violence." Simon J. Williams, *The Politics of Sleep: Governing (Un)Consciousness in the Late Modern Age* (New York: Palgrave Macmillan, 2011), 68. Williams suggests that sleep deprivation in prisons may be particularly cruel because sleep is a rare opportunity for an incarcerated person to mentally escape the conditions of imprisonment. Jonathan Crary argues that sleep and sensory deprivation were used jointly as torture and interrogation techniques at Guantánamo Bay and other extrajudicial prisons in order to "fabricat[e] a world that radically excludes the possibility of care, protection, or solace." Crary, *24/7,* 8. Incarcerated people within the United States have also argued that the prison system deploys sleep deprivation purposefully to harm prisoners, often in the guise of welfare measures like suicide checks that wake prisoners up every half hour. Sal Rodriguez, "'Suicide Checks' Lead to Extreme Sleep Deprivation at Pelican Bay Prison," *Solitary Watch* (blog), January 21, 2016, https://solitarywatch.org.

9. John Fuegi argues for Margarete Steffin's significant contributions to the text of *Mother Courage and Her Children,* particularly in the character of Kattrin and her death scene, which are the focus of my reading. John Fuegi, *Brecht and Company: Sex, Politics, and the Making of the Modern Drama* (New York: Grove Press, 1994), 380–81.

10. Unless otherwise noted, my source for all descriptions and images of Galindo's artwork is the artist's professional website: "Regina José Galindo," accessed September 19, 2022, https://www.reginajosegalindo.com. Translations from Spanish are my own.

11. Regina José Galindo and Madeline Murphy Turner, "On the Violence of the World: A Conversation with Regina José Galindo," trans. Jane Brodie, *Magazine | MoMA* (blog), January 12, 2021, https://www.moma.org.

12. Rebecca Schneider, *The Explicit Body in Performance* (London: Routledge, 1997), 20.

13. Schneider, *Explicit Body*, 184.

14. Karen Gonzalez Rice, *Long Suffering: American Endurance Art as Prophetic Witness* (Ann Arbor: University of Michigan Press, 2016), 1.

15. Lilian G. Mengesha, "Defecting Witness: The Difficulty in Watching Regina José Galindo's PERRA," *TDR: The Drama Review* 61, no. 2 (Summer 2017): 145.

16. Foucault, *Discipline and Punish*.

17. Klein, *Shock Doctrine*, 294.

18. Galindo and Turner, "On the Violence of the World."

19. Artpace was founded in the 1990s by artist, philanthropist, and contemporary art collector Linda Pace, daughter of the inventors of Pace Foods' picante sauce. Appropriately for a sleep performance, Artpace describes itself as a "laboratory of dreams." "About," Artpace San Antonio, accessed January 13, 2023, https://artpace.org; Erika Arredondo-Haskins, "Linda Pace: Artist, Entrepreneur, and Philanthropist," *Handbook of Texas Online*, August 27, 2020 (updated October 24, 2022), https://www.tshaonline.org.

20. Galindo and Turner, "On the Violence of the World."

21. Galindo and Turner, "On the Violence of the World." Artistic decisions made based on the need to care for young children—and the conflicts between childcare and theatrical and artistic production schedules—also show up in the work of Peggy Shaw (chapter 2) and Caryl Churchill (chapter 3).

22. Talbot, "Lost Children."

23. Williams, *Politics of Sleep*, 66.

24. Talbot, "Lost Children."

25. Ruth Wilson Gilmore defines the carceral theory of incapacitation as a "geographical solution that purports to solve social problems by extensively and repeatedly removing people from disordered, deindustrialized milieus and depositing them somewhere else." Gilmore, *Golden Gulag*, 14. While Gilmore refers primarily to the domestic U.S. criminal-legal system, her description can also be applied to the U.S. system of immigrant detention, which holds migrants in place—neither the place they came from nor the place they want to be—while figuring out what to do with them. See Serena Parekh, "Refugee Camps and Urban Settlements: The Problem We Have Created," in *No Refuge: Ethics and the Global Refugee Crisis* (New York: Oxford University Press, 2020).

26. Talbot, "Lost Children."

27. Talbot, "Lost Children."

28. The Haitian children in U.S. detention in Guantánamo Bay were kept in solitary confinement and staged hunger strikes. Brianna Nofil, "Family Separation Is Officially Over, but History Suggests the U.S. Won't Find a Good Solution for Migrant Children," *Time*, June 28, 2018.

29. Davis, *Are Prisons Obsolete?*, 65–79.

30. Angela Y. Davis, *Freedom Is a Constant Struggle: Ferguson, Palestine, and the Foundations of a Movement* (Chicago: Haymarket Books, 2015), 105–6; Paisley Currah, "Incarceration, Identity Politics, and the Trans-Cis Divide," in *Sex Is as Sex Does: Governing Transgender Identity* (New York: New York University Press, 2022), 119–42; Mariame Kaba, *We Do This 'til We Free Us: Abolitionist Organizing and Transforming Justice* (Chicago: Haymarket Books, 2021), 30–53; Women of ACE (Aids Counseling and Education), Bedford Hills Correctional Facility, "Prison Issues and HIV: Voices," in *Women, AIDS, and Activism,* by ACT UP/New York Women and AIDS Book Group (Boston: South End Press, 1990), 143–55; Bree Carlton and Emma K. Russell, *Resisting Carceral Violence: Women's Imprisonment and the Politics of Abolition* (Cham, Switzerland: Palgrave Macmillan, 2018).

31. Gilmore, *Golden Gulag,* 16–17.

32. Klein, *Shock Doctrine,* 59.

33. Iris Marion Young, "The Logic of Masculinist Protection: Reflections on the Current Security State," *Signs: Journal of Women in Culture and Society* 29, no. 1 (2003): 1–25.

34. Franny Nudelman, "Interlude: Sleeper Agent," in *Fighting Sleep,* 63–90. On parents and children in undocumented immigrant families in the United States, see Karla Cornejo Villavicencio, *The Undocumented Americans* (New York: One World, 2020).

35. Caroline Rodrigues, "Performing Domination and Resistance Between Body and Space: The Transversal Activism of Regina José Galindo," *Journal of Media Practice* 12, no. 3 (December 2011): 291–303.

36. Nofil, *Migrant's Jail,* 220, 226. Nofil notes that ICE then maneuvered around the county's decision in order to contract directly with a private prison company, so immigration detention continues under different auspices in Williamson County, Texas.

37. Regina José Galindo, *America's Family Prison,* 2008, standard-definition video (color, silent), 54:49 min., MoMA Media and Performance, https://www.moma.org.

38. Diana Taylor, "Performing Gender: Las Madres de La Plaza de Mayo," in *Negotiating Performance: Gender, Sexuality, and Theatricality in Latin/o America,* ed. Diana Taylor and Juan Villegas (Durham, N.C.: Duke University Press, 1994), 275–305. See also Gilmore, *Golden Gulag,* 181–239.

39. Amy Littlefield, "The New Red Meat," *The Nation,* August 21–28, 2023.

40. "President Bush Acts to Promote Strong Families, Safe Children," president's remarks, press release, White House, January 17, 2002.

41. The Brecht Collective play *The Mother* presented working-class German women with the model of Pelagea Vlassova, a mother who becomes a revolutionary activist after her adult son is executed by the state. *Caucasian Chalk Circle* expands the category of motherhood beyond the biological, presenting the servant Grusha Vashnadze as the "true" mother

of the child of a deposed state leader because Grusha has cared for the child rather than trying to claim him as a possession.

42. Bertolt Brecht, *Mother Courage and Her Children: A Chronicle of the Thirty Years' War,* trans. Eric Bentley (New York: Grove Weidenfeld, 1963).

43. The rise of feminist performance studies as a scholarly field occasioned significant reappraisals of the feminist possibilities and limitations of Brecht's work, including his representation of women characters as political actors, the uncredited contributions of women coauthors to his plays, and his usefulness for feminist theater companies and critics. See Karen Laughlin, "Brechtian Theory and American Feminist Theatre," in *Re-Interpreting Brecht: His Influence on Contemporary Drama and Film,* ed. Pia Kleber and Colin Visser (Cambridge: Cambridge University Press, 1990), 147–60; Gay Gibson Cima, "Making a Difference," in "Brecht/'Brecht': A Symposium," *Theater* 25, no. 2 (1994): 24–41; Diamond, "Brechtian Theory/Feminist Theory"; Carol Martin, "Brecht, Feminism, and Chinese Theatre," *TDR: The Drama Review* 43, no. 4 (1999): 77–85.

44. Sara Lennox, "Women in Brecht's Works," *New German Critique* 14, no. 14 (1978): 86, 89.

45. Iris Smith, "Brecht and the Mothers of Epic Theater," *Theatre Journal* 43, no. 4 (1991): 495.

46. Kim Solga, "'Mother Courage' and Its Abject: Reading the Violence of Identification," *Modern Drama* 46, no. 3 (2003): 349.

47. Brecht, *Mother Courage and Her Children,* 119.

48. Solga, "'Mother Courage' and Its Abject," 352.

49. Brecht, *Mother Courage and Her Children,* 116.

50. See Galindo's participatory performances *Crisis Cloth* (New York: Exit Art, 2009) and *Crisis Blood* (Prague: Karlin Studios, Futura, Centre for Contemporary Art, 2009).

51. Rodrigues, "Performing Domination and Resistance," 299.

52. Loïc Wacquant, *Punishing the Poor: The Neoliberal Government of Social Insecurity* (Durham, N.C.: Duke University Press, 2009), 290.

53. Galindo and Turner, "On the Violence of the World."

5. Dreams from the Sickbed

1. Caryl Churchill, "A Poem for Irene Fornes," in *Conducting a Life: Reflections on the Theatre of Maria Irene Fornes,* ed. Maria M. Delgado and Caridad Svich (Lyme, N.H.: Smith and Kraus, 1999), xiv.

2. In a somewhat confrontational panel on lesbian literature, novelist Bertha Harris directly questioned Fornés on her sexuality, and Fornés replied, "I'm a lesbian." The panel moderator pressed the issue, but audience members later pushed back, seeing Harris's question as intrusive. In the same panel, Fornés described herself as "a Hispanic" who felt "a great difference between being from the United States and being a Hispanic." María Irene Fornés et al., "On the Beginnings of Lesbian Literature in the United States," in *Queer Representations: Reading Lives, Reading Cultures,*

ed. Martin B. Duberman (New York: New York University Press, 1997), 351. Yet playwright Caridad Svich, Fornés's student, has said that Fornés did not typically call herself Hispanic or Latina and "acknowledge[d] her debt to Chekhov, Ionesco, and Brecht before linking her work to the Iberian or Latin American masters." Caridad Svich, "Conducting a Life: A Tribute to Maria Irene Fornes," in Delgado and Svich, *Conducting a Life,* xvi. As noted previously, during her lifetime, Fornés published under the name Maria Irene Fornes (without accents).

3. Bruce Weber, "María Irene Fornés, Writer of Spare, Poetic Plays, Dies at 88," Obituaries, *New York Times,* October 31, 2018.

4. Marc Robinson, ed., *The Theater of Maria Irene Fornes* (Baltimore: Johns Hopkins University Press, 1999).

5. Peter Littlefield, director, writer, and stage manager, in Delgado and Svich, *Conducting a Life,* 187–88.

6. See William B. Worthen, *Modern Drama and the Rhetoric of Theater* (Berkeley: University of California Press, 1992), 187–94; Martin Puchner, *Stage Fright: Modernism, Anti-Theatricality, and Drama* (Baltimore: Johns Hopkins University Press, 2011), 81–118.

7. Susan Sontag, "Notes on 'Camp'" (1964), in *"Against Interpretation" and Other Essays* (New York: Picador, 2001), 280.

8. José Esteban Muñoz, *The Sense of Brown* (Durham, N.C.: Duke University Press, 2020), 126–27.

9. Evelyn Nakano Glenn, "From Servitude to Service Work: Historical Continuities in the Racial Division of Paid Reproductive Labor," *Signs: Journal of Women in Culture and Society* 18, no. 1 (1992): 3.

10. Lisa Lowe, *Immigrant Acts: On Asian American Cultural Politics* (Durham, N.C.: Duke University Press, 1996), 159–60.

11. María Irene Fornés, *Enter THE NIGHT,* in *Plays for the End of the Century,* ed. Bonnie Marranca (Baltimore: PAJ Publications, 1996), 121–80. All parenthetical page citations refer to this edition.

12. Marsha Kinder, review of *Jamón Jamón,* directed by Bigas Luna, *Film Quarterly* 47, no. 1 (Autumn 1993): 34.

13. Fornés, quoted in Robinson, *Theater of Maria Irene Fornes,* 221. Fornés's resistance to Freudian interpretation echoes Sontag's famed argument in "Against Interpretation," including her concluding call for an "erotics" rather than a "hermeneutics" of art. Sontag, *"Against Interpretation,"* 14.

14. Sedgwick, "White Glasses," 204.

15. Sontag, "Notes on 'Camp,'" 279–80.

16. Julia Lesage, "Artful Racism and Artful Rape in *Broken Blossoms,*" *Jump Cut,* no. 26 (December 1981); Naomi Greene, *From Fu Manchu to Kung Fu Panda: Images of China in American Film* (Honolulu: University of Hawai'i Press, 2014).

17. Greene, *From Fu Manchu to Kung Fu Panda,* 25–26. See also Robert G. Lee, *Orientals: Asian Americans in Popular Culture* (Philadelphia: Temple University Press, 1999); Barry Keith Grant, *Shadows of Doubt: Ne-*

gotiations of Masculinity in American Genre Films (Detroit: Wayne State University Press, 2011).

18. Esther Kim Lee, *Made-Up Asians: Yellowface During the Exclusion Era* (Ann Arbor: University of Michigan Press, 2022); Sheng-mei Ma, *Off-White: Yellowface and Chinglish by Anglo-American Culture* (New York: Bloomsbury Academic, 2020).

19. Lee, *Made-Up Asians,* 3.

20. Anne Anlin Cheng, *Ornamentalism* (New York: Oxford University Press, 2019), 4, 127.

21. Sheila Rabillard, review of *Enter THE NIGHT,* by María Irene Fornés, *Theater Journal* 46, no. 2 (1994): 283–84.

22. Glenda Frank, review of *Enter THE NIGHT,* by María Irene Fornés, *Back Stage: New York* 40, no. 52 (December 31, 1999): 37; Barry Johnson, "'Enter the Night': The Dream World of Maria Irene Fornes," *Oregon ArtsWatch* (blog), January 28, 2015, http://www.orartswatch.org.

23. David L. Eng, *Racial Castration: Managing Masculinity in Asian America* (Durham, N.C.: Duke University Press, 2001), 139, 165–66. See David Henry Hwang, *M. Butterfly* (New York: New American Library, 1989).

24. Summarizing the history of women of color working in domestic service in the United States in the twentieth century, Glenn writes, "A white woman's status comes from her relationship to a white man . . . she gains privileges from the relationship that blinds her to her own oppression, and . . . she therefore willingly participates in and gains advantages from the oppression of racial-ethnic women." Glenn, "From Servitude to Service Work," 17.

25. Robin Bernstein, "Staging Lesbian and Gay New York," in *The Cambridge Companion to the Literature of New York,* ed. Cyrus R. K. Patell (Cambridge: Cambridge University Press, 2010), 204.

26. Charles Ludlam died of AIDS in 1987. His *New York Times* obituary, written by a theater reporter, was the first for which the *Times* had permission to say the subject had been "suffering from AIDS." The obituary describes the New York theater community as "struggling daily—mostly, until now, in private, personal ways—with the devastation of AIDS." Jeremy Gerard, "Charles Ludlam, 44, Avant-Garde Artist of Theater, Is Dead," Obituaries, *New York Times,* May 29, 1987.

27. Rabillard, review, 284.

28. Brett Neilson, "Inside Shangri-La / Outside Globalisation: Remapping Orientalist Visions of Tibet," *Communal/Plural* 8, no. 1 (2000): 95–112. See also Greene, *From Fu Manchu to Kung Fu Panda,* 151–63.

29. Neilson, "Inside Shangri-La," 95.

30. Cheng, *Ornamentalism,* 2.

6. A Dormant Trans/Queer Archive

1. Sarah Kane, *4.48 Psychosis,* in *Complete Plays* (London: Methuen Drama, 2001), 203–45. All parenthetical page citations refer to this edition.

2. David Greig, "Introduction," in Kane, *Complete Plays,* ix–xviii.

3. Kim Solga, "*Blasted*'s Hysteria: Rape, Realism, and the Thresholds of the Visible," *Modern Drama* 50, no. 3 (2007): 369n1. See also Elaine Aston, *Feminist Views on the English Stage: Women Playwrights, 1990–2000* (Cambridge: Cambridge University Press, 2003); Elaine Aston, "Feeling the Loss of Feminism: Sarah Kane's *Blasted* and an Experiential Genealogy of Contemporary Women's Playwriting," in *Contemporary Women Playwrights: Into the Twenty-First Century,* ed. Penny Farfan and Lesley Ferris (Basingstoke: Palgrave Macmillan, 2013), 17–34.

4. Cristina Delgado-García, "Subversion, Refusal, and Contingency: The Transgression of Liberal-Humanist Subjectivity and Characterization in Sarah Kane's *Cleansed, Crave,* and *4.48 Psychosis,*" *Modern Drama* 55, no. 2 (2012): 241.

5. Although *trans* and *queer* have distinct definitions and histories, here I adapt Eric A. Stanley's term "anti-trans/queer violence," which names how "gendered and sexualized violence emerge together yet unfurl differently." Eric A. Stanley, *Atmospheres of Violence: Structuring Antagonism and the Trans/Queer Ungovernable* (Durham, N.C.: Duke University Press, 2021), 4. *4.48 Psychosis* is certainly an archive of anti-trans/queer violence. Moreover, I read *4.48 Psychosis* as an archive of trans/queer life and strategies of survival that also emerge together in the face of this violence and in the hope for something different.

6. Carolyn Dinshaw, *How Soon Is Now? Medieval Texts, Amateur Readers, and the Queerness of Time* (Durham, N.C.: Duke University Press, 2012), 10. For trans/queer readings of hostile or disinterested archives across temporal distance, see also Heather Love, *Feeling Backward: Loss and the Politics of Queer History* (Cambridge, Mass.: Harvard University Press, 2007); Zeb Tortorici, *Sins Against Nature: Sex and Archives in Colonial New Spain* (Durham, N.C.: Duke University Press, 2018); Saidiya V. Hartman, *Wayward Lives, Beautiful Experiments: Intimate Histories of Social Upheaval* (New York: W. W. Norton, 2019).

7. Dinshaw, *How Soon Is Now?,* 43.

8. James Macdonald, "'They Never Got Her,'" Stage, *Observer,* February 28, 1999.

9. Graham Saunders, *"Love Me or Kill Me": Sarah Kane and the Theatre of Extremes* (Manchester: Manchester University Press, 2002); Laurens De Vos, *Cruelty and Desire in the Modern Theater: Antonin Artaud, Sarah Kane, and Samuel Beckett* (Madison, N.J.: Fairleigh Dickinson University Press, 2011); Aleks Sierz, *In-Yer-Face Theatre: British Drama Today* (London: Faber and Faber, 2001).

10. Tinker, "This Disgusting Feast of Filth"; Michael Billington, "How Do You Judge a 75-Minute Suicide Note?," Stage, *The Guardian,* June 29, 2000.

11. Greig, "Introduction," xvi.

12. Ryan Claycomb, *Lives in Play: Autobiography and Biography on the Feminist Stage* (Ann Arbor: University of Michigan Press, 2014), 98–104.

13. Stanley, *Atmospheres of Violence,* 98, 93–94.

14. Kane does not use slashes in this text; I use them in quotations to mark line breaks.

15. Paisley Currah, "'If Sex Is Not a Biologic Phenomenon," in *Sex Is as Sex Does,* 44, emphasis added.

16. Hil Malatino, *Trans Care* (Minneapolis: University of Minnesota Press, 2020), 24, 5.

17. Malatino, *Trans Care,* 57.

18. Philip Venables, *4.48 Psychosis: A Chamber Opera in One Act After Sarah Kane* (London: Ricordi, 2016). Descriptions of the *4.48 Psychosis* opera in performance refer to the Prototype Festival / Royal Opera production directed by Ted Huffman at the Baruch Performing Arts Center in New York City in January 2019. Parenthetical page citations continue to refer to the edition of Kane's text cited above.

19. Sarah Kane, *4.48 Psychosis,* directed by James Macdonald, Royal Court Jerwood Theatre Upstairs, London, July 3, 2000, British Library Sound and Moving Image Collection. Sound design for this production was provided by Paul Arditti.

20. On other stagings of *4.48 Psychosis,* see Elzbieta Baraniecka, *Sublime Drama: British Theatre of the 1990s* (Berlin: De Gruyter, 2013); Glenn D'Cruz, "Teaching/Directing *4.48 Psychosis,*" *Australasian Drama Studies,* no. 57 (October 2010): 99–103; Martin Harries, "Still: Sarah Kane After Beckett and Joy Division," *Modern Drama* 60, no. 1 (2017): 1–24.

21. Arvind Gaur, quoted in Sumati Mehrishi Sharma, "Mind Games," *Indian Express,* December 31, 2005.

22. Delgado-García, "Subversion, Refusal, and Contingency," 246–47.

23. Philip Venables, *A Short Introduction to the Music of Philip Venables* (2017), YouTube, https://www.youtube.com/@philipvenables.

24. Pamela Demory, "Queer/Adaptation: An Introduction," in *Queer/Adaptation: A Collection of Critical Essays,* ed. Pamela Demory (Cham, Switzerland: Palgrave Macmillan, 2019), 1–13.

25. Andrew Sutherland, *Queer Opera* (Lanham, Md.: Lexington Books, 2023), 269.

26. Tim Ashley, "4.48 Psychosis Review—Venables Brings Sarah Kane's Savage Text to Musical Life," Music, *The Guardian,* May 25, 2016. See also Marc Bridle, "Philip Venables: 4.48 Psychosis," *Opera Today,* April 25, 2018.

27. *Queer Maximalism × Machine Dazzle,* September 10, 2022–February 19, 2023, Museum of Arts and Design, New York, https://madmuseum.org; Sissi Liu, "Designturgy, Being Queer: Taylor Mac Wears Machine Dazzle in 24 Decades," *Theatre Topics* 30, no. 3 (2020): 169–85.

28. Naomi Adele André, *Black Opera: History, Power, Engagement* (Urbana: University of Illinois Press, 2018), 20.

29. Stanley, *Atmospheres of Violence,* 95.

30. For a musicological reading of the use of percussion in this scene, see Tom Crathorne, "'Just a Word on a Stave and There Is the Opera': The

Interaction Between Music and Libretto in Philip Venables' *4.48 Psychosis*," *Tempo* 75, no. 298 (October 2021): 63–77.

31. Kane's use of "slept" echoes Tracey Emin's in her title *Everyone I Have Ever Slept With*. Kane and Emin were somewhat parallel figures in the provocative worlds of London theater and art in the 1990s; their first major pieces (Kane's *Blasted* and Emin's *Tent*) debuted only two years apart and attracted similar rage from reviewers.

32. Ashley, "4.48 Psychosis Review."

33. Catherine Clément, *Opera, or the Undoing of Women* (London: Virago Press, 1989), 3, 5. Although Clément's opening phrase is conventionally spelled "Lasciatemi morire," I maintain her spelling here. "Lasciatemi morire" is a repeated lyric in the recitative "Lamento d'Arianna," the only piece of music that has survived from Monteverdi's lost opera *L'Arianna* (1607–8), a retelling of the story of Ariadne/Arianna (soprano) and Theseus/Teseo (castrato). The libretto was written by Ottavio Rinuccini and survives in its entirety. While Clément cites this line from the early seventeenth century, the majority of her examples of women dying on opera stages come from nineteenth-century operas.

34. Wayne Koestenbaum, "The Queen's Throat: (Homo)Sexuality and the Art of Singing," in *Inside/Out: Lesbian Theories, Gay Theories*, ed. Diana Fuss (London: Taylor & Francis, 1991), 211; Corinne E. Blackmer and Patricia Juliana Smith, "Introduction," in *En Travesti: Women, Gender Subversion, Opera*, ed. Corinne E. Blackmer and Patricia Juliana Smith (New York: Columbia University Press, 1995), 2; Samuel D. Abel, *Opera in the Flesh: Sexuality in Operatic Performances* (Boulder, Colo.: Westview Press, 1996), 180.

35. The *Semiramide* anecdote opens Blackmer and Smith's introduction to *En Travesti*; the undergraduate lesbian is anonymous. On gender and voice type, see Felicia Miller, "Farinelli's Electric Hermaphrodite and the Contralto Tradition," in *The Work of Opera: Genre, Nationhood, and Sexual Difference*, ed. Richard Dellamora and Daniel Fischlin (New York: Columbia University Press, 1997), 73–92; Camille Rogers, "Listening for a Queer Utopia: Unexpected Pleasures in Baroque Castrato Roles," *Whatever: A Transdisciplinary Journal of Queer Theories and Studies* 2, no. 1 (2019): 71–96.

36. Koestenbaum, "The Queen's Throat," 230. Delightfully, Rand says she became interested in opera when it held her attention and kept her awake in the audience at a young age: "I saw my first opera at four and a half years old, didn't fall asleep as [my mother] expected and left the opera house, telling her that's what I wanted to do." "Talking to Acclaimed Soprano Gweneth-Ann Rand Who Rejects Elitism in Opera: Currently in *24 Italian Songs and Arias* at BAC," *Alt A Review*, March 8, 2022, https://alt-africa.com.

37. Robin Elliott, "Blacks and Blackface at the Opera," in *Opera in a Multicultural World: Coloniality, Culture, Performance*, ed. Mary I. Ingraham,

Joseph K. So, and Roy Moodley (New York: Routledge, 2015), 34–49. On otherwise-white opera stages, starting in the 1920s, Black singers were initially cast only in particular roles, typically in Orientalist narratives set in places that had been colonized by European nations. Lakmé, for example, is a Hindu priestess, and Aida is an Ethiopian princess enslaved in Egypt. Black American opera companies offered an alternative to this limited casting practice, and their casting of Black sopranos predated that on European stages by more than fifty years. On Leontyne Price playing Aida, see André, *Black Opera,* 17–20; see also Twila L. Perry, "Race on the Opera Stage," in *The Routledge Companion to African American Theatre and Performance,* ed. Kathy A. Perkins, Sandra L. Richards, Renée Alexander Craft, and Thomas F. DeFrantz (London: Routledge, 2019), 77–82.

38. André, *Black Opera,* 13.

7. Rest in Power

1. "Real, Sleep Science from Mayim Bialik," advertisement for Nectar Sleep mattress, November 2018.

2. A few words on names: Although the title *Best Place to Sleep* is usually used to refer to Yamaoka's solo nap performances, and *Come with Me* to group performances, Yamaoka uses the titles somewhat interchangeably. I use *Best Place to Sleep* to refer to all performances from this series. Similarly, *Black Power Naps* and *Siestas Negras* have both been used as titles depending on the language(s) of the host site; I use *Black Power Naps* to draw out the relationship between Black Power and power napping. During the 2018 and 2019 installations of *Black Power Naps,* the artists were credited as niv Acosta and Fannie Sosa. For the 2023 installation *Black Power Naps: La Biblioteca Is Open,* they were credited as Navild Acosta and Sosa (mononymic).

3. Janine Francois notes, "A growing amount of research has found that Black Americans experience significantly less slow-wave sleep—the kind required for actual, rejuvenating rest—than white Americans. The lack of slow-wave sleep can cause serious mental and physical health issues, including premature death." Janine Francois, "Reparations for Black People Should Include Rest," *Black Power Naps Magazine,* no. 2 (2019), n.p., reprinted in *Vice,* January 8, 2019, https://www.vice.com.

4. Judy Wajcman, *Pressed for Time: The Acceleration of Life in Digital Capitalism* (Chicago: University of Chicago Press, 2015), 164.

5. Muñoz, *Cruising Utopia,* 98–99.

6. Michel de Certeau, *The Practice of Everyday Life* (Berkeley: University of California Press, 1984), 30, 38–39.

7. Eva Feder Kittay, with Bruce Jennings and Angela A. Wasunna, "Dependency, Difference and the Global Ethic of Longterm Care," *Journal of Political Philosophy* 13, no. 4 (December 2005): 453. On feminist ethics of care, see also Virginia Held, *The Ethics of Care: Personal, Political, and Global* (New York: Oxford University Press, 2006); Eva Feder Kittay and

Ellen K. Feder, eds., *The Subject of Care: Feminist Perspectives on Dependency* (Lanham, Md.: Rowman & Littlefield, 2002).

8. Sosa and Navild Acosta, "Una guía para instituciones blancas que reciben artistas racializades y a sus públicos" (artists' statement for *Siestas Negras,* Matadero Madrid, 2018), *Black Power Naps Magazine,* no. 1 (2018), n.p. All translations of quotations from this Spanish-language magazine are my own.

9. Glenn, "From Servitude to Service Work," 1–43.

10. Sharma, "Biopolitical Economy of Time," 439–44.

11. Arlie Russell Hochschild, "Love and Gold," *Scholar and Feminist Online* 8, no. 1 (Fall 2009), https://sfonline.barnard.edu.

12. Leah Lakshmi Piepzna-Samarasinha, *Care Work: Dreaming Disability Justice* (Vancouver: Arsenal Pulp Press, 2018), 33. Piepzna-Samarasinha acknowledges that reciprocal care work is often unfairly distributed, insufficient, and exhausting. Her vision of collective care attempts to enact a new model against caregiver burnout and toward a sustainable future.

13. Sakiko Yamaoka, *Come with Me vol. 2* (last modified April 23, 2009), YouTube, https://www.youtube.com.

14. Sakiko Yamaoka, "Sakiko Yamaoka (Tokyo, Japan)," LIVE2011 Biennale of Performance Art, last modified September 15, 2011, https://livebiennale.ca.

15. Rebecca Walker, "Fill/Flash/Memory: A History of Flash Mobs," in *Culture Jamming: Activism and the Art of Cultural Resistance,* ed. Marilyn DeLaure and Moritz Fink (New York: New York University Press, 2017), 300–321; John H. Muse, "Flash Mobs and the Diffusion of Audience," *Theater* 40, no. 3 (2010): 9–23.

16. Diana Taylor, *The Archive and the Repertoire: Performing Cultural Memory in the Americas* (Durham, N.C.: Duke University Press, 2003), 28, 33.

17. Dalih Sembiring and Rizky Sasono, eds., *Spiritual Renewal: Performance Art Urban Festival* (Perfurbance # 3), trans. Rachel Saraswati (Yogyakarta, Indonesia: Performance Klub, 2007), 207.

18. Quoted in Sembiring and Sasono, *Spiritual Renewal,* 325.

19. Piepzna-Samarasinha, *Care Work,* 108.

20. Sakiko Yamaoka, *Sakiko Yamaoka Performance on the Street "Come with Me" 09 Ginza5, Tokyo* (last modified March 13, 2009), YouTube, https://www.youtube.com.

21. Bertolt Brecht, *Brecht on Theatre: The Development of an Aesthetic,* ed. Steve Giles, Marc Silberman, and Tom Kuhn, trans. John Willett (London: Hill and Wang, 1977), 104–5, 121.

22. Jean-Luc Nancy, *The Fall of Sleep,* trans. Charlotte Mandell (New York: Fordham University Press, 2009), 17.

23. Rachel Hann, *Beyond Scenography* (New York: Routledge, 2019), 9.

24. Navild Acosta and Fannie Sosa, "The Fundamentals of Black Power Naps," *Black Power Naps Magazine,* no. 2 (2019), n.p. Unless otherwise cited in endnotes, all further quotes from Acosta and Sosa are from this essay.

25. James B. Maas, with Megan L. Wherry, David J. Axelrod, Barbara R. Hogan, and Jennifer A. Blumin, *Power Sleep: The Revolutionary Program That Prepares Your Mind for Peak Performance* (New York: William Morrow, 1998). The *Oxford English Dictionary* attests to the use of "power nap" in Toronto's *Globe & Mail* as early as 1980—to speculate that a live performer used a ninety-minute break in a performance to take a nap offstage. "Power, n.[1]," *OED Online,* last modified 2006, http://www.oed.com.

26. Piepzna-Samarasinha, *Care Work,* 65.

27. "Vanity, n.," *OED Online,* last modified 1989, http://www.oed.com; "Procrastinate, v.," *OED Online,* last modified 2006, http://www.oed.com.

28. Gerard Manley Hopkins, "Pied Beauty" (1877), in *Poems of Gerard Manley Hopkins,* ed. Robert Bridges (London: Humphrey Milford, 1918).

29. jamilah malika, "Rest/Woke," *Black Power Naps Magazine,* no. 2 (2019), n.p., reprinted as jamilah malika, "A Poem for the Anxious and Exhausted," *Vice,* January 11, 2019, https://www.vice.com.

30. Taylor, *Archive and the Repertoire,* 20.

31. Francois, "Reparations for Black People."

32. Francois, "Reparations for Black People."

33. Francois, "Reparations for Black People."

34. "The Best Bed for Better Sleep | Casper®," Casper Sleep, accessed May 28, 2019, https://casper.com.

35. In the 2010s, psychologists described an influx of patients on a "perfectionistic quest for the ideal sleep in order to optimize daytime function." The condition has been dubbed *orthosomnia,* reflecting not actual lost sleep, as described by the term "sleep gap," but instead an "unhealthy preoccupation" with perfected sleep. Kelly Glazer Baron, Sabra Abbott, Nancy Jao, Natalie Manalo, and Rebecca Mullen, "Orthosomnia: Are Some Patients Taking the Quantified Self Too Far?," *Journal of Clinical Sleep Medicine* 13, no. 2 (February 2017): 351.

36. Mitch Goldstein, "Welcome to Soft-Space," Soft-Space, Buffy, 2019, https://softspace.buffy.co.

37. Karl Marx, *Capital,* vol. 1, *A Critique of Political Economy,* trans. Ben Fowkes (London: Penguin Classics, 1992), 342.

38. Marx's analysis of surplus value is buttressed by medical investigators' reports on sleep deprivation among nineteenth-century laborers: "The work of a London journeyman baker begins, as a rule, at about eleven at night. At that hour he 'makes the dough.' . . . He then lies down upon the kneading-board, which is also the covering of the trough in which the dough is 'made'; and with a sack under him, and another rolled up as a pillow, he sleeps for about a couple of hours" before returning to work. Journeyman bakers "rarely reach the age of 42." Marx, *Capital,* 359–61.

39. Acosta and Sosa, "Una guía," n.p. Sosa later created a digital, English-language iteration of this guide; see Fannie Sosa, "A White Institution's Guide for Welcoming Artists of Color and Their Audiences," *Galerie Galerie* (blog), accessed May 29, 2024, https://www.galeriegalerieweb.com.

40. Heather Agyepong, quoted in Tom Seymour, "MoMA Apologises to Artist Heather Agyepong, Who Was Ejected from Exhibit Intended as Safe Space for Black Visitors," *Art Newspaper,* March 28, 2023, https://www.theartnewspaper.com; Isabella Segalovich, "Fallout Continues After MoMA Removed Black Visitor from Exhibition," *Hyperallergic,* October 22, 2023, https://hyperallergic.com.

41. niv Acosta, "Save Black Power Naps," created September 1, 2023, GoFundMe, https://www.gofundme.com.

42. Piepzna-Samarasinha, *Care Work,* 107.

Coda

1. Readers familiar with *Cymbeline* will recall Imogen's sleep not only in act 2, scene 2 but also in act 4, scene 2, when Imogen/Fidele's drugged, sleeping body is mistaken for dead and laid to rest alongside Cloten's beheaded corpse, and act 5, scene 4, when the imprisoned Posthumus's true parentage is revealed to him in a staged dream that includes the god Jupiter descending on an eagle. William Shakespeare, *Cymbeline,* ed. Martin Butler (Cambridge: Cambridge University Press, 2005). All parenthetical citations of act, scene, and line(s) refer to this edition.

2. This line from *The Rape of Lucrece* is one of many allusions to narratives of voyeurism and rape threaded through Iachimo's long monologue.

3. Mulvey, "Visual Pleasure and Narrative Cinema."

4. A significant caveat comes from bell hooks, who points out that Black women also watch films and other popular media, and in doing so, they have developed a critical "oppositional gaze" that is not so easily taken in by cinematic manipulations of the viewer's desires. bell hooks, "The Oppositional Gaze: Black Female Spectators," in *Black Looks: Race and Representation* (New York: Routledge, 2015), 115–31.

5. Hélène Cixous, "Aller à la mer" (1977), trans. Barbara Kerslake, *Modern Drama* 27, no. 4 (1984): 546.

6. Christen A. Smith, "Counting Frequency: Un/Gendering Anti-Black Police Terror," *Social Text* 39, no. 2 (147) (2021): 35.

7. After writing the song, Tines noticed how the improvised lyrics echo the line "Where there is darkness, let me sow light," from the Peace Prayer of Saint Francis. In interviews, Tines has identified the first performance of "Vigil" as having been recorded for a short film for the Los Angeles Opera in 2020. "Vigil" repurposes Tines and Dieudonné's composition "Chorale" and was later performed in a streamed concert with the Louisville Orchestra, as an immersive audio installation at Lincoln Center, and as the closing benediction in Tines's full-length concert *Recital #1: MASS.* Davóne Tines and Shira Kagan-Shafman, email correspondence

with author, May 12, 2025; Simret Aklilu, "Opera Singer Pays Tribute to Breonna Taylor," *CNN* (blog), September 30, 2020, https://www.cnn.com; Nate Chinen, "A Conversation with Davóne Tines, Before His 'Recital No. 1: MASS,'" *WRTI* (blog), February 24, 2023, https://www.wrti.org; *Program: The Philadelphia Orchestra,* November 6, 2021, https://www.philorch.org; Davóne Tines and Teddy Abrams, hosts, *Vigil: Screening and Conversation,* Lincoln Center for the Performing Arts, 2021, YouTube, https://www.youtube.com; "Q&A with Davóne Tines: Healing Through Citizen Artistry," Interlochen Center for the Arts, October 26, 2020, https://www.interlochen.org.

8. Several versions of "Vigil" are available online, and several have been performed live. My reading focuses on the version in the film *Vigil (an exercise in empathy),* composed by Igee Dieudonné, Davóne Tines, and Matthew Aucoin, 2021, YouTube, https://www.youtube.com/@dtines.

9. Tines and Abrams, *Vigil: Screening and Conversation.*

10. Kathomi Gatwiri and Virginia Mapedzahama, "Pedagogy or 'Trauma Porn'? Racial Literacy as a Prerequisite for Teaching Racially Dignifying Content in the Australian Social Work Context," *Journal for Multicultural Education* 16, no. 3 (2022): 272–82; Esther O. Ohito, "'I'm Very Hurt': (Un)Justly Reading the Black Female Body as Text in a Racial Literacy Learning Assemblage," *Reading Research Quarterly* 57, no. 2 (June 2022): 609–27.

11. Jennifer C. Nash, *The Black Body in Ecstasy: Reading Race, Reading Pornography* (Durham, N.C.: Duke University Press, 2014); Heather Berg, *Porn Work: Sex, Labor, and Late Capitalism* (Chapel Hill: University of North Carolina Press, 2021); Amia Srinivasan, "Talking to My Students About Porn," in *The Right to Sex: Feminism in the Twenty-First Century* (New York: Farrar, Straus and Giroux, 2021), 33–72.

12. Srinivasan, "Talking to My Students," 64, emphasis added.

13. Sampada Aranke, *Death's Futurity: The Visual Life of Black Power* (Durham, N.C.: Duke University Press Books, 2023), 4–8.

14. Saidiya V. Hartman, *Scenes of Subjection: Terror, Slavery, and Self-Making in Nineteenth-Century America* (New York: Oxford University Press, 1997), 20. Hartman goes on to say that white spectators' claims to empathetic understanding of Black suffering led to misreadings of this very pain as cheerful performance, as when enslaved people's work songs were construed as evidence of joy in forced labor.

15. Michel Foucault, *The History of Sexuality,* vol. 1, *An Introduction,* trans. Robert Hurley (New York: Pantheon Books, 1978), 138.

Index

Danielle Drees is Marsted Curatorial Fellow at the Wadsworth Atheneum Museum of Art in Hartford, Connecticut. Her writing has been published in the *Journal of Dramatic Theory and Criticism*, *Signs*, *Frontiers*, *Performance Research*, *Theatre Journal*, and *TDR: The Drama Review*.

Printed and bound by CPI Group (UK) Ltd, Croydon, CR0 4YY

13/08/2026

14941850-0001